THE SILVER SPITFIRE

THE SILVER SPITFIRE

The Legendary WWII RAF Fighter Pilot
In His Own Words

WING COMMANDER TOM NEIL

Weidenfeld & Nicolson
LONDON

First published in Great Britain in 2013
by Weidenfeld & Nicolson

3 5 7 9 10 8 6 4 2

© Tom Neil 2013

A CIP catalogue record for this book
is available from the British Library.

ISBN: 9780297868132

Typeset by Input Data Services Ltd, Bridgwater, Somerset

Printed and bound by CPI Group (UK) Ltd, Croydon CRO 4YY

The Orion Publishing Group's policy is to use papers
that are natural, renewable and recyclable and made
from wood grown in sustainable forests. The logging
and manufacturing processes are expected to conform to
environmental regulations of the country of origin.

Weidenfeld & Nicolson

Orion Publishing Group Ltd
Orion House
5 Upper Saint Martin's Lane
London, WC2H 9EA

An Hachette UK Company

www.orionbooks.co.uk

For my beautiful wife,
the former Flight Officer Eileen Hampton, WAAF,
who not only provided me with three wonderful sons but who
has also loved, guided, encouraged and supported me
throughout 68 years of married life.

Contents

Contents

Author's Note

Throughout 1944, as a 23-year-old Squadron Leader of the Royal Air Force, I flew and served with the 100th Fighter Wing of the 9th United States Army Air Force.

As the 9th Air Force was new and in the process of forming, I and several other experienced RAF pilots, whose assistance had been requested by the Americans, were posted to them for an indefinite period. Arising from this attachment, in this book I describe flying and other experiences with the 100th Fighter Wing, together with accounts of further incidents occurring shortly thereafter.

Although I had occasionally spoken and written of my flying adventures over the years, when I was invited by the Orion Publishing Group to record some of them in a book entitled *The Silver Spitfire*, I was reluctant to do so for a number of what I considered to be valid reasons.

First, as a 91-year-old author, I was not altogether in favour of any arrangement which would result in my being sentenced to two years' hard-labour writing a book! Second, it would involve me in an arduous memory exercise, trying to recall a host of unrecorded facts relating to events and incidents that occurred 70 years before. And finally, almost all of the people about whom I would be writing would now be dead and therefore unable either to confirm or to challenge my assertions.

There were, moreover, other factors to consider.

In 1982, I had written a rather light-hearted account about my finding, and later flying for at least a year, a Spitfire belonging to some unknown squadron, which had apparently been left on a French airfield in August 1944. This unusual story, which was published in the aviation press, had then 'gone round the world'.

The result, in the main, was total disbelief! No one, it was argued, in any disciplined organisation, would be allowed to take possession of a military aircraft, employ it as a private armed taxi for many months and use thousands of gallons of government fuel, without being discovered and then brought to account.

But, I am happy to add, this particular culprit was not brought to account and, surprisingly, did in due course agree, even at 92 years of age, to write a book entitled *The Silver Spitfire*.

However, there are other facts a reader should understand.

When the Air Ministry sent me to join the Americans, it appeared, to me anyway, that they completely washed their hands of me, believing no doubt that having carried out the transfer, I would be subject to the orders and control of 9th USAAF, or more precisely those of the 100th Fighter Wing. This feeling was confirmed in my mind when, for 12 months, I did not receive a single visit or written instruction from any RAF department or representative.

The Americans, from the first, and somewhat to my surprise, accorded me more respect than I merited or deserved, the Headquarters element of the 100th Fighter Wing, a new and unblooded organisation of which I became a member, treating me, despite my youth, with an undue measure of awe and deference, with the result that throughout the year I was with them I was allowed to do more or less as I pleased – flying, travelling, performing and speaking without constraint. In short, it was a novel experience and despite the fact that I always tried to behave responsibly and conform to American methods and rules, for most of the time I was a free agent and thoroughly enjoyed the experience.

There are, in addition, other matters I feel ought to be mentioned.

In these days of instant communication, when every ten-year-old is now equipped with a mobile telephone containing an inbuilt camera, it may be difficult to understand that for much of the Second World War those of us in the RAF, if not forbidden, were certainly not expected to take photographs of what was happening around us. Only the official photographers were permitted to do that, and then only occasionally. Similarly, for security reasons, many important details of what was said or took place were never properly recorded.

I am therefore especially indebted to Messrs Alan Wright and Edward Sergison of Kent, together with the Editor of *Aeroplane Monthly*, all of whom collected most of the photographs used in this book. Also to 'Bob' Ogley of Westerham, Kent, and my old and late lamented friend, Charles Bowyer, a Norfolk neighbour, the former for details of the 'V' weapons attack on Britain and the latter for the many facts and observations contained in his book, *The Air War Over Europe*.

And lastly, and in particular, I am indebted to the young Polish historian Wojtek Matusiak, who spent countless hours endeavouring to discover the final fate of 'The Silver Spitfire'.

So, I hope and trust that the events, incidents and situations you will now read about will be viewed and enjoyed, but only when set against the background I have described.

Chapter 1

Genesis

Late November 1943. Bitterly cold throughout the United Kingdom, the visibility was unseasonably clear beneath a thin but solid layer of pearl-grey cirrus at 25,000 feet. A fairly normal day but one I would have cause to remember.

As the CFI (Chief Flying Instructor) of No. 53 Spitfire OTU (Operational Training Unit) flying out of RAF Kirton-in-Lindsay in Lincolnshire, I was leading a formation of 12 Mark 2 Spitfires at 20,000 feet. All, apart from one flight commander and me, were young student pilots learning their trade, engaged on what would be one of the final flights of their 14-week course.

Before take-off, I had briefed them all with stern words and a warning finger. Absolute radio silence throughout the whole trip – understood? Not a single word or order to be passed.

First, three finger-four battle formations would make a fast ascent at maximum climbing power. Then, for an hour, rate-four turns at combat speed, wheeling and turning, rising and falling, crossing over, above and underneath. Kids' stuff low down, of course, but much harder and dangerous four miles high, with Merlin engines panting hard in the thinner air and everyone becoming tired and losing concentration.

So concentration was key. Concentration, a focused mind, and always the will and enthusiasm to engage and *fight* the enemy. And all the time, naturally, with eagle eyes looking for 'Huns in the sun!'

After that, however, there would be a period of relaxation: a lull during which we would amuse ourselves by throwing our aircraft around, just for the joy of flying – a game of follow the leader, in fact. A few rolls and loops and whatever else I, in front, might decide. I would signal long-line-astern by rocking my wings and the formation would spread out, with not less than 200 yards between aircraft, each pilot then imitating my actions. Finally, feeling like pieces of chewed string, no doubt, we would all form up again and return to base, having completed about 95 minutes of pretty serious aviation. Everything crystal clear? Nods and smiles all round.

An hour later, the serious stuff being concluded, it was only when I sensed everyone properly in line behind me that I felt ready to proceed. A glance at my altimeter and the small rear-view mirror above my head: 8,000 feet, about, and 12 exhaust banks trailing thin white streamers of vapour into the frigid air. Everyone nicely in place and ready to go. Splendid!

First a slow roll. I dropped the nose of my Spit a trifle, pulled up and turned the aircraft over, barrelling the manoeuvre slightly to prevent my engine being flooded with fuel as the result of negative G, before slowly resuming my normal upright position. A glance in my mirror to see in the far distance several pointed wings rising and falling as those behind imitated my actions. I remember nodding to myself. All right so far!

Now a high loop, followed possibly by a nice smooth 'roll off the top'. I glanced around to check that there were no other aircraft anywhere in the area. After which, I adjusted the throttle and engine speed: at this height about 4lb boost and 2,650 revs, which would give those behind plenty of power to play with.

Down then, with the nose and about 275 on the ASI (airspeed indicator). The controls of my aircraft tighten and I lift my Spitfire up until I am in a vertical climb, with the nose pointing straight towards the white-grey cloud above, gradually losing speed. Another glance left and right to check that the wings are exactly at right angles to the horizon. After that, slowly over the top, my head bent back as I look for the rising line of the earth and sky. Then, after a brief silence, down! The airspeed mounting ... 150 ... 200 ... 300! In a vertical dive now, the hiss of the slipstream rising to a shrill scream. Everything going well, until ... *Oh, Jesus!*

My scream was more a prayer than a blasphemy as I observed another aircraft within feet, no, inches, of me! Another Spitfire in plan view, its green and brown camouflage and coloured roundels massively close and completely unaware it was underneath me, flying straight and level, preparing to start its own loop.

A metallic bump and a violent shudder as I snatched at the controls and tried to avoid it. My God, had I hit it? My own aircraft was lurching sideways in a massive skid, my heart racing.

For seconds that felt like hours, I flew almost aimlessly into the distance, testing my controls to see if they worked, meanwhile looking hopefully about for the aircraft I might have hit. In the middle distance, two, three, four Spitfires were climbing away and soaring into the heavens – was my victim one of them? I hoped to God it was. Perhaps I had succeeded in avoiding it, the bump and violent lurch resulting from my hitting its slipstream. Oh, Lord! What a terrible thing to happen and it was my fault. *My fault!* I had miscalculated and made a horrible mistake. I just hadn't seen it.

The next planned manoeuvre entirely forgotten, for several minutes I strove to recover my composure, my heart rate reducing as a small group of aircraft, their loops completed, began to form up on my left and right. Eventually, and with vast relief, I counted twelve, including myself. All safe and sound. Thank God for that! I breathed a prayer and looked over the side. Far below were the green and brown fields of the Lincolnshire countryside, plus the grey huddle of a distant town – Lincoln itself, probably, with its ancient, beautiful cathedral. Suddenly, everything began to seem normal again. Phew! But what an upsetting thing to happen.

Fifteen minutes later, we were all down to 1,500 feet and circling Kirton-in-Lindsay – three sections of four in echelon-starboard formation. With wheels lowered and flaps down, each section slid separately across the boundary fence to touch down like swans alighting on a lake. As Kirton is a grass airfield, I found my aircraft bouncing and lurching slightly as I slowed up and, for the hundredth – or was it the thousandth – time experienced the sweet, pungent tang of exhaust smoke as I opened the throttle to turn and taxi to my own hardstanding outside my office. Finally I was able to brake, and my engine fitter placed chocks beneath my wheels and helped me with my straps.

Noticing my silence, he asked, 'Everything all right, sir? You look a bit wan.'

Smiling, I shook my head but sat there, suddenly feeling very weary, recognising that it was my fifth major collision incident. These incidents include one that had resulted in four of my colleagues being killed and injured, and the nasty occasion when I came back to earth at the end of a parachute.

Later still, I was struggling out of my Mae West and flying suit when my flying wing adjutant knocked at my office door and entered, smiling.

Flying Officer 'Jimmy' Smithers, a nice non-flying man, was 39, rather plump, wore glasses, and ran the orderly room very efficiently. A competent and perceptive officer, he noticed immediately my glum expression.

'If I may say so, sir, you look a bit green about the gills. Any particular problems?'

As I provided brief details of my near-fatal flight, he listened gravely and then said without a smile, 'This, then, is clearly not to be your day, sir, as the station commander has just asked to see you.'

'What about? Did he say?' I was thinking: Surely he can't have heard about my incident so soon.

'No, sir. Just that he wanted to talk to you.'

I thought: Oh Lord! After dicing with death, a telling-off was all I needed.

Glancing at my watch, I saw that it was about 3.30 p.m. and relaxed a little – getting on for teatime, anyway.

A little later, suitably spruced up and with my forage cap properly in place, I walked the 400 yards to station headquarters and the Group Captain's office. Little did I know that I was within 15 minutes of being given instructions that would affect my service career for the following 12 months and, indirectly, my life for many years to come.

As I entered the station commander's room and saluted, I said a little stiffly, 'I understand you sent for me, sir.'

Ever the gentleman, Group Captain John Hawtrey rose to his feet and waved me to a chair.

'Rest your nether quarters, dear boy' was his rather unusual response. 'I did not *send* for you, dear heart, but merely suggested that you might wish to join me to have a chat.' Then, casting a benevolent smile in my direction, 'I trust you weren't offended.'

I silently signified that I wasn't. The Group Captain had only assumed command at Kirton a month or so before and I hardly knew him. I was certainly unfamiliar with his manner of speech and frequent 'drollisms'; I only later learnt that he never invited a visitor just to 'sit down', but always instructed his companion to 'park his bustle', 'rest his bum' or perhaps 'ease his secret parts' – to quote but a few exhortations – while all instructions were accompanied by such friendly appellations as 'dear heart', 'old fruit' or the more usual 'dear boy' or 'old chap'.

At the time, John, an Old Etonian, was about 40 years of age and a single man; and, I was informed, being distantly related to the Edwardian actor Sir Charles Hawtrey, he was something of a thespian. Apparently, he had also been personal staff officer to a certain government Air Minister, a multi-millionaire of Middle Eastern extraction, who, with no visible lady in his life, was also the owner of a vast mansion in Kent (more recently employed as No. 1 Squadron's officers' mess) where, it was alleged, 'naughty' parties frequently took place.

All of which, when John Hawtrey turned up, caused a few eyebrows to be raised among several of the more worldly members serving at Kirton-in-Lindsay. However, I have to add that the Group Captain was also known to fly a Spitfire now and then – though only, it was said, to keep up appearances.

After a few further pleasantries had been exchanged, I sat, a little on edge, wondering why I had been summoned until, finally, my senior went into 'priest at prayer' mode and, with hands spread on his desk and eyes closed, asked, 'Now, dear lad, what does the third week in November signify?'

I returned a blank look. 'Nothing that I can recall. Did something special occur?'

The Group Captain shook his head. 'Wrong answer, dear boy. Cudgel your brains, there's a good chap.'

I considered solemnly but, my mind going blank, merely added, 'I flew that day, I'm pretty sure. I may have even had a headache – I can't remember.'

My senior grimaced. 'You really are a tiresome young man; I shall award you no marks out of ten for history.' Then, after a moment's pause, 'Thursday, 25 November 1943, dear heart: Thanksgiving Day. Surely you've heard of it?'

I continued to look woodenly in his direction. Thanksgiving Day ... I had indeed heard of it but couldn't recall in what context.

Feigning exasperation, the Group Captain continued. 'Always the fourth Thursday in November! When our American cousins gorge themselves to bursting point on turkey drumsticks and cranberry sauce, in celebration of the end of the "starving time" of their forefathers. Desperately short of food, because they were really a pretty hopeless lot, the so-called Pilgrim Fathers who had landed in the *Mayflower* a year or so before had little idea of how to grow things, and nearly all croaked. Then, when they were on their last legs, two Red Indian chaps named Samoset and Squanto walked out of the forest and advised them, in very tolerable English, how to plant corn and things, showing them how to dig holes in the ground and manure the seed with fish heads, and, of course, saving the colony.'

I found myself frowning in disbelief. 'Oh, surely that's all nonsense, sir. If they were aboriginals and just out of the forest, how on earth were they able to speak English?'

But my senior was in full flood. 'Because these Pilgrim Father chaps, dear boy, were by no means the first in that neck of the woods. You see, fishermen from the Baltic area, Britain and other places had been fishing off what is now Newfoundland for yonks and, in order to preserve their catches, find water, feed themselves and repair their wooden ships, they had been landing in North America for ages. At which times, of course, they had obviously taken some Indian chaps back to Europe – and presumably taught them English. As clear as a pikestaff in my mind.'

I recall smiling at the time and shaking my head. 'All fascinating stuff, sir. But I really don't see what all this has to do with me. There are no Red Indians on the present course, and we are all reasonably well fed at the moment.'

'Ah, but it does involve you, dear lad. It does! And in the biggest possible way.'

He picked up a paper from his desk. 'I've just received a signal, which I will read out to you.' He paused to clear his throat. 'Here we are: "79168 S/L T F Neil to attend interview soonest P2 Dept. Air Ministry London pending posting to 9th USAAF w.e.f. January 1944."'

There was a brief, horrible silence as my mouth, I imagine, fell open. After which I heard my own voice uttering a strange noise. 'Americans! Me? I don't know anything about Americans.'

Looking up, I saw the Group Captain smiling in my direction. 'That's what it says here, dear boy. And who knows, it may do your history a power of good.'

Later, I recall glancing down at my two-guinea RAF watch: 5 p.m. on the day I nearly killed myself in a mid-air collision, and here I was being posted to the bloody *Americans*!

I went by train to London on 13 December – which was a Monday – and took a room in the Regent Palace Hotel. Not the most splendid of venues, it had, however, the twin advantages of being comparatively inexpensive and within spitting distance of Piccadilly Circus. It also served a whopping great breakfast, of which I was reminded when I visited the dining room the following morning and was confronted by a sea of uniforms and the usual wedge of small, fat, foreign-looking chaps with crinkly hair who somehow never seemed to get into the war.

Partly for the exercise but also to calm my nerves, I walked to Adastral House in Kingsway. The weather being cold, foggy and horribly damp, and there being stark evidence of three years of bombing throughout the West End of London, it was not a thirty-five-minute hike I can say I enjoyed.

In the Air Ministry, I filled in the customary pink form and was conducted by an elderly ex-serviceman along a seemingly endless corridor to the P2 Department.

My interviewing officer, a rather harassed-looking wing commander of about 40, greeted me civilly and, after examining my credentials, nodded with obvious approval before seating himself comfortably with a mug of tea. He signified that I might have one if I wished, but he did not offer to order one for me, so I was obliged to sit there with a rapidly drying mouth, waiting for something to happen.

My senior then started off by asking me if I knew anything about the 9th USAAF. When I silently shook my head, he set off on an explanation that not only lasted a good five minutes but also had the effect of utterly confusing me.

The 9th United States Army Air Force was in the process of establishing itself in Britain but, unlike the 8th USAAF, which was already well grounded in East Anglia, it would be a tactical air force, not a strategic one. In short, its role would be to provide close support for any invading US army by destroying the enemy on the ground and in the air, disrupting communications and generally causing mayhem, all this with a large force of fighters and short-range medium bombers.

Only too aware that most of its new air force would consist of non-regular, unblooded personnel, the American hierarchy had asked for small groups of specialist RAF officers to assist in several areas, namely, the operational flying side, in the intelligence sphere and with the provision and supply of equipment, or materiel, as they termed it. In response to this request, the Air Ministry had selected several small teams of three and, it appeared, I was to be the flying operations member of the first.

Somewhat dazed by all this information, when I asked what precisely I might be expected to do, the Wing Commander waved an airy hand and gave a Continental-type shrug, suggesting he didn't really know. The job was what I was able to make of it: I was just to look pretty and help out in every way possible, basically. As there was no job specification ... well, it would all be up to me.

I must have looked pretty unconvinced because after we had

exchanged a few silent glances, he went on to say that he had decided
to send me to a little village called Boxted, which he thought was in
Essex – or it might just be in Suffolk. A new temporary airfield had
just been created there and the Yanks were apparently moving in
some aircraft and personnel. If I called on them and saw precisely
what they were up to, I could report back, at which time he could
decide on my next move. He suggested that the following morning I
go by train to Colchester, where he would arrange transport for me
and I could properly 'case the joint', to use an American expression.

I have to say that whilst I was trudging back in the rain towards
my meagre room in the Regent Palace Hotel and my crinkly-haired
companions, my morale was not exactly high.

Early the following morning I set off in somewhat better spirits and
started a day that I can only describe as memorable.

From Liverpool Street station, my puffer train wended its way
slowly northwards through the wilderness that was East London,
a vast area shattered by three years of constant bombing, before
making several creaking stops, at and between several stations.
It took more than two hours to make the 50-mile journey and I
arrived to find Colchester bitterly cold and shrouded in a thick mist.

When the travelling crowd had cleared sufficiently, I wandered
around, searching for the ordered transport, but there was nothing
to be seen. The platforms finally became empty; the waiting room
was cheerless and without a fire, and there was no one to consult
other than one miserable-looking ticket collector guarding a single
telephone in a dingy office.

Approaching him, I immediately sensed resistance. The man
– obviously a card-carrying, left-wing class warrior – exuded an
aura of belligerent defiance. When I asked to use his telephone, all
I received was a hostile nod and I was told, 'There's a public one
outside.' When I asked politely, 'Where outside?' I received another
nod: in the general direction of London.

That did it! I was cold, wet and unhappy. The man and I
exchanged stares. Then, with a straight face and patting an empty
raincoat pocket, I told him quietly, 'You can see I am heavily armed.

I shall probably have to shoot you if you do not allow me to use your phone. D'you understand?'

I saw the man's eyes widen. Then there was uncertainty – did this fascist pig of an officer really mean what he said? Finally, with another nod in the direction of the telephone, the miserable creature turned away.

I would like to say that everything went well after that. But it didn't.

Using the telephone number I had been given in the Air Ministry, I was connected fairly promptly to my intended destination. The response was unusual.

An American voice said jocularly, 'Ar-right! So speak to me!'

Surprised and a little put off my stroke, I asked, 'Is that the airfield at Boxted?'

The voice: 'I can't say.'

'Why can't you say?'

'Because I'm not allowed to.'

'But why not, for heaven's sake?'

'Because it's restricted information, that's why.'

'Restricted information! But Boxted is just a tiny village in Essex! What makes it so important?'

The voice again: 'Listen, bud. It's restricted information and, as far as I'm concerned, that's good enough for me. OK? I just go by the book.'

I took a deep breath and tried another tack. 'Look, I'm a senior officer in the Royal Air Force and I've been invited by your commanding officer to help you out today. I was expecting to be met by a car at Colchester station, but I've been waiting here an hour and it's very cold. So please get someone to do something. And quickly!'

The voice said somewhat suspiciously, 'What's your name, bud?'

'Bud'! Closing my eyes, I winced, but controlled myself and gave him my name and rank. After which there was a subdued background conversation, presumably with a senior, followed by a ripple of laughter.

Then the voice again, this time more cheerfully: 'OK, buddy

boy! We'll try to get something down to you. Where d'you say you were?'

After about half an hour, I telephoned again and said that if they didn't send some transport soon, they should redirect their driver to the nearest hospital, where they would probably find me in A&E. This seemed to goad them into a frenzy of activity, as only 25 minutes later, an open-topped jeep swung into the station approach, driven by a bulky work-stained NCO chewing on an unlit cigar. Clad in denims with more stripes on his arm than the national flag, he wore a baseball cap with the peak turned up, which sat jauntily on the back of his head.

Seeing me pale and rigid on my seat, he came in my direction and called out in pure Brooklynese, 'Hey! You de guy look'n fer me?'

Conversation during our 25 minute drive was monosyllabic. When I asked if it had been raining recently, my driver merely grunted past his cigar, 'All the time.' When I enquired if the present heavy mist had been a problem, his reply was a brief 'Yup'.

My first impression of the airfield at Boxted was of a sea of glutinous mud, a glimpse of a thin ribbon of concrete perimeter track and at least one aircraft, which, through the thick winter mist, looked like a North American P.51 (Mustang).

Mud was clearly the by-product of everything American. During the brief period I was there, I watched it being manufactured by a multitude of enormous eight-wheeled trucks, and then ploughed through unendingly by jeeps and every type of wheeled vehicle known to man. No American, it seemed, ever walked. Mud-making clearly their speciality, they had succeeded in reducing this quiet and delightful corner of John Constable's England into something resembling the Passchendaele battlefield of the First World War.

Outside a large marquee, which was sagging under pools of accumulated rain, I was decanted into ankle-deep mud and invited into a dark interior littered with trestles, tabletops, chairs, blackboards, and impedimenta of every type, size and description.

I was greeted unsmilingly by an American major with a few captains in attendance and several hangers-on. Was I the operations guy he'd been hearing about? If so, boy, was he glad to see me – or anyone, in fact, who could make sense of what he described as all this 'crap!', waving a despairing arm.

Stiff with unease, I weighed up the situation at a glance and explained that in the RAF 'operational people' meant aircrew who flew aircraft in battle, not chaps who ran operations rooms. Such people were termed Control and Reporting Personnel, and I was not one of those. No, this definitely was not my line of business and I would have to speak immediately to my superiors. So, if he would kindly recall my driver ...

I left hurriedly, caked with mud, the major and his henchmen looking woefully at my retreating form like a line of dogs waiting to be put down.

Back in London I reported to my 'P' Staff wing commander that Boxted was a disaster area and that I would only agree to go there under the threat of death. Furthermore, they were looking for chaps with C and R experience, which I most definitely did not have. Clearly, we would have to think again.

I heard my senior mutter, 'Oh, dear' under his breath. Then, after a moment's pause, 'I think it would be best if you returned to Kirton-in-Lindsay and waited there until I sort something out. Do that and I'll keep you informed.'

Which is how I came to spend the rest of December 1943, including Christmas Day, back in Lincolnshire, in a comfortable officers' mess, among many old friends and in front of roaring coal fires.

In fact, it was not until 9 January 1944 that I received word from my wing commander that I had been officially posted to the 100th Fighter Wing, 19th Tactical Air Command, 9th USAAF, with effect from 10 February 1944.

Somewhat relieved, I replied that I would be honoured to serve in such a distinguished organisation, provided there was no mud and I was not expected to organise their operations room.

So I took a spell of leave until 22 January 1944 when, as my flying logbook reveals, a Flight Lieutenant Lucarrotti, the OTU's navigation officer, flew me down to RAF Northolt in the Dominie.

Chapter 2
My First Americans

The 100th Fighter Wing headquarters occupied a large cluster of corrugated-iron-topped Nissen huts a stone's throw from RAF Ibsley, near Ringwood, in Hampshire. I have no recollection of how I got there, other than that I arrived safely and remember there being the usual stream of jeeps and trucks going in and out like a line of ants. But, thank heaven, no mud! I even observed one or two Americans actually on foot.

I was greeted cordially by a tall, pleasant-looking young man who introduced himself as Major de Fehr. A little later, we did a quick tour of the base in his jeep.

On the airfield of RAF Ibsley, Mark 6 Spitfires of No. 616 Squadron were parked in the distance. As we drove by, my companion explained that he often used the RAF officers' mess at Ibsley, as 'a cute little WAAF officer' with whom he was hoping to make his mark lived there. Also, the several aircraft at present used by the 100th Fighter Wing headquarters were kept on the airfield on what he termed 'the line', a term then new to me.

As we wandered around the local area, de Fehr became quite chummy. We exchanged Christian names and he explained that the Willys jeep in which we were travelling had originally been called a 'peep', but the macho military had thought the name too 'cissy' and had ordered it to be changed to 'jeep', after a Popeye cartoon character. He also said that the Wing headquarters had only a single Spitfire and a few light aircraft to fly, but others were expected by the day.

Unhappily it was rumoured that they might be getting a Bell P.39 (to me an Airacobra), in which case he, de Fehr, would immediately put in for a transfer, as the P.39 was the 'darnedest aircraft he had

ever flown'. Not only could you never keep the thing serviceable
but also in certain conditions of flight it would tumble. No kidding!
It would actually go 'ass over tit', he would swear to God! He knew
because it had happened to him. I found that story a little difficult to
swallow, but made no mention of my doubts at the time.

I deduced that, when complete, the 100th Fighter Wing would
be broadly equivalent to an RAF Tactical Group (No. 83 Group,
for example) and would eventually comprise four or five American
fighter groups. Each fighter group would normally consist of three
squadrons, and each squadron usually flew 16 aircraft in battle
(not 12, as the RAF did). However, only part of the Wing headquarters was in existence at present and the squadrons were only
now beginning to arrive in dribs and drabs. Also, it looked as though
their aircraft would be P.51s (Mustangs) and P.47s (Thunderbolts),
with some Lockheed P.38s (Lightnings) being used in the tactical
reconnaissance role.

The numbers involved quite took my breath away. Clearly there
was going to be much more to my job than I had expected, as with a
force of several hundred fighter aircraft in the Wing, a lot of explaining and talking lay ahead of me. Flying, too, I hoped.

I made my first flight that day from Ibsley in a tiny Taylor Cub,
my new companion, de Fehr, acting as pilot. After we had landed,
he confided in me that he would soon be going on attachment to
Italy, to 'get me some combat experience'.

He left almost at once and I never saw him again, as he was
killed within days. A West Point officer and my first American
friend, he was an able and delightful person and, at 23, the same age
as me.

Although I did not know it at the time, we were to remain in the
Ibsley area for almost three months. I now look back on that period
with enormous pleasure, as much happened to me that was different. Very, very different – my goodness!

My first day in the shadow of the Stars and Stripes left me wide-
eyed, amused, a bit breathless and not a little overfed.

The morning after my first and indeed only flight with the

unfortunate de Fehr, I awoke early after a restless night and went in search of breakfast. Despite double British Summer Time – as decreed by government – it was still barely light when I came across a wooden structure on which was rather crudely scrawled 'Mess Hall'.

Inside, the entrance broadened out into a largish room flanked by a long bar-like structure, behind which several denim-clad figures moved around, attending to their private chores.

A youngish GI hailed me. 'Hi there! Are you the new English guy they're talking about?'

I smiled, indicating that I probably was.

The man waved an arm. 'If it's coffee you're after, it's over there. Never short of coffee 'round here. Enough coffee to float a ship! With doughnuts, pastries and cheese, if you want 'em.'

Then, after a pause and whilst polishing the bar, 'So what do we call you?'

I offered my name but not my rank.

'OK, Tom,' said my interrogator cheerfully. 'And how d'you style yourself? Sergeant, "Lootenant" or what?'

I replied, 'Well, I'm a sort of "Lootenant", except that I'm called Squadron Leader.'

'Squadron Leader? What's that, Tom?'

'Well, in the RAF, I fly fighter aircraft and lead a squadron. I'm a sort of major.'

The polishing stopped abruptly. 'Major! No kiddin'! You a major?' Then, 'Boy! You don't look old enough to be even a "Lootenant". Well, whaddya know 'bout that!' The man shook his head in wonderment before apparently becoming lost for words.

I attempted to bridge the gap. 'So, what do I do about breakfast?'

The man almost shook himself out of his shocked reverie. 'OK, sir. Breakfast comin' up. Whaddya want? Juice, hotcakes, bacon, eggs, toast, anything. We got the lot.'

'Do I sit down anywhere, or what?'

'Yessir, you certainly do. Being a major I guess you rate the top table. That's it over there. Next to the stove. The Old Man – the Colonel, that is – likes to make his own toast, so we give him an old beat-up toasting fork. You sit down there and I'll bring it across, OK?'

As my now respectful companion went about his business, other people of indeterminate rank filtered in. Most grinned in my direction and said 'Hi!' or 'What's the word?' as they passed on to seats further down the room. All continued to wear their hats – round hats, slouch hats, crushed hats and the peaked variety I imagine were used for baseball – leading me to conclude, even at that stage of my association with the 100th Flying Wing, that hats were the most important item of clothing in the American wardrobe and likely to be worn even in bed.

When my breakfast was finally put before me, I probably looked a little dismayed. First, there appeared a small mountain of butter that was possibly equivalent to my parents' fat ration for two years, a pile of pancakes about five inches high, surmounted by four strips of bacon and several eggs, hovering above which was my talkative GI companion, waving a tall jug of maple syrup.

I heard myself protesting faintly, 'Steady on! You're not going to pour that over my eggs and bacon, are you?'

But he was, and he did! I sat there, motionless, for some moments, only to be 'saved by the bell' when a group of more senior officers arrived at my table, obliging me to stand up, introduce myself and talk.

It was at that moment, too, that I became aware of a more decisive, metallic voice, causing me to turn and face an older arrival, who was plainly the 'head man'.

My first thought was: My god, a Mexican gunslinger! For I was confronted by a wiry person of middle height, with a balding head, gimlety dark eyes and a villainous-looking pencil-thin moustache, who was grinning in my direction.

The figure rasped, 'You must be our new RAF expert! They didn't say you had ginger hair.'

I felt myself smiling in response. 'Good morning, sir. But my hair's not ginger, it's Titian.'

'Titian? What the hell's that?' The smile was still there.

'Well, I would describe it as a sort of orange marmalade colour.

Robertson's Golden Shred, not the Silver Shred variety.'

The man's eyes widened but he kept on grinning and, looking towards others in the group around us, tapped his head. 'Jesus! Looks like we're getting a Limey nut in the Wing!' After which he turned away and shouted, 'Hey, Kollenfrath, where are you? Where the hell's my toasting fork?'

That was the first occasion I met Colonel (later Brigadier General) Homer L. Sanders, the commanding officer of the 100th Fighter Wing. And I'm bound to say, on looking back, I was not immediately impressed.

Following the sad demise of Major de Fehr, the section known as A3 was taken over by a new operations officer, Major Jim Haun.

Haun, a slow and deliberate ex-National Guardsman, was a dyed-in-the-wool southern boy. As he in no way presented a fighter-type appearance, I was surprised to learn later that he had spent a short time flying Spitfires with 485 New Zealand Squadron at RAF Biggin Hill, an attachment, apparently, he did not particularly enjoy, as he felt himself out of his depth. Even so, he was a pleasant, capable officer who habitually smoked a big pipe and went around cocooned in a blue fog smelling powerfully of Mackintosh's toffee – all American pipe tobacco at the time seemed to be similarly perfumed.

One day he disappeared and returned with a P.47 (Thunderbolt), the first one to arrive in the headquarters flight. Apparently, it was Haun's initial trip on the type and, with his pipe severely polluting the atmosphere, he announced that it was just like sitting in his 'Grandpappy's li'l ol' rockin' chair'. After which, and within the hour, I was invited to have a go.

To me, indeed anyone experienced on even the larger Griffon-engined Spitfire, the P.47 seemed positively huge, which indeed it was, weighing almost 7 tons when fully loaded.

When I first climbed into the cockpit, I felt quite overwhelmed by space and switches; it was so unlike any fighter I had ever flown before. The instruments seemed scattered about; there was no tidy group of primary 'blind flying' dials, as found in all RAF fighters from the Gloster Gladiator onwards. Nor was there a comforting

Sutton harness with its leg and shoulder straps; instead there was merely a 'belly band', which enabled a pilot to lean forwards unrestricted. Have that on a Spit, I thought bitterly, and the pilot would be minus a face in no time!

There were other differences, too. American aircraft had a 24-volt electrical system (not 12-volt, as in the RAF), and employed exhaust-driven superchargers, powerful hydraulic foot brakes, piston-grip control columns, and inertia starters for their engines, which produced a crescendo of whirring noise inside before a clutch was engaged and the engine turned over – all this and much else besides.

Somewhat daunted, I began to question my mentor, who was leaning over me, puffing his pipe and regarding the correct amounts of oil, fuel and other pressures and temperatures, telling me off-handedly just to 'keep everything in the green'.

'In the green'? To me, a new expression. I then saw that almost every instrument was marked with little coloured lines indicating the proper range of operating temperatures and pressures. What a super idea! I was absolutely in favour and have been ever since. Surprisingly, it was something the RAF, in my time anyway, never adopted.

Under instruction, I did everything required and, after much internal whirring, the big Pratt & Whitney engine of more than 2,000 horsepower rumbled throatily into life. The massive four-bladed airscrew settled down to a comfortable mechanical beat in front of me, everything as smooth as silk. Haun then climbed down from the wing, waved a negligent hand, and I set off – carefully!

Of that first flight, I have little to report. The P.47 was indeed like sitting in a 'li'l ol' rockin' chair': easy to control, thoroughly amiable. I did not feel, though, that I was flying it; rather, it was flying me. I was merely part of the payload.

Landing without incident, I taxied in, thinking as I did so that if I was going to war in this type of aircraft, I would jolly well have to put in a great deal more practice.

That soon became obvious. Taking off from another airfield to fly the P.47 back to Ibsley a few days later, I could not get the airscrew out of fine pitch. The control was electrical, and having pressed and experimented with everything I could find, I was obliged to return some 50 miles, with the engine screaming its head off. Apparently, I was meant to operate some circuit breaker or other that no one had told me about. I decided then that, for me, there was such a thing as too much electricity and too many switches. Flying a P.47 was like playing a Wurlitzer organ.

A few days later still, I was invited to collect another P.47 from Andover and bring it down to Ibsley. It was explained that the aircraft was brand new and that I would be expected to 'slow-time' the engine. Unfamiliar with both the term and the practice, I was told that this meant taking off using the minimum throttle opening compatible with safety, and not 'pulling' more than 30 inches of boost thereafter. All this for the first ten hours of engine life.

The difference in recording boost was immediately revealed. Whereas in the RAF boost was measured in pounds per square inch, American instruments displayed in inches of mercury, olbs boost roughly equating to 30 inches and 18lbs boost to 66 inches. For some obscure reason, American pilots always 'pulled' whatever boost they required, which immediately set my mischievous mind at work, speculating what might happen if they 'pushed'.

Having been flown up to Andover in the Airspeed Oxford, I was confronted by a gleaming silver monster with the latest type of bubble canopy. This apparently was a P.47D, ours at Ibsley being the older 'C' model. Not only that, but the engine had 'water injection', an arcane expression I had heard before but knew little about, except that it meant that water and other magic additives were apparently injected into the cylinders to cool them down at high levels of boost.

Minutes later, and very much aware that Andover was a small grass airfield and that I was flying a brand-new type of aircraft I knew little about, with an engine, too, that had 'water injection' and had to be 'slow-timed', I taxied gingerly to the far end and tucked my rear into the hedge. Then, checking over my scattered instruments, I took a deep breath and opened the throttle.

The P.47 set off like a trotting hippo, and I was already halfway across the airfield when I realised that unless I did something fairly drastic, I would be through the far hedge and still not airborne. Then – horror of horrors! – I flashed a glance at my instruments and saw that I was 'pulling' only 27 inches of boost. Galvanised into action, I thrust open the throttle to its extremity, whereupon the Thunderbolt jerked into life and I flashed across the airfield boundary, heading like a dart for the Milky Way.

It took me a full minute to sort things out, raising the undercarriage, reducing power and the revs, and regaining my composure. I then saw that I had taken off using the full 66 inches of boost the engine was capable of delivering – water injection and all – and that the 27 that had so impinged itself on my mind had actually been 2,700 engine revolutions. Had someone altered the position of the instruments? If they had, no one had told me!

Riddled with guilt and feeling that I had damaged the engine beyond repair, I turned the aircraft towards the south and, well throttled back, almost glided the rest of the 40-mile journey.

During the ensuing weeks, I flew various P.47s many times, but I never really felt truly at home in the aircraft – it was just not me. In fact, I was later to be involved in one other very nasty flight that almost frightened the life out of me.

In the following months I would be presented with a variety of other communications aircraft which regularly turned up on 'the line'. These included a Percival Proctor, a Stinson L.5 and, somewhat later, a Cessna UC-78 (Bobcat), a North American AT6 (Harvard), a Douglas C-53 (Dakota) and, later, a fat and ungainly Noorduyn Norseman. All these beside a Mark 5 Spitfire, an Airspeed Oxford, and a Lockheed P.28 (Lightning) which turned up for a short time and was really rather special.

I very much liked the single P.38 I encountered, although, remembering my successful engagements with Messerschmitt Bf 110s during the Battle of Britain, I did not feel it had much of a future as a fighter in Europe. I recalled that our own A&AEE (Aeroplane and Armament Experimental Establishment) at Boscombe Down had rejected it a year or two earlier, believing the model they tested not to have the performance or the manoeuvrability they required. In spite of this verdict and the fact that it did not turn too well, I was very impressed with this later version of the aircraft.

Like the P.47, it had exhaust-driven superchargers, those on the Lightning being mounted on the top and rear of the each engine nacelle. As this did away with the conventional ejector exhausts, as fitted on the Spitfire and the P.51 (Mustang), the Allison engines on the P.38 emitted a delightful humming noise rather than the usual raucous, staccato snarl of the others. Also, because it had counter-rotating airscrews, the aircraft did not swing on take-off or deviate directionally when power was applied in the air.

On the other hand, I felt somewhat exposed in a cockpit that had both engines alongside me and not very much in front. A personal phobia perhaps, but I always liked to think that in the event of a wheels-up landing or a full-blooded crash, I would hit any hard obstacle after and not before the engines. In the P.38, this was barely the case.

Moreover, the superchargers, whizzing around at perhaps 30,000 rpm and glowing cherry-red, were plainly visible from the cockpit, particularly in poor light and at dusk, and that was a sight that never much appealed to me. Engines, I always felt, were best hidden away and left to get on with their own private affairs.

Meanwhile, I was gradually acclimatising myself to all things American, making new friends and forming fresh relationships, many of which were to endure for 60 years and more. I mixed with scores of colleagues, and although the names of some are now lost in the mists of time, many colleagues I recall clearly even now, some of them being very special indeed.

During those first several months of 1944, the two senior officers who influenced me most were Colonel (later Brigadier General) Homer L. Sanders, the commanding officer of the 100th Fighter Wing, whom I had met at breakfast on my first morning, and his immediate senior, Major General Elwood Quesada, the titular head of the 19th Tactical Air Command.

I encountered Sanders – variously referred to as 'the Colonel', 'the Old Man', or just plain 'Tex', and by one disgruntled officer from the north (who shall be nameless) 'that snotty-nosed southern bastard' – almost daily and Elwood Quesada many times during and after 1944.

The two men were about the same age and from roughly similar backgrounds. Quesada was the more agreeable and sophisticated person, while Sanders endlessly cultivated a hard-man image. With a penetrating voice and a flow of picturesque language, the Colonel bit the end off his cigars in the approved cowboy style and, with his hands dangling ominously by his sides, adopted the gait of a Dodge City gunslinger, seeming always to be treading on red-hot bricks.

In spite of his eccentricities, however, he had a gentle and kindly side to his nature, and I grew eventually to like and admire him. A fearless and capable pilot, he flew every aircraft we had, and possessed great talents as an innovative do-it-yourselfer, constructing strange machines in his spare time, using light-aircraft engines and airscrews he always managed to obtain from 'undisclosed sources'.

He also, now and then, demonstrated acute delusions of grandeur, modelling himself on our own General Montgomery, who, in 1942, conducted his affairs in the Western Desert from a comfortable furnished caravan, thus persuading Sanders to do the same. With the result that later, after the D-Day landings in France, the 100th Wing Headquarters often managed to find itself in some broken-down French chateau in which there were vast if horribly damaged bedrooms and lavatories – although, it must be said, the lavatories were always facilities that were especially welcomed by me!

It soon became obvious to me that Quesada and Sanders were cast in the same mould, so that they frequently struck sparks from each other. I particularly recall one occasion when they met on the airfield at Ibsley and Quesada, having ridden madly around the perimeter track on a motorcycle, immediately challenged Sanders to follow suit, which, of course, he did, with wild gestures and whoops of excitement – obliging me, a wide-eyed foreign onlooker, to watch two 40-year-old senior officers demonstrating childish acts of one-upmanship that were almost too embarrassing to behold.

As a young RAF officer of 23, who had been flying a fighter aircraft for almost four years, I had infinitely more war experience than the other 30-odd officers and senior NCOs who worked with and around me during those early months, despite the many 'rubber' medal ribbons some of them wore on their uniforms. Aware that I had flown throughout the Battle of Britain, in the Siege of Malta and more recently in the bitter duels that had taken place over the English Channel, they viewed me with perhaps exaggerated respect, tolerating my strange remarks and habits and always acquiescing to my whims, whether or not they agreed with them. In short, everyone – including Colonel 'Tex' Sanders – dealt with me generously and very circumspectly and, not to put too fine a point on it, I took advantage of their good nature.

Such then was the situation at the end of my first month with the 100th Fighter Wing. I was flying a great deal, had made many good friends and was more than satisfied with my lot. I could even cope with maple syrup being poured over my morning eggs and bacon. Yes, life was pretty good. Not bad at all, in fact!

Chapter 3
Early Days

As spring 1944 approached, I found myself busily employed lecturing successive groups of pilots and others on the geography and history of England and the near Continent, air warfare during and since the Battle of Britain, fighter tactics in general and the capabilities of the Luftwaffe.

I was especially careful to point out that, unlike the USA, Britain had already been at war for almost five years. The citizens of England, therefore, with their property and animals, having been showered from the heavens with the debris of battle, deserved some consideration; courtesy when flying was the least they should expect. Furthermore, a German invasion having long since been averted, it was now unnecessary to drive around the country lanes like dingbats or go about armed to the teeth, expecting an enemy face to appear round every hedge.

All my talks were quietly and courteously received, but one in particular lives on in my memory; indeed the whole day turned out to be rather special!

On that occasion, my lecture was attended by no less than the top brass: Major General Elwood R. Quesada of the 19th Tactical Air Command, and Colonel Homer 'Tex' Sanders of the 100th Fighter Wing, both of whom sat in the front row looking a trifle pensive, I thought, wondering no doubt how well I would perform. Behind them, in the vast, silent space of No. 1 hangar, RAF Ibsley, sat about 50 officers and others, plus several rows of faceless characters at the back.

They need not have worried, as my talk went down splendidly and was received in pin-drop silence; in fact, I was quite bucked to be given a generous round of applause when I concluded after a full hour of non-stop talking. After which, of course, came a short break and questions, most of them to the point and very pertinent, and others I can only describe as being a little facetious, even bizarre – where, for example, did Robin Hood and Maid Marian live in Sherwood Forest, and was King Arthur's round table still to be seen in some local castle?

There were also some conversations relating to the antecedents of some of those present. I well recall a Captain Isaac Isador Azimow hinting that his forebears may have come from Scotland, and my straight-faced response that with a name like his it was highly unlikely. Later, I amused myself by visualising the captain in his MacAzimow tartan kilt, striding across the Perthshire hills!

'Tex' Sanders, after congratulating me on my talk, asked, 'Say, that Queen you were talking about: who was she again?'

'Boadicea,' I explained. 'Queen Boadicea of the Iceni tribe, who lived in East Anglia about 2,000 years ago. There is a statue of her, driving her chariot, on the Thames Embankment next to Westminster Bridge.'

'And she actually knocked off 65,000 Roman soldiers?'

'Well, that's what the history books tell us.'

My senior paused, giving it some thought, before giving a lewd wink and shaking his head in apparent admiration. 'Yup! She was certainly some gal! Probably had hair on her chest.'

And I remember smiling to myself and thinking: What an extraordinary man this is!

Towards 4 p.m. on the same day, I received a telephone call asking me to get in touch with a Colonel 'Anonymous', who was lodging in the White Hart Inn in nearby Ringwood. I say 'Anonymous', as he was a complete stranger and we met for so short a time that it is perhaps understandable that, almost 70 years later, his name escapes me.

A 'bird' Colonel, from I imagined at the time 9th USAAF headquarters (or possibly that of the 3rd US Army), he declared himself to be a peacetime academic from Cambridge, Massachusetts, which suggested to me that he was on the faculty at Harvard University,

although he never at any time said so. Apparently he had been one
of the faceless people in the back row during my lecture. Interested
in what I had said, he wished to meet me, as his speciality was
history and his particular brief was to keep a running diary
during the forthcoming invasion of Europe and, as an official
archivist, to chronicle events as they occurred. About 52 years of
age, he seemed a most cultured and pleasant man, and I was most
impressed.

After he had fed me a stiffish Bourbon whiskey, which I did not
enjoy particularly but which loosened my tongue, we ate a simple
five-shilling fish-pie meal and began talking. His questions were
fairly predictable. Was it a culture shock being a single blue dot in
a sea of brown? Was I being treated with consideration? How did I
find the quality of my colleagues, compared with those in the RAF?
What US aircraft had I flown and how did they measure up? And
other questions that were broadly similar.

Naturally, I replied quite truthfully that I was very happy and had
no complaints. However, I was surprised a little on two grounds:
that pretty well all my headquarters colleagues came from the
southern states, and that they all roundly despised and loathed
President Roosevelt, their Commander in Chief. Which, considering the esteem in which the President was held in Britain and the
fact that our Prime Minister, Mr Churchill, held him in such high
regard, was to me a most unusual and rather unpleasant attitude to
take and even hinted at disloyalty.

The Colonel took some to time to consider his reply but finally
answered fully and with vigour.

No, he was not in the least surprised that the bulk of the 100th
Wing headquarters staff came from the south. He had not had the
opportunity to meet many of my colleagues personally but he would
wager a bet that there would not be a black face among them, nor
even a coloured pilot in any of the Wing's fighter squadrons. The
Mason–Dixon line was not just a geographical landmark of what
was perceived to be the northern and southern states of the eighteenth century: it also created a cultural divide, which still existed.
The entrepreneurial north was more industrialised, possessed a

powerful work and profit ethic, and only thought about military issues when forced to do so. In the view of many in the north, service life was for those incapable of earning a living any more sensible way.

For the southern states, however, life in the services was an honourable profession among a people who, only eighty years earlier, had come second in a particularly bloody civil war and who were still muttering and seething in defeat. Although the war was fought in the main to abolish slavery, there was still a colour bar in many southern states, and a much-diminished Ku Klux Klan was still carrying out its vile operations, though now to a far lesser degree. In short, the people of the south and north were just plain different, and would remain so until the present war, and the vast upsurge of movement throughout the country that would inevitably take place because of it, caused a merging of population and ideas and brought about lasting change.

About Franklin Delano Roosevelt, the Colonel prefaced his remarks with the rather surprising information that he had been a peripheral associate of the President for more than fifteen years. And, furthermore, that you did not have to be someone based in the south to dislike him, as Roosevelt had all the unfortunate baggage that went with being a member of a very wealthy and highly politically motivated family: he was an able lawyer who exhibited leftish, liberal views, but also a hard-nosed Yankee businessman who always demanded cash for goods delivered or services rendered. For three terms of office, the President had won the respect of most – though certainly not all – of the nation, for his leadership in restoring the USA to a sort of equilibrium after the horrors of the stock market crash of the early 1930s. However, employing his newly introduced 'fireside chats', he not only had the annoying characteristic of believing he could convince most people of pretty well anything but was also, unfortunately, a man of obsessions. No, FDR was by no means everyone's cup of tea.

As regards his relationship with Mr Churchill, the two were certainly friendly and cooperative but each had axes to grind. The Prime Minister and Britain needed Roosevelt and the USA to guarantee Britain's security and eventual winning of the war. However, FDR had long held a vision of the United States becoming *the* supreme world power, in which case the immediate threat from Germany would have to be removed, using Britain as an essential island base from which to launch a final assault. In the Colonel's view, Roosevelt, coming from Dutch and French stock, had no special affection for Britain; in fact he saw the British Empire, against which he was obsessively opposed, as already in the process of disintegration and was determined by every means within his power to hasten its end.

It was against that background that the Colonel saw Churchill and Britain being gently sidelined by Roosevelt in the months ahead, to be replaced by Stalin's Russia, which, though communism was always to be deplored, had the massive manpower and ruthlessness to be a successful ally. That he, Roosevelt, would eventually be able to 'civilise' the loathsome Stalin and his poisonous creed was, in his mind anyway, not in doubt.

As a completely non-political young man of 23 at the time, the Colonel's words and the information they imparted came to me, as something of a shock and I listened, more than a little disturbed, to his monologue.

If the Colonel was correct, how could Mr Churchill be so misled by the President's apparent friendliness and cooperation? Or was he, Mr Churchill, and of course the British government, as naively deceived and misled as they appeared? To me, so lacking in wisdom and experience, and finding diplomacy and politics such arcane subjects, clearly only time would tell.

The surprises continued, as the Colonel suddenly changed tack and asked me several most unusual questions: was I in any way religious and did I believe that there was such a thing as divine intervention? When he saw me wide-eyed and unable to give an immediate answer, he smiled and helped me out by explaining his own views on the subject.

Apparently, his first American relation was a German mercenary soldier who fought in the British Army in the American War of Independence and was wounded and then captured at Saratoga in

1777. Recovering later but choosing not to be repatriated, his forebear remained in America, a resentful and bitter immigrant.

According to the Colonel, the Battle of Saratoga was a battle the British Army should never have lost. The overall plan, devised by the British General John Burgoyne, was absolutely sound and was being carried out, admittedly with many difficulties, with some success. There would be a three-pronged attack that would split the rebellious colonies in two, one driving southwards from Canada in the north, a second eastwards from Lake Ontario along the Mohawk Valley, and the two finally joining up at Albany on the Hudson River with major elements of General Sir William Howe's relieving force, which would march northwards from New York. But Sir William, an unpredictable man, for reasons of his own, split his command, marched the major part of his army southwards towards Philadelphia and left Burgoyne stranded with a rapidly weakening force, obliging him finally to surrender.

Similarly in 1781, under the able leadership of General Lord Cornwallis, the British Army, having won a series of lesser victories, was gradually weakened by losses, exhaustion and lack of supplies. Finally, in the face of growing opposition on land and sea, not least from the opportunist French, Cornwallis retreated to Yorktown on the shore of Chesapeake Bay, where he waited in expectation of support and rescue by the Royal Navy – support that never materialised, resulting eventually in final surrender and the loss of the American colonies.

Clearly, in each case, defeat could mostly be ascribed to sound plans and properly considered courses of action being changed by unforeseen circumstances or ignored in the heat and stress of battle. More difficult to explain, however, were the changes of heart and mind among both leaders and led – on both sides – that brought about such changes: changes that could never properly be identified or explained, and that might almost be described as baffling, even mysterious.

Finally, no doubt aware of my involvement in the Battle of Britain, the Colonel used it as another example to further emphasise his conviction.

In the autumn of 1940, the Luftwaffe, very much superior in terms of numbers, was more than holding its own against RAF Fighter Command during the preliminary phase of the German invasion plan and causing very significant losses among the defending Spitfires and Hurricanes. Suddenly, however, as the result of a series of quite trifling RAF bombing attacks on mainland Germany, Hitler had apparently flown into a rage and ordered a change of plan. The new intention, he ordered, would not be to destroy Fighter Command but to break the morale of the British people by bombing their cities to rubble. His senior generals protested strenuously but he vetoed their objections. The result? The Battle of Britain was lost for Germany, the invasion of Britain postponed indefinitely and the course of the Second World War dramatically altered in favour of the Allies.

Was Hitler's change of heart really the result of a minor fit of rage, the Colonel wondered? Or was it not something considerably more than a mere act of fate?

I well recall the Colonel talking to me into the night and me retiring eventually to my iron-roofed Ibsley bedroom in no easy frame of mind. What was I to make of the man? What was I to make of his seemingly outlandish theories? He seemed a reasonable, even impressive sort of officer, but was he just some sort of educated fantasist? My own knowledge of the war situation being less than comprehensive, I would clearly have to spend a lot of time in the local libraries, as there was very much more to learn.

I did not sleep for quite some time that night. A thought passed constantly through my head: 'There is a Divinity that shapes our ends. Rough hew them how we will.'

As best I can recall, my meeting with the Colonel occurred during the second week in February 1944. A year later, almost to the day, Germany was in the throes of defeat and a meeting was being held of the 'Big Three' at Yalta in the Crimea, to determine how a beaten Germany would be divided up and governed, and by whom. It was also agreed at the time that Russia would come into the war against Japan when the German war was formally declared over, a decision welcomed by the Americans, who anticipated enormous casualties without Russia's involvement.

A famous photograph was taken during that Yalta conference: of Churchill, Roosevelt and Stalin sitting together in a line, surrounded by their military advisers. The faces of the three tell a poignant story. On the right of the group, Stalin, whose massive armies were at that very moment rolling back the Germans towards Berlin, sat with a smug smile of success on his face, whilst on the extreme left, Churchill sat frowning and seemingly glumly isolated, the personification of a nation no longer in control of events, exhausted in treasure and manpower by six years of bitter conflict. And in the middle was Roosevelt, the major player, representing authority and the powerhouse of the Allies.

But on Roosevelt's face was the drawn and haggard look of death Within weeks, on Thursday, 12 April 1945, at the age of 63, Franklin Delano Roosevelt collapsed and died at his home in Warm Springs, Georgia, while having his portrait painted. A new president took over immediately, a chirpy little character called Truman – Harry Truman – as different from Roosevelt as chalk is from cheese. And immediately, new leaves began to be turned.

Sadly I was never to see or hear of the Colonel again. I so wished to have been able to discuss his beliefs and forecasts of the future with him further, and his views on divine influence, but it was not to be – which has always saddened me greatly.

I see from my flying logbook that, following my encounter with the Colonel, I spent the next several weeks engaged in little else but flying, visiting and generally amusing myself. However, my apparently frivolous activities were to prove most profitable.

My more frequent flights enabled me to become far better acquainted with the NCOs of 'the line', the rather tightly knit group of sergeants – the USAAF didn't seem to go in for any rank lower than sergeant – who were to service the aircraft I flew for the next twelve months; indeed, they became good if not intimate personal friends.

The crew chief, Top Sergeant Smedley, was a beanpole of a man, 6 feet 4 inches of silent acquiescence. Smedley never conversed and seldom spoke. He always listened, thought, nodded and then mostly did what he was asked to do. If he didn't agree with you, there was only a silent glare of disapproval. But a nice man withal; I never had any complaints.

My crew chief, however, had another side to his cooperative demeanour. Every several months, it would be as though a dam, long held in quivering restraint, burst forth and flooded its banks. Smedley would take a few days' leave – usually in London – go berserk, hit someone and get himself arrested, and then appear before his commanding officer, under guard and suitably penitent. After which he would be 'busted', to use the current term, to spend the next month or so languishing in the 'doghouse', only to be re-established within weeks to take up his former duties. During our time together, this happened on several occasions – he never seemed to learn.

This business of 'busting' an NCO, seemingly so prevalent in the USAAF, was quite foreign to me. Having been a commanding officer myself, I knew only too well that in the RAF to severely censure any senior NCO almost required an Act of Parliament. But not so with 'Tex' Sanders, it would appear.

Smedley's deputy, the incomparable Sergeant Carter, was big in every sense of the word. In his mid-thirties, he was large, physically, with hands to match, but a sound technician even so, capable of the most delicate and intricate work.

Although I was always cooperative, I have long held a picture in my mind's eye of him shaking his head, smiling broadly in my direction, whilst regarding me, I suspect, as a rather wayward schoolboy engaged in practices that verged on the illegal and irresponsible. In short, he was for ever tolerant of my strange ways and methods, and I always seemed to amuse him – even at 4 a.m. on the most miserable of mornings, when I occasionally became involved in some of my less impressive airborne dawn forays.

I was always aware that he had serviced Spitfires when serving with the first US fighter squadrons to be based in Britain, and both he and Smedley were later to be of great assistance to me when a Spitfire, quite by chance, fell into my hands.

Of the remaining three NCOs that formed 'the line' group, two were inconveniently named Smith, requiring me to identify them as 'Smitty Major' and 'Smitty Minor'. The third, considerately, bore the name Johnson.

About twenty-three, the same age as me, Smitty Major was an absolute gem of a young man, one of those priceless individuals who can turn his hand to almost anything. Although I was never able to identify his exact trade, he was always my expert when it came to electricity, American switches (the bane of my life), radio or indeed anything not actually concerned with piloting an aircraft. Because he so enjoyed being airborne, he eventually used to accompany me as a substitute second pilot whenever I flew the bigger twin-engined aircraft to which I graduated later on. An endearing characteristic was that he seldom wore one of those comic, crushed denim hats to which most other American servicemen seemed to be so passionately devoted.

Smitty Minor was altogether different. A more simple, 'homely' individual than the others, he had an unfortunate speech impediment, which made him the butt of jokes from time to time, but he was always diligent in an unsmiling way and more than pulled his weight during 'the line's' day-to-day duties. He was a serious, helpful man and I always got on well with him.

Of Johnson I have only distant memories, my recollections of his contribution to the flight being mainly associated with the business of refuelling and starting the many aircraft we possessed. I still see his face and his figure quite distinctly, but more than that, very little.

My memories, then, of the NCOs of 'the line' are of an agreeable, helpful and workmanlike group, quietly efficient and always willing to meet any demand I made of them. Until, very sadly, a few months later into 1944, my relationship with them – and indeed their own happy association with each other – was overtaken by misfortune and tragedy.

The first days of March saw the arrival of the two remaining members of the three RAF 'experts' promised to the 100th Fighter Wing by the Air Ministry: the intelligence officer, Squadron Leader Raymond Carr, and a flight lieutenant equipment officer, whose name I do not recall.

Carr, a quiet but delightful man with a wonderful sense of humour, was a volunteer reservist who had formerly been a solicitor practising in Brighton, and the equipment officer, somewhat out of character, a brisk down-to-earth businessman. Carr was to remain with me for almost a year but the equipment officer disappeared the day the Wing left to invade in July, his tasks no doubt completed. I got on well with them both and like to think that as a trio we made a worthwhile contribution during the Wing's rather haphazard formative weeks.

In early March I also re-established links with my old colleagues at Kirton-in-Lindsay. Rather to my surprise, since leaving Kirton in January, Group Captain John Hawtrey had kept in touch, and he had invited me more than once to visit my old OTU in Lincolnshire to allow them to have a sight of 'at least one of those streamlined bricks' the Yanks were now flying around England. So during that first week in March, I accepted his invitation and flew north in my P.47 on a day that was windy, bitterly cold and threatening snow.

And snow it did with a vengeance, so that when I reached Kirton, the grass airfield there was covered with a thick white blanket, obliging me to divert to Hibaldstow, a satellite airfield some 3 miles away.

Landing with difficulty into a pretty violent cross wind on the single usable runway, I finally skidded to an ungainly halt, profoundly thankful that I had arrived in one piece, to find the Group Captain waiting to greet me, having apparently driven over from the main airfield. True to form, he was uniquely different. Wearing his gold-tipped service dress hat but dressed incongruously in a long woolly cloak affair that stretched from shoulder to toe, and standing there shivering with cold, he so looked like an ancient Briton chieftain, or some character out of *The Last of the Mohicans*, that all he needed was a spear and a dash of woad, or a bow and arrow, to complete the quite ridiculous illusion.

As we greeted each other he saw me grinning, and he said, a

trifle testily, 'Don't snigger, dear heart! My late friends, the Kurds of northern Iraq, had an altogether more sensible response to winter than we have in civilised Britain, and dressed accordingly. And if you find my coat a little "pongy", it's because my batman's tomcat finds its way into my car now and then and pees on it, the horrible, ghastly creature. I keep threatening to shoot the wretched animal but my chap said he will leave if I do, and he's such a good cook, I can't afford to take the risk.' Then shaking his head theatrically: 'The terrible dilemmas we station commanders sometimes have to contend with, dear boy!'

Later, as we drove somewhat erratically the 3 miles through country lanes heaped and ridged with snow, the Group Captain explained that he had recently taken over the large six-bedroomed station commander's married quarters, where he now lived – rather grandly, it appeared – with several other senior officers. He added that I would be staying with him and not in the officers' mess, and that he had arranged a small dinner party that night, during which he was quite sure I would be given ample evidence of his batman's cooking expertise.

All of which pleased me enormously, as knowing my senior's background and rather expensive tastes, I had visions of a comfortable evening and night, with good food and pleasant company amid an ambience of wine, warmth and gently flickering coal fires – all a far cry from my spartan iron-topped living quarters in Ibsley, with its primitive mess hall, bare wooden tables, gauntly black stoves and unfamiliar, if more than ample, menus.

And I was not disappointed; indeed my visit to Kirton as a whole turned out to be an event I had cause to remember for the rest of my service career.

The reason for my including this anecdote is that it gives me the opportunity of introducing one of my dinner companions that night, Wing Commander E B Hughes, the OTU's Chief Technical Officer, who for several years had been a rather unusual friend of mine.

I had met 'Bert' Hughes fleetingly during the first several years of the war and it was only when we served together for six months

at Kirton-in-Lindsay that I came to know him intimately. With me
the chief flying instructor and him the chief technical officer, we
naturally had much to do with each other, and I soon came to value
his knowledge and advice and to admire him for his sheer down-to-
earth ability and good sense. Moreover, not only was he an excellent technician, but as President of the Mess Committee, he also ran
the RAF officers' mess very successfully, maintaining an extraordinary level of excellence there whilst demanding a high standard
of discipline from the many specialist NCOs, airmen and WAAFs
involved.

As he and I formed an increasingly close relationship, to others
we must have appeared a very odd couple indeed. I was a young
'flying type', fair-complexioned and 6 feet 3 inches tall, whilst he
was very much a 'ground type', positively tiny – not more than
5 feet 3 inches – dark-haired and, at around 45 years of age, a generation older.

A lowly flight mechanic in the RFC and RAF during the latter
part of the First World War, Bert wore the MBE and the two usual
'Mutt and Jeff' (Victory and General Service) medal ribbons on his
uniform, plus the Long Service and Good Conduct award, the latter
in recognition of twenty-one years of undetected crime – or so it
was often jokingly alleged.

Rising through the ranks between the wars, he was commissioned in the late 1930s and by the time we met again in 1943, he was
a senior wing commander with a lifetime's experience of servicing
all types of aircraft.

He had a delightful wife, who, like him, was positively wee,
but they were unhappily childless and I often suspected that Bert
regarded me as the son he had never been able to father: he was
kind to me beyond belief. I will always remember him as a generous, uncomplicated man with smiling, deep-set eyes in a face I can
only describe as very well lived in. I had liked him enormously from
the start and we would never exchange a cross word throughout
our many years of friendship.

And when I was leaving Kirton the day after our very pleasant
evening as the Group Captain's guests Bert drew me aside and

whispered that he would shortly be moving on down south, probably to the RAF fighter station at Ford, near Arundel, on the south
coast.

Ford! Not too far from me. I made a mental note of his casual
remark – and it would prove to be just as well that I did.

Chapter 4

A Testing Time

I have always regarded the last two weeks in March 1944 as a testing time, as not only did I fly everything the 100th Fighter Wing had to offer, but I was also called upon to fly aircraft of other organisations and in other places.

In our Ibsley mess hall at about noon, on a date I do not exactly recall, I was manfully tackling a heap of Hungarian goulash spread over a mound of potato and sweetcorn when I was called to the telephone and summoned to the front entrance.

There I was confronted by an RAF officer who, after stiffening to attention, announced himself respectfully as Flight Lieutenant Gunn (probably not his correct name but it will suffice), the engineer officer in charge of a small maintenance unit offshoot stationed at RAF Stoney Cross airfield, a few miles north and east of Ibsley.

Then, properly at ease and bending his knees like a pantomime policeman, Gunn began to explain.

Apparently his small unit collected most of the lesser-damaged aircraft that had force landed or crashed within a 50-mile radius of Stoney Cross and, if possible, repaired them. The work completed, each aircraft then had to be flight tested before it could be collected and flown away, and thus far he had usually called upon a pilot of No. 616 Squadron, then stationed at Ibsley, to help him out. However, as 616 had since left the area, and having been told that I was living with the Americans and might possibly be available to assist, he felt ... Well, he just felt he had to ask.

I found myself smiling. New aircraft to fly! Why not, for heaven's sake?

'So what aircraft are you expecting to have?' I heard myself asking.

I detected a slight hesitation in Gunn's reply. 'Well, I've a Lysander ready and waiting right now, sir. With one or two others in the pipeline.'

Hearing the word 'Lysander', the smile died on my face, as I recalled a nasty incident at Ringway aerodrome in 1939 that had nearly ended my flying career before it had begun.

'Lysander!' I felt myself frowning. 'I don't really know. I've never flown one of those wretched things and I'm not sure I want to have my first go on an aircraft you've just built up from scrap.'

But, smiling now, Gunn clearly felt he was on firm ground. 'You have my word, sir, that this aircraft is absolutely guaranteed. Anyway, a chap with your experience should have no problem with a clapped-out old Lizzie!'

At which point, I have to admit, my pallid resistance crumbled.

The 100th Fighter Wing provided a 'recon' – a reconnaissance vehicle, a two-ton soft-topped truck – to transport me to Stoney Cross. It was driven by yet another sergeant, whose appearance and accent marked him down immediately as a Kentucky farm boy. For some obscure reason, but probably because we were never properly introduced, I privately christened him 'Kaintucky Zeke', and would always remember him as such.

A large and primitive man with fingers like an assortment of newly gathered parsnips, Kaintucky Zeke had, I was soon to learn, an eye permanently focused on a 'passel' of 'bottom land' bulging with 'corn, 'bacca and 'trawberries'. To Kaintucky Zeke the world struggle against Nazi tyranny was little more than an inconvenient interlude and I listened, not for the first time with an indifference only just within the bounds of courtesy, to the man's juvenile ecstasies as the recon pursued an erratic course around the side roads of Hampshire.

Flight Lieutenant Gunn was waiting on a hardstanding to greet me, his face registering a mixture of surprise and relief as I appeared. A Lysander, painted in various shades of earth-brown and green in addition to black, stood silent and brooding in the background.

'So why the coat of many colours?' I enquired.

'It came from the cloak-and-dagger boys at Tangmere,' Gunn explained. 'It was caught on the ground and the chap in the back shot. Fortunately the pilot was only winged and managed to take off and get back across the Channel. After that he force landed on Chesil Beach, wiped off part of the undercarriage, and damaged the fuselage and part of the wing.' Then, glancing mischievously in my direction, he said, 'However, we've removed all the bloodstains and replaced everything else that was necessary. And the engine seems to be all right.'

'What d'you mean, "seems" to be all right?' I asked suspiciously. 'You sound as if you're not quite sure.'

At this Gunn smiled a secret smile, no doubt believing he had this young whippersnapper squadron leader a little rattled.

'No, what I mean is, we didn't have to change the engine. We gave it the usual once-over but everything was within limits.' Then, clearly not wishing to ruffle me more than was absolutely necessary, he added encouragingly, 'But we did replace the airscrew, so everything should be OK.'

Together, we walked forward and inspected the aircraft, with me – not having been within a mile of a Lysander for many years – feeling as though I were inspecting a pterodactyl.

However, I then signed the form 700, signifying acceptance of the aircraft, and began struggling into my parachute harness. After which, from a slightly stooped position, I glanced without enthusiasm towards the cockpit.

'Right, if you'll now show me how to get into the cockpit, we'll get this hen coop into the air.'

Climbing with difficulty on to the wheel housing, by a devious route I found my way into the cockpit, being pushed in the rump by a cooperative Gunn, who delivered terse words of advice from somewhere underneath.

Settling myself eventually into the pilot's position, I felt at least a mile from the ground, totally unprotected and surrounded by glass, and nakedly accommodated in a bucket seat with two wings sprouting from my ears. There was nothing much in front either: it was quite unlike a Spitfire, whose nose reached out ahead the length of a cricket pitch. Moreover, the control column didn't break in the middle like that of a fighter, but grew like a stalk out of the floor. There was also a mass of space, instruments everywhere, and a rather peculiar non-fighter-type smell – old spies, I concluded with a ghost of a smile. I waggled the controls and kicked the rudder bar, which, because the brakes were on, hissed back at me like a couple of truculent cobras.

Meanwhile, Gunn, who had been clambering up behind me, arrived beside my left ear, breathing heavily. Clutching the edges of the cockpit framework and balanced precariously on the junction of the wing strut and wheel housing, he began to point out the various controls.

'First, this Lizzie has a constant speed airscrew. OK? Most of 'em are fitted with the old two-pitch.'

I nodded.

Gunn helped himself to another deep breath. 'Right. Petrol cocks here, on the left. Primer over there – four strokes will do in this weather, and don't forget to screw it up afterwards. It starts on that button there. All the other controls and instruments pretty normal. No radiator, of course, on these. Cooling gills are operated by that gizmo there on the end of that stick thing. Have them open for taxiing and when the temperature gets above normal. Otherwise have them at trail, as the Yanks say, or closed – suit yourself.'

I put in, 'And what's normal?'

Gunn was dismissive. 'Oh, just somewhere in the middle.'

'The middle! The middle of where?'

'The middle of the dial!' Gunn frowned. 'Where was I? Oh, yes. Radials are a bit more fussy about oil temperature than in-line engines. Don't attempt to take off with the oil like glue as you do with the Merlin, although the book says you can, I believe. Let it get to about 15 degrees to be on the safe side. Those things there are the heating controls, which you can use on the run-up. That knob there! That's right. Pull it out but don't forget to push it back before take-off. What else? Oil pressure 80 to 90lbs, the usual bit. Oh, and the fuel contents are behind you.'

'Where?'

'Behind you. Through that hole. Silly place, really. But that's life, isn't it? The tank's full anyway, so forget about it.'

'And what are these wheels for?' I enquired, feeling left and right of my seat.

'Which? Oh, those! The one you're holding adjusts your seat and the other is the tail trimmer. And watch out: it really does trim the tail. The whole caboodle wanders about at the back end, so treat it gently. And the seat sometimes gives way and you fall into the bottom of the cockpit. But . . .' he waved his hand airily.

At this point Gunn fell silent, gazed around vacantly for a moment, and said, 'Well, that's about it, I think.' He then tried to change feet, lost his foothold, and disappeared from sight with a strangled cry.

I looked down to where the man was picking himself up.

'Are you all right? And is that all?'

Recovering, he limped away, muttering, 'Ready when you are.'

As there seemed little else to do, I unscrewed the Ki-Gas primer, adjusted the selector, first to 'carburettor' and then to 'engine', and squirted in jets of fuel. Then, setting the throttle to what I thought was a sensible amount, I switched on the magneto and ignition switches and pressed the starter button.

Ahead, one finger of the airscrew jerked into motion and, with a rumble and a cloud of blue smoke that spread around like a gas attack, the engine caught and everything in sight began to shake. On the instrument panel a few dials came to life, and a little pointer appeared from nowhere and began hopping rapidly up and down in the oil pressure gauge.

When everything had finally quietened down, I sat for a time collecting my thoughts, after which, just a trifle on edge, I waved away the chocks and inched forward the throttle.

The Lysander, its engine bubbling throatily, trundled off, with me feeling totally exposed and as though I were on stilts. I immediately tried the brakes and was relieved to find they worked before wriggling my rear more comfortably into its parachuted bucket seat. Then, feeling a little more relaxed, as everything seemed to be in good working order, I was able to raise a smile. All right so far!

I turned right at the perimeter track but, after taxiing for 100 yards or so, discovered I was heading in the wrong direction. Rather than admit my error, I resolved to do a complete circuit of the airfield and was happy to let the aircraft amble ahead, kicking it around the corners with the aid of the two cobras hissing amiably at me at feet level.

After a good ten minutes' meandering around rural Hampshire, I reached a runway that appeared to be the one in use. Braking to a standstill, I tidily replaced all the knobs I had previously pulled out, checked my instruments and settings, and gave an extra tug to tighten my straps. Then, taking a deep breath, I opened the throttle to test the engine before turning into wind.

In front, nothing happened. I opened the throttle further. No response. Finally, I shoved it open all the way, but the engine continued its subdued bubbling and the airscrew resolutely refused to rotate any faster.

Perplexed, I closed the throttle and tried again. A third open. Then half open. Finally, fully open. But nothing. The engine seemed hell bent on just ticking over and doing precisely nothing.

I sat there frowning and feeling an utter passenger before shrugging resignedly. A pox on all Lysanders and this one in particular! I then bent forward and switched off. The airscrew flicked almost to a standstill but then set off again stubbornly as the engine gave out a series of strangled, smoking coughs. That, however, proved to be the end of its protest, for it finally jerked to a stop with a metallic click, before ticking at me meanly as I sat there at an altitude of 12 feet, in splendid and isolated silence.

Two minutes later a jeep arrived and, with a squeal of tyres, braked to a standstill alongside me. Flight Lieutenant Gunn's face appeared at the open window.

'What's the matter?'

'It won't go,' I replied.

Gunn got out, looking pained, and shouted up to me, 'Something wrong?'

'It just won't go,' I repeated, articulating clearly as though speaking to a half-wit.

'Have you coaxed her?'

'Coaxed her!' I felt my brows gathering. 'Look, I'm not discussing treaty rights with a ruddy engine. Either it goes when I tell it to or we cease to be friends. I've had the throttle wide open twice and it won't go faster than a tick-over. Something must be stuck,' I added in a more conciliatory tone, remembering a Hurricane in Malta which had exhibited approximately the same symptoms when sand had insinuated itself into the works.

Gunn scrambled up and arrived, panting, within inches of my head.

'Must remember not to fall off this damn thing,' he muttered darkly to himself. Then, for my benefit, added, 'Look, sir, I should have told you. These Mercury radials tend to coke up if you leave them ticking over too long. Fuel and oil ...' He suddenly clutched wildly at the open window. 'God! I nearly did it again, didn't I?' He gave a near hysterical giggle before continuing between gulps, 'Right. Fuel and oil coke up, particularly in the bottom cylinders. You've got to clear them out – jolly them along. Catch the engine on the throttle, but for God's sake, don't make it blow back whatever you do, or I shall have a cracked exhaust ring on my hands and there isn't another one between here and Inverness. OK?' He backed down carefully. 'Are all the switches off?'

I nodded.

'Right. I'm going to turn her over to see if she's not hydraulicking.'

'You're going to *what*?'

'To see if she's not ... Oh, never mind!'

Gunn disappeared somewhere in front and the airscrew began to move round in jerks. As it did so, I sat there for a minute, still feeling like the passenger I so obviously was, until Gunn reappeared, wiping his hands on a handkerchief.

'All right? Don't prime her, for Pete's sake. Just give her about an inch of throttle and try her again on internals. If she won't take it, I'll have to go back and get a battery.'

Half hoping the engine would not start, I set the throttle, switched on, pressed the starter button and, to my surprise and embarrassment, after one revolution of the airscrew, the monster in front burst into life with a roar.

Feeling about an inch high, I throttled back but in response to Gunn's silent mouthings to 'Run her up!', I gingerly opened the throttle again as instructed, whereupon the big Mercury's rumblings crescendoed, setting up a whirlwind straight ahead which, to my quiet satisfaction, plucked off Gunn's hat and sent it floating away like a leaf.

I then tried the magneto switches in turn and the revs fell obligingly, but well within limits. Well, how about that? The wretched engine was as sound as a bell! Why on earth didn't it do that before?

Stung into retaliation by the intransigence of my mount, I turned swiftly into wind and, without further ado, opened up. The engine in front thundered away in a rumbustious but pleasing basso profundo, and the built-in hurricane started up again. The Lysander accelerated swiftly along the runway and, with tail down, hopped into the air like a goosed angel – a current and much favoured expression in the 100th Fighter Wing.

At 50 feet, with the airfield rapidly dropping away behind, I became convinced that I was airborne in a Matilda tank. The long stick of the control column seemed rooted to the centre of the cockpit, so that even the slightest lateral movement required both hands. However, always one to resolve my problems singly, I trimmed the aircraft into a climb, adjusted the throttle and airscrew pitch controls to what I considered to be respectable settings, and kept the aircraft straight. In front, with the engine thundering away reassuringly, we all went up like a lift.

At 1,000 feet, I throttled back and took stock. For one horrifying moment, I thought that someone had left the control locks on the ailerons. Such things did occur from time to time. I well remembered a chap at FTS (Flying Training School) at Montrose attempting a dive-bombing sortie in an old Audax, only to return to the airfield complaining that the aircraft appeared to be jolly heavy in the climb and dive. It certainly must have been, as the two wooden slats, clipped on to the elevators to prevent them flapping about in a wind, had been left in place. Everyone laughed themselves sick over that, of course, and christened the pilot 'Muscles', a name he was known by for years to come. But, like having your car stolen, that sort of thing was much funnier when it happened to someone else.

Meanwhile, the Lysander seemed quite content to bumble ahead and, feeling like a child in a high chair, I began to enjoy the splendid, uninterrupted view. I flew over Ringwood and then down towards Bournemouth, where the sea glinted at me, all silver and grey; and on the dashboard, the instruments all registered unobjectionable amounts and quantities, apart from the little oil pressure pointer, which kept jumping up and down like a hiccupping sprite.

After that, and quite by accident I suppose, my gaze eventually focused on the cylinder-head temperature gauge, an instrument with which I was barely familiar, having only rarely flown behind big radial engines and certainly not one as moody as the brute in front of me.

As Gunn had been singularly unhelpful as regards the proper temperature at which to run it, I decided at first to adhere to the age-old principle that if something does not show signs of either expiring or kicking up a fuss, you leave it alone. There was certainly nothing to complain about thus far, the temperature needle being as steady as a rock.

On the other hand, I would be a poor specimen indeed if I didn't play about with the gills a little, just to see what happened. So I worked the appropriate control and the cowling gills fanned out obligingly.

At that moment, however, the aircraft was facing south-west, so that the sun, slanting in from the left, made silhouettes of several of the cylinders beneath the cowling; and, to my horror, I saw valve springs hopping up and down like mad, so that I had a creepy feeling that someone had just laid bare my heart and entrails and that I was watching my very life-supporting system operating. With a shudder, I wound the gills shut again. Engines, like internal organs, were best left alone to get on with the job for which they were designed.

Returning towards the New Forest area, I picked out the old sailing-ship construction yard of Bucklers Hard before banking towards Stoney Cross. The airspeed indicator showed 140 miles per hour and the altimeter 3,800 feet. I inched back the throttle, the engine note died to a whisper and I began to lose height.

After floating downwind I turned on to my crosswind leg and felt automatically for the undercarriage lever. It was missing!

For a good five seconds I looked around the cockpit, before catching a glimpse of the projection on one of the undercarriage housings. Of course! Fool that I was! The wheels were permanently down. I found myself grinning sheepishly into my face mask, thankful that no one had been witness to my stupidity.

Before me, the main runway stretched ahead, more than a mile of it. I throttled back further and the speed dropped to 100 miles per hour ... then to 90 ... The tail began to sink but the aircraft went floating on ... and on ... and on ... and on! The flaps – where were the ruddy flaps? I hunted around the cockpit for them but no flaps were evident.

I looked up. Lord above! I was already halfway across the airfield in an aircraft I was supposed to be able to land on a sixpence.

I was down to about 80 miles per hour when something fell out with a detectable clatter. As my mind groped for an explanation of this new phenomenon, I cast an anxious glance to my left and was intrigued to observe the flaps sneaking into the open like mice from a hole. What in heaven's name was happening?

I gave a quick look over the rumbling engine and saw New Forest trees almost within touching distance. Recognising the need for instant action, I thrust open the throttle and was mightily relieved when the whirlwind in front started up again and the Lysander climbed away steeply, requiring me to trim forward with considerable dispatch to keep the rising nose in check. Wow! Deep, deep breath!

Back at 1,000 feet, I throttled back and looked around. This brute was part of a conspiracy: first the engine and now this! I was being frightened to death.

Breathing deeply to calm myself, I flew straight and level and gave the matter some thought. Then, closing the throttle, I hauled up the nose – which felt like lifting a pail of wet cement – and, taking care to keep my feet level, let the speed die away, trimming meticulously meanwhile.

At something below 90 miles per hour, some of the slats at the end of the wing began to flutter in and out. A few moments later, others closer to the cockpit began to appear, in company with the flaps, which drooped into sight hesitantly and with obvious reluctance. Finally, as the speed decreased, everything settled down in the fully extended position, after which it was all plain sailing.

Confident now that I had got the hang of things, I inched open the throttle again, and with the tail well down and the aircraft's nose in the air, I maintained height in the slow-flying attitude, with the ASI showing 65 miles per hour.

Eureka! Lysanders were splendid aircraft. Well ... almost splendid!

Five minutes later, I floated in on my final approach, the nose of the aircraft well up and the big Mercury bubbling quietly.

As I crossed the threshold of the runway, I was so engrossed with the action of the slats and automatic flaps that I quite neglected to note that I was still six feet up.

Suddenly, the Lysander decided to stop flying and, tilting a wing with evil intent, fell to earth like a shot grouse. As it crunched into the tarmac, my seat shot to the bottom of its travel, depositing its very surprised pilot instantly and painfully into the bottom of the cockpit. Simultaneously, there was a crash as a window flew open (or out, I didn't know which, exactly). My nerves in shreds, I could barely summon sufficient concentration to keep the aircraft straight.

With the two cobras hissing frantically beneath my feet, the Lizzie squealed to a halt, whereupon the engine gave three greasy, blue coughs and expired.

After that, there was only the malevolent ticking of the contracting exhaust ring and the sound of my heavy breathing.

For a good several minutes I sat motionless, gathering myself at first and then attempting to raise myself from the floor on which I had been so unceremoniously dumped. Looking around finally,

I saw Gunn's small car racing in my direction and, a little shame-faced, awaited its arrival.

When he had alighted, together with his corporal deputy, the engineer officer wiped his hands on his much-soiled handkerchief and, exhaling deeply, announced with admirable restraint that it might be necessary to 'check the slow running again on that engine'.

The Corporal, to whom his remarks were directed and who appeared rooted to the spot in expectation of another major repair job, nodded in agreement, adding that it might also be necessary to give the undercarriage another close inspection.

It was only at that point that I was able to relax a little, comforting myself that any landing that didn't draw blood or from which you could walk away was more than acceptable to me under the circumstances.

Chapter 5

More Challenges in the Air

Two days later, having returned to Ibsley after my undistinguished performance on the Lysander, I was more than a little surprised when I received yet another telephone call requesting my test-piloting skills. This came from Chattis Hill, a small horse-training gallops airfield I had never heard of. A distant unknown voice enquired: would I be available to test fly a Spitfire the following day, or if not then, as soon as possible?

I was soon to learn that Chattis Hill was within 10 miles of Salisbury and therefore in my local area, and that the Spitfire I was expected to fly was a Mark 8, a type on which I had no experience but one about which I knew a great deal.

The Mark 8, I was aware, was the planned successor to the Mark 5, which by 1943 had been totally outclassed by the German Focke Wulf 190 and relegated to being flown in a supporting role by RAF squadrons not in the front line. To bridge the gap, the Mark 9 had been quickly introduced. It was basically a Mark 5 with one of several more powerful Merlin 60-series engines to be installed. In fact, the Mark 9b with a Merlin 66 – the LF Mark 9, as it was officially referred to – was so successful that the Mark 8, which was altogether a more modern version of the Mark 9, was only employed in the Mediterranean area and the Far East and never used in Britain.

I had known Jeffrey Quill, the Supermarine Company's experimental test pilot for some years, and, as I recall, it was he who informed me of the Mark 8's history.

Apparently, in view of the growing importance of the Middle East, the Mark 8 was more or less earmarked as the aircraft to be employed in that area. Consequently, it was designed to incorporate a full tropical conversion, additional fuel tanks holding about

50 extra gallons, plus many other important modifications to wings, fuselage and armament. However, according to Jeffrey Quill – and a most controversial point, this – the first Mark 8s were fitted with extended wings, similar to those used on the Mark 6s and 7s, which were then regarded as specialist high-level interceptor aircraft, and were only ruled out after the strongest objections from Jeffrey himself, who always saw the Mark 8 as a splendid air combat fighter at medium heights. As a result, the new type, in his view, was not only the most delightful aircraft to fly but eventually the best Merlin-engined Spitfire ever produced.

With his plaudits in mind, I was naturally very keen to fly the aircraft. I was arranging to fly the Oxford up to Chattis Hill the following day, when I was confronted by Patterson, the second-string doctor on the headquarters staff, who, a trifle shyly, asked permission to fly with me in the second pilot seat, a request I was happy to grant.

Captain Robert A. Patterson (shortly to be promoted to Major) I had known only fleetingly since my arrival. I was well aware, even so, that over the preceding weeks, he had often sought my companionship, as he quite rightly recognised me as a means of getting himself airborne.

A qualified surgeon, Patterson was 29 years old and 6 feet 5 inches in height, sported a flat-top crew-cut hairdo and, because of rather poor eyesight, wore thick-lensed spectacles, always bringing to my mind the bottom of a Guinness bottle. He was passionately interested in aircraft and flying, but because of his impaired vision he was unable to fly operationally (or so he insisted), and eventually insinuated himself into the flying fraternity as an aviation medicine specialist. I was aware that he was fairly inexperienced, but as the 100th Fighter Wing line-up of communication aircraft included a variety of types, including a Mark 5 Spitfire, I naturally assumed he had enjoyed at least some experience on most, if not all, of them.

We flew up to Chattis Hill the following morning, to find a small grass landing area, apparently an offshoot of the Supermarine Company, where a small number of aircraft were being assembled and test flown. With the weather fine and clear, a brand-new Mark 8 Spitfire had been run out for my inspection and approval, accompanied by two white-coated ground staff.

The aircraft was freshly painted and looking immaculate, and Patterson and I walked around it beaming with appreciation and patting it reverently. Alongside, the white-coated assistants looked on, smiling, checking panels and fasteners, and positioning the starter battery and chocks.

After signing the paperwork and passing a final word, I climbed into the cockpit and settled down, rejoicing in the newness of it all and the perfume of the paint that was peculiarly Spitfire. Super! This was going to be fun.

I had no trouble with the cockpit, as it was almost identical to that of the Mark 9, with which I was totally familiar. So, starting up, I went through my cockpit drill, taxied away and then, turning into wind, took off.

Climbing up, with the Merlin howling like a dervish in front of me, I experienced anew the thrill and excitement of being airborne in such a thoroughbred aircraft, the curved wings with their brave cockades left and right of me, and the controls responding instantly to my slightest touch.

I flew first over Andover, and then turned south over Salisbury Plain, eventually curving towards the town and the 404-foot steeple of the elegant cathedral, experiencing the strange phenomenon of my stomach leaving me briefly when, flying close enough to the tall pointed spire, it connected me to the ground far below. How very unsettling and odd!

Then several aerobatics. First two slow rolls, with the engine pausing briefly as I introduced a touch of negative G. Then two of my favourite loops, with me standing the aircraft on its tail and waiting until the speed fell off into complete silence, so that the Spit either fell over backwards or silently toppled forwards, the latter manoeuvre leaving my stomach rising in its wake, the speed then rapidly increasing – 150 ... 200 ... 250 ... then 300 plus, the controls tightening as the aircraft dropped like a stone, the airflow hissing in my ears.

After that, the airfield again. I reduced speed around the circuit, lowering the wheels when 180 showed on the ASI. Then the curved approach, with 140 on the clock, which enabled me to lower the flaps – all or nothing at all on a Spit – heralding the near boundary fence, which flashed suddenly beneath my wheels, followed by the flattened spring-green grass of the airfield.

I held off, and waited ... and waited ... until the faint bump of landing occurred, followed by the final rocking jog that proved conclusively that I was down ... Down and safe, yet again. For the thousandth time, was it? Probably many more than that.

After taxiing in and closing down, I climbed out and chatted with the two white coats, telling them of my brief trip and thanking them for their assistance. I then turned towards Patterson, who was watching from a distance, a smile of envy on his face.

He called out, 'So how was it?' Then, when I made a favourable grimace, added, 'Lucky old you!'

To which I replied lightly, 'Want to have a go yourself?'

I saw him brighten immediately. 'Are you kidding?'

I returned a smiling shrug and, without thinking, replied, 'I'll ask the owners if you like.' Then, walking in their direction, I enquired, 'Might my American friend have a turn in your aircraft? Just a circuit or two? I've only been up half an hour, so it won't need refuelling beforehand.'

I saw the two exchange glances and their body language suggested that they didn't really care one way or the other – after all, they appeared to imply, it wasn't their Spitfire, was it?

So, after that most casual of arrangements, I found myself assisting Patterson into the cockpit, helping to adjust my parachute around his more ample middle and pointing out the controls. What is more, it never occurred to me at the time that I was doing anything either remotely naughty or ill considered. It just seemed a friendly thing to do.

As I watched, and somewhat to my surprise, it seemed to take an age for Patterson to sort himself out in the aircraft before managing to start the engine, with the help of the two white coats, and slowly taxi away; then an even longer time waiting at the far end of the landing field, preparing to take off – so long, in fact, that I began to fear that something might be amiss.

However, after a lengthy spell, I saw the airscrew dissolve into a blur of motion and the distant Spitfire gather speed. After which, after a minute or so, it was airborne and, with its wheels safely tucked away, it disappeared at low level into the distance.

The Spitfire having departed, the two white overalled assistants walked off, leaving me alone to take full advantage of a pleasant spring day.

A little distance away from our parked Oxford, I sat on the grass, and then lay back, looking up at the scattered drifting clouds and appreciating the scents and balmy silence of the Hampshire countryside. I glanced down at my watch. Patterson would be about 20 minutes, I reckoned. Time for a few moments' shut-eye.

After 25 minutes at least, I rose to my feet and looked about, faintly – just faintly – concerned. There was no sign of the Spitfire, and the terrible realisation began to dawn: had I been rash in suggesting that Patterson should take to the air in what was to us all a brand-new type of fighter? Had he the experience to cope with such an aircraft? His long delay in taking off was not exactly reassuring.

After some 35 minutes, I really began to worry. My apprehensions were clearly shared by the two white overalls who, I observed, were walking determinedly in my direction. When they arrived, their smiles were courteous but their question pointed: what had happened to my American friend and their rather important Spitfire? I don't think they found my explanation altogether convincing.

On tenterhooks, I was obliged to wait another fifteen minutes until, to my vast relief, Patterson returned, his aircraft appearing suddenly over the brow of a local rise, as though the pilot had suddenly come across the airfield quite by accident.

After circling the landing area at far too low a height, the Spitfire was brought in much too fast and was obliged to go round again. The delinquent doctor's second attempt, however, was rather better and the aircraft made what was usually described as a 'now me, now you!' landing: a series of minor kangaroo leaps, not exactly dangerous but not the sort likely to gladden the heart of any experienced pilot.

But the Lord be praised: the Spitfire was down. I found myself, eyes closed, thanking Providence for even that small mercy.

Aware that I was very cross with Patterson but not wishing to vent my displeasure in front of even a minor audience, I resolved to stand back initially and let him finish his brief conversation with the white overalls. However, when he finally joined me, I let fly, though in an undertone.

'Patterson, where in God's name have you been? You've been gone almost an hour and I've been worried sick.'

In an equally low voice, Patterson replied, 'OK, so I was lost! Your cotton-picking country is so covered with small towns, villages and crossroads, all looking exactly alike, I was lost within minutes. Why don't you guys have a desert, a range of mountains or something decently prominent round here, so that we dumb Americans can find our way about?'

I wasn't keen to let him off the hook, however. 'But weren't you aware that you must have been running short of fuel?'

'Short of fuel? I didn't look!'

'You didn't look! Not even at the fuel gauge on the dashboard?'

'No, I didn't look at the fuel gauge on the dashboard because I was far too busy flying the gol-darned aircraft! After all, I'd never flown one before!'

'*What?* You'd never flown a Spitfire before?' I could hardly believe my ears.

'Well, that's the long and short of it. Back at Ibsley, Jim Haun only allows me to fly the light, single-engined stuff. Those and twins like the Oxford. But only as second pilot, even on the Oxford.'

I felt my blood run cold. Lord above! The awful consequences resulting from Patterson crashing the Mark 8 beginning to dawn, I felt my knees turning to jelly. Had there been a chair within reach, I could well have been forced to sit on it.

★

When, some days later, Flight Lieutenant Gunn telephoned from Stoney Cross, inviting me to fly an Armstrong Whitworth Albemarle, my immediate reaction was one of dismay. My ploy was to play the idiot whilst I thought rapidly of a suitable excuse.

'Albemarle?' I echoed. 'What's that, a pub?'

Gunn, a reply already rehearsed, oozed unction. 'A lovely aircraft, sir. Absolutely straightforward. Tricycle undercart. Two big, fool-proof engines. A grown-up Anson, in fact. You'll be carried away.'

My suspicions in no way allayed by the words 'carried away', I enquired darkly, 'How grown-up?'

'Well ... roughly ... a biggish sort of Blenheim. A failed bomber, really. Too good-natured to drop bombs on people. Used for glider-towing now. We're giving them away to the Russkies, incidentally. Which rather proves my point, doesn't it? They'd have to be pretty simple for those chaps to fly them.'

But I persisted. 'What d'you mean by "biggish"?'

'Biggish? Well ... sort of Wellington size – more or less.'

'Wellington! But that's as big as a house!' I shook my head. 'No, I couldn't fly one of those things. Not first go. My total twin experience, I would have you know, is a couple of circuits and bumps in an Oxford. And that was after an alcoholic lunch.'

But Gunn was remorseless, bringing up his reserves. 'What about that Yankee P.38 you fly? That's a twin, isn't it? Or are my eyes deceiving me?'

This last remark rather floored me – I had forgotten all about the P.38 (Lightning) and was forced into: 'Ah, well! That's a fighter, isn't it? That doesn't really count.'

'Listen, sir.' Gunn lowered his voice and glanced around furtively, like a bookie contemplating escape. 'Little slips of girls in the ATA fly Albemarles all the time. On their own. Standing on their heads.'

I was determined to be unimpressed. 'What ATA girls do standing on their heads or in any other position is entirely their business. I'm a one-engine man! That much I can keep an eye on. And that's how it's going to stay.'

But, in my heart, I knew I was beaten.

The following day, I took Major Jim Haun, the section leader of

A3, to Stoney Cross. We found the Albemarle in a hangar and stood beneath it. It really was a whopper, all glass up front and at the back, with two thumping great airscrews attached to a pair of enormous Hercules engines. Huge, silent and above small iridescent pools of oil, it crouched there on its tricycle undercarriage, a menacing, darkly camouflaged shape.

'Jeez!' breathed Haun, removing his pipe for a moment to show how deeply he was moved. 'Are you aimin' to fly this, buddy boy?'

'We,' I corrected him evenly. 'That's why you're here, major mine!'

'Not me, old buddy!' Haun shook his head emphatically. 'No, sir! I'm not going to risk my butt in that hen coop. What did they do?' he asked incredulously. 'Make it up from a kit?'

I recall pulling a face. 'Oh, very droll, I'm sure. Is that your last word?'

'It sure is. Include me out!'

'What about the Atlantic Alliance, and all that?'

'To heck with the Alliance,' declared Haun. 'Get Patterson, the lunatic medic, to help you out. He'll be more use to you when they're digging you out of the wreck.'

When I explained my plan to Patterson, he replied immediately with spurious solemnity, 'OK, Squadron Leader, I'm your man. Let's go get it!'

The following day was bright and clear. With Patterson, I drove out to Stoney Cross, where the Albemarle had already been run out on to a hardstanding.

To me, it looked no less formidable than before. Patterson, on the other hand, viewed it with a keen and professional eye, much as he would a body to be dissected.

I confronted Flight Lieutenant Gunn. 'I do this under protest,' I complained, not exactly serious. 'If I prang, not only will I haunt you but my couple of hours in an Oxford are not going to look very convincing on the 765c accident form.'

Gunn, however, remained cheerfully unimpressed. 'I have the greatest confidence in you, sir.'

I then started on my usual external inspection, aware that not only did I not know what I was looking for, but the important bits were probably far too high up for me to see anyway.

Having made a circuit of the aircraft and observed very little, I aimed a kick at the tyres before signing the form 700 and placing my signature in a local authorisation book that happened to be handy.

After that, a bright idea suddenly occurred to me. Turning to Gunn, I asked, 'Tell me, who knows most about this aircraft?'

After a short debate, it was finally agreed that Corporal Jackman and Leading Aircraftman Gunter were the experts, Jackman on the airframe and Gunter on the engines.

'Right,' I said, suddenly decisive. 'They come with us, or the trip's off.'

The news was passed to the airmen concerned who, far from registering alarm, seemed pleased to be so honoured. As we all moved out to the aircraft, I whispered an aside to Patterson. 'Quite extraordinary! These chaps are possibly going to their deaths and all they can do is grin like fools. They must be on drugs.'

As there appeared to be no suitable entrance, clutching my parachute and gazing around perplexed, I asked, 'And how do we mount this charger – if you will pardon the expression?'

Gunn explained, 'There's a hole up front but we don't usually use it, as people tend to knock things off pushing past. Instead, we drop in through the roof.'

'Drop in through the roof?' My face registered disbelief. Then, shrugging, 'How silly of me! I might have known.'

Gunn motioned for a ladder. 'Up here, sir. Then through that hole just behind the cockpit.'

Exchanging surprised glances, Patterson and I scrambled first on to the wing, and then the fuselage, before letting ourselves down inside.

As we moved forward into the cockpit, which to me, accustomed to fighters, seemed absolutely vast, I heard myself breathing, 'Blimey! The Albert Hall!' After which, turning to Paterson, 'Front stalls or circle? Take your pick.'

As with difficulty we settled ourselves into our seats, me on the left and Patterson on the right, we seemed to be surrounded by

acres of glass, through which the two enormous engines and airscrews leered at us like robbers about to break in. At which point
I suddenly felt quite sick and began to think how I could decently
break a leg or otherwise render myself *hors de combat.*

Patterson, however, with the childish inquisitiveness of the ignorant, began moving levers, working the controls and playing with
every switch within reach.

I remember growling at him, sourly, 'Retract the wheels before
we even start, you medical misfit, and you're for the knacker's yard!'
At which Patterson, unsmiling, gave a nod, and tried without success to put his hands in his pockets.

Then the Corporal appeared and began to help with the straps.

'I hope you know what goes on around here,' I heard myself
admitting with a brave attempt at *sang froid*, 'because we don't.' To
which Patterson added loudly, 'That's for goddamn sure!'

The Corporal smiled modestly and in five minutes we managed
to identify most of the various levers, knobs, gauges and switches.

Then LAC Gunter was suddenly on hand and, following his
instructions, I turned on everything that was necessary, primed the
engines and started up.

Unaccustomed to having a monster radial engine on either side
of me, I was almost unnerved by the drama of the start. Each in
turn, the big motors shook themselves like a couple of Gordon set-
ters shedding water and, amid a fog of blue smoke, the airscrews
whirled into huge discs, seemingly within inches of our noses.

Numb with foreboding, I turned my attention to the gauges
and waited until all the temperatures and pressure registered what
seemed to me sensible amounts. Remembering the Lysander and its
wretched engine, I offered up a prayer for divine cooperation before
opening the gills, then shutting them, then leaving them halfway
open when I couldn't decide which was the better arrangement. If
in doubt, I opined, compromise was the best policy.

After that, I ran up the engines in turn and carefully tested the
switches – no problems there, thank the Lord. I then went through
the mnemonics of my fighter cockpit drill, adding a few more letters for good measure and whatever else I could think of.

Finally, when I had run out of ideas, I shrugged my shoulders in Patterson's direction and said, 'Well, unless you have anything else to suggest, that's about it, I think.'

Away to the left, Flight Lieutenant Gunn watched the proceedings with apparent indifference. Then, when I waved away the chocks, he gave us a broad wink before putting up his thumbs. I let off the brakes, which gave a cheerful hiss, and the great beast lumbered forward, the engines bubbling sonorously and great gobs of blue smoke hurrying astern.

The half-mile waddle around the perimeter track to the runway in use was uneventful and, having negotiated the first two corners, I was beginning to enjoy myself. Alongside, his eyes gleaming behind his spectacles, Patterson silently took it all in, nodding with encouragement as I squeezed around each bend, the engines responding with roars and crackles as the throttles were advanced and retarded.

Finally, turning the aircraft on to the main runway, I braked to a standstill. Methodically, I then went through my improvised cockpit drill for the umpteenth time before beckoning to the Corporal, who by this time had found a hole for himself up front.

'Have I missed anything out?'

'We'll soon see, sir.' The Corporal kept a straight face.

Not amused, I chilled the man with a glance and said, 'OK, everyone. Tie yourselves down and we'll have a go.'

In the distance, at the far end of the runway, a row of trees sat like dragon's teeth poised for a bite. I found myself swallowing and suddenly felt quite sick. Patterson was looking in my direction. Everyone was waiting, it seemed, including the Albemarle.

Remembering the Lysander and praying for inspiration, I opened the throttles gingerly and the engines began to throb and roar in earnest.

At olbs boost, the massive airscrews thrashed a gale of air towards the back end so that the twin tails danced prettily in anticipation of the take-off. Listening to the even beat of the motors, I kept the brakes tightly applied. Then, in a moment of decision, I let go, at the same time pushing firmly on the two levers in the throttle quadrant.

The Albemarle seemed to give a minute hop before moving off ponderously down the runway, gathering speed, the engines thundering mightily. Momentarily observing the boost surging towards the 6lbs mark on each of the two gauges, and looking up from my instruments, I found myself gripping the yoke of the control column and hanging on to it like a drunk to a lamppost.

Somewhere in front, the nose wheel started to clank dismally as the oleo leg flexed in protest, while underneath, the concrete strip accelerated swiftly beneath my feet until it became a grey blur.

On and on! On and on! The dragon's teeth came nearer and nearer. Not exactly a Spitfire take-off, this!

Come on, come on, you brute, get your bum into the air! I tried lifting the nose, but it wouldn't come. By George, it was going to be close. So close that a horrible thought suddenly struck like a dagger: *flaps!* Of course! I should have put down 20 degrees of flap. But I'd forgotten, hadn't I? *Forgotten!* More power? There wasn't any! The throttles were wide open.

Then ... the nose slowly beginning to lift, after a further 100 yards, I was finally able to coax the howling monster into the air. Relief! Utter, but utter, God-given relief!

As the Albemarle flashed across the airfield boundary, the dragon's teeth snapped at us, but just beyond reach, and amid all the noise, vibration and tension of the moment, I heard Patterson shouting excitedly, 'Ride him, cowboy!' At the same time, I applied the brakes to stop all the rumbling, and then raised the wheels before trimming the aircraft into a slow climb, the engines meanwhile bellowing noisily.

Moments later, having recovered my breath, I throttled back a mite and coarsened the pitch of the airscrews, so that the engine notes changed. Lord, above! But what would I do now if one of the motors stopped?

Chilled by the mere possibility of any such calamity arising and trying hard to banish the thought from my mind, I kept the aircraft climbing, praying meanwhile that I would not be confronted by such a crisis.

In front, the Corporal's face appeared round a corner, mouthing something in my direction, but I was too busy to embark on any lip-reading exercise. I was relieved, however, to see that the man was grinning and nodding, which suggested that everything was probably all right. Phew!

At 1,000 feet, I emerged from my mild state of shock to look carefully around. Patterson was sitting with his hands on his knees, nodding and looking intently at the instruments. Up front, the Corporal had disappeared down his hole and, on each side, the engines drummed out a disconcerting 'whum! – whum! – whum!'

Although synchronising engines had not been a major feature of my past flying experience, I recognised the problem immediately and carefully set about adjusting the pitch controls until the 'whum-whums' died away and the engines seemed altogether more content. I then trimmed the aircraft carefully, fore and aft – or tried to – and, after adjusting everything within reach, gave a deep sigh and sat back. It was then, as I loosened my grip on the control column, that I noticed my hands were still shaking. Lord, what a business!

The Albemarle, meanwhile, lumbered on with a peculiar cork-screwing motion, so that I felt that I was riding on the back of a very indecisive whale, which couldn't make up its mind whether it wanted to stay on the top of the water or dive into the depths. It was not particularly unpleasant but decidedly odd – at least to me it was odd – as I found that no amount of trimming the elevators or rudders helped very much. But perhaps all Albemarles were the same? No wonder they were giving them away to the Russians.

After a time, I turned and we climbed and corkscrewed our way towards the south coast, with me gaining confidence by the minute. Provided none of the more important parts fell off or stopped, I felt that I was home and dry. Coaxing the Albemarle back on to the ground, I felt, was not likely to be too much of a problem, particularly with a tricycle undercarriage: I was always one of those chaps much more concerned about taking off, and, of course, keeping the aircraft I was flying in the air, than landing. Everything came down sooner or later, I reasoned; it was the staying aloft bit that usually presented the problems.

At 4,000 feet, and flying straight and level, I remember relaxing and nodding in Patterson's direction. 'OK, sawbones! She's all yours. You've got her.' I then sank back into my seat and began to survey the landscape and coastal scenery.

Patterson, quietly delighted, flew westwards for some time, before executing a slow right-hand turn, which brought us inland to an area I knew very well indeed – I had flown many times around the Warmwell area of Dorset during the early part of the Battle of Britain. Then and later, I had regularly partnered my flight commander friend, James Nicolson, who was shot down over Southampton on 16 August, an engagement which later resulted in his being awarded the one and only Victoria Cross earned by a pilot of Fighter Command during the Second World War.

The area also reminded me – with some amusement – of another close colleague and friend, Michael Constable-Maxwell of 56 Squadron, who seemed to have spent half his service career crash-landing bent and damaged Hurricanes in Dorset and Essex – so frequently, in fact, that several of us in 249 Squadron had often light-heartedly suggested that we would all be better off if Michael fought on the other side.

It was during this quiet period of reflection that I found myself searching for familiar landmarks, scanning the countryside with narrowed eyes, the memories rich and clinging, when, like a blow to the head, it suddenly occurred to me that the ground was much closer that it ought to have been. Shooting a quick glance at the altimeter, I saw to my horror that it was registering 1,400 feet – and reducing. The climb-and-descent instrument was also showing us losing altitude at more than 300 feet a minute: although the aircraft's nose was more or less on the horizon, we were dropping fast. Patterson, totally unconcerned, was gazing into the distance. Something was most definitely wrong.

Trying desperately to control the panic that was rising in my breast like liquid up a tube, I took in the engine instruments at a glance. The motors seemed to be all right – 2,000 revolutions per minute on each engine – but one cylinder-head temperature was right down. Oh, Lord!

Instinctively, I put my right hand to the throttle quadrant – and found one of the levers missing. It was almost in the fully closed position. Oh, God! The starboard engine was giving virtually no power and was being lugged around by the other one, thus keeping the revs respectable. Somehow, the throttle had gradually slipped back in its quadrant and Patterson, in his ignorance, had been quietly trimming out the foot load to his own satisfaction.

Reacting immediately, I pushed forward the right-hand lever with a decisive movement and the engine responded with a heartening surge, so that the nose swung smartly to the left. As I almost snatched the control column, Patterson, nonplussed, raised his hands in the air and regarded me with wide-eyed surprise.

'What's wrong?' My companion's gaze behind his spectacles registered interest but very little concern.

'The ground, you mutt!' I said shrilly at him. 'Can't you see? It's coming up at us! You let the throttle close. Find and tighten the friction thing!'

Patterson, shrugging and surprised, obediently bent to his task.

The engine working properly again and the aircraft back in trim, we climbed to 2,500 feet before I decided to head for home. As we wended our way towards Stoney Cross, we discussed the throttle-closing incident with so much relieved laughter that the Corporal's head appeared from his hole up front to discover the cause of all the merriment.

Approaching the airfield, I reduced our altitude to circuit height, and, after a wide turn, settled carefully into our downwind leg. Mentally going through the vital actions for landing, I braced myself before selecting 'wheels down'. There was brief yaw as the undercarriage emerged and a small cluster of red lights appeared. Continuing to fly straight ahead and carefully noting my speed, I waited for the clunk that normally signified the wheels locking in the 'down' position, and the accompanying green lights. But I detected no clunk and one red light continued to glare malevolently in my direction.

When it became clear that it was not going to change to green, I muttered 'Oh, no!' and selected 'wheels up' again. The aircraft promptly went into its shimmying routine, after which everything was silent. Finally, all the lights went out.

I turned to Patterson, who was watching with detached interest. 'Lucky old us! The starboard main wheel is not locking down. Can you see anything your side?'

Patterson craned his neck and then shrugged. 'Not a damn thing at the moment.'

I replied peevishly, 'You won't at the moment, will you? The wheels are up at present. What I mean is: can you see anything when they're supposed to be down?'

Seeing that I had overshot the airfield, I selected 'wheels down' again. This time the red lights came on, followed by one green light only – the nosewheel. Oh, Lord! Things were going from bad to worse. Next time, there would probably be no green lights at all.

I found the Corporal at my shoulder and produced a helpless shrug for his benefit. 'D'you know what's happening? Because I don't.'

The Corporal looked doubtful and shook his head. 'Could be the microswitches, sir – anything. You've got loads of pressure in the accumulator.' He pointed to a gauge on the far side of the cockpit.

I asked, 'Can you see the wheels from where you were? Or from anywhere else, for that matter?'

'Not properly, no, sir. Though there's a visual indicator up front for the nosewheel.'

'But that doesn't help very much, does it? The nosewheel's the only one that seems to be working. It's the main wheels I'm worried about. Go forward and have another look.'

The Corporal's backside disappeared through the hole beside the dashboard, and I waited, killing time by increasing and synchronising the engine revs yet again. Presently, the man returned, breathing hard with all the bending and exertion.

'The front one's down, all right,' he announced. 'The others I can't see properly. I'm pretty sure, though, it's the microswitches, which means the main wheels are probably down. The system's working, anyway.'

Frowning, I gave myself a few minutes to think, before turning to the Corporal again. 'Tell me, have you got a book of words which tells you how to fly this thing?'

I saw a shadow pass over the man's face. 'You mean . . .?'

'You're dead right. That's exactly what I do mean. Have you a copy of the Pilot's Notes anywhere?'

'Pilot's Notes! I wouldn't have any of those, would I? I'm a technician, not a pilot.' The Corporal's face registered injured dignity; clearly he believed reason to be on his side.

I conceded, 'All right, no Pilot's Notes, and no book of words. Can you tell me, then, what the emergency method is of lowering the undercarriage? Because there must be an emergency system somewhere.'

The Corporal's face took on a set expression. 'There's a hand pump, but that only does what the engine pumps are doing already.'

'But there has to be a separate emergency system . . .' I would have pressed the point further had not the face of LAC Gunter appeared enquiringly just behind me. Followed by another face – totally unfamiliar.

'Who's he?' I heard my voice rise to a falsetto.

I saw the Corporal looking sheepish and was about to question him further, when a third head appeared.

'Great God! The never-emptying taxi! How many more have we got back there?'

'Don't know, sir.' The Corporal's face had gone stiff. 'A few got on, I believe.'

'What's a few?'

'Can't say, sir.' The man's face was now a mask. 'I haven't been down to the back end.'

Stiff with annoyance, I was about to take issue with him when I recognised the futility of continuing the interrogation. Instead, I put on my sternest squadron leader face.

'We'll discuss this later,' I announced grimly. 'For the moment, let's concentrate on getting this brute back on the ground. Corporal?'

'Sir?'

'Let's check the wheels again.'

Corporal Jackman dutifully went forward once more and I, more in hope than expectation, selected 'wheels up', followed by 'wheels down', but the single red eye continued to stare at me balefully. It was just no good. The thing was determined not to work.

Presently, Jackman's face reappeared. 'I'm almost certain they're down.' He gave an apologetic grimace. 'That's the best I can do, I'm afraid.'

As I set off on yet another wide circuit, Patterson sat quietly behind his glinting spectacles, his hands on his knees, waiting for something to happen.

Deciding immediately on my next course of action, I announced, 'Right, we're going across to Ibsley. If I'm going to bend this aircraft, I'm going to do it on my home ground. I'll bounce the wheels on the runway, which might sort things out.'

'What if it doesn't?' Patterson enquired with a sudden show of interest.

'Then we'll just have to do a wheels-up landing. Unless, of course, you want to jump out.'

'Jump out! Are you kidding?' Patterson's voice had risen an octave. 'In any case, what about those characters in the back? Do they have jump-sacks?'

As the Albemarle corkscrewed its way back to Ibsely, my mind remained a blank. The Corporal kept disappearing and then returning to put his thumbs up, until I began to wish the damn things would fall off. At the same time, a succession of faces, wearing a variety of expressions, kept appearing in the hole behind my shoulder. But I ignored them all, my brain mesmerised by the single unwavering red light.

I brought the aircraft in on a wide turn, which brought me over the town of Ringwood, the grey strip of runway slanting obliquely in the distance. As I put the airscrew pitch controls into fully fine, the engines howled back at me and I began trimming the Albemarle into a long, low approach.

A mile or so short of the airfield, I lowered the flaps by degrees – the hydraulics were certainly working – and then, with them fully extended, opened up the two engines to a throbbing grumble, bringing up the nose meanwhile.

Patterson, from his side of the cockpit, asked quietly, 'Are you OK?'

I nodded, my hands firm on the control column. 'Tighten your straps!'

The final run-in seemed interminable. Finally, as the boundary hedge flashed by, I reduced power as much as I dared and held the aircraft off. As I did so, the undercarriage warning horn began to blare like some dreadful Gideon, making me jump as though a hatpin had been stuck into my nether regions. Blast and damn the noise! But I continued doggedly, and amid all the tension and din, the Albemarle settled down like a hen alighting on eggs ... lower ... lower ... and lower. Until, with a subdued screech, the two main wheels struck the tarmac – and the red light stayed on!

As I immediately and very firmly pushed open the throttles, both engines bellowed in unison and the warning horn expired. Wallowing uncomfortably under the influence of full flap, the aircraft lifted off and climbed away painfully with me trimming furiously meanwhile. I then brought up the flaps, bit by bit, and several minutes later, we were back again at 1,000 feet.

With the Albemarle once more on an even keel, I considered the situation with some concern. There was nothing for it: we would just have to take a chance.

With the Corporal and LAC Gunter in attendance, I said, without preamble, 'We're going to land here, now. If the undercarriage folds, it folds. Tie yourselves down and get whoever is in the back to do the same. Find the hatches and decide what you're going to do if we catch fire.' I glanced into the distance. 'I see the fire engine and ambulance are out, so they seem to know what is going on.'

The two airmen disappeared with almost indecent haste and Patterson began to tidy up the cockpit in the manner of a housewife preparing to depart on holiday.

I set the aircraft off on a further circuit and we were soon steady again on our final approach. I was just a little surprised that I felt no anxiety, only interest. The aircraft seem so large and impregnable that I felt confident that I could fly it safely through a couple of brick walls.

For the second time, I began to hold off as the boundary hedge approached, to the raucous accompaniment of the blaring warning horn. As if conscious of the need to behave itself, the Albemarle then settled down like a lamb, so that the first touch, when it came, was almost imperceptible. I held the nose as high as I could but it fell almost immediately with a thump, with everyone cringing and bracing themselves for the grinding, slithering collapse.

But it didn't come. With the horn still blaring and one red eye staring balefully in my direction, the Albemarle ran steadily ahead, deviating not so much as a centimetre, the two engines crackling away happily. Still gripped with tension, I braked gingerly to a final, squealing standstill. At which point, everyone breathed their own personal sigh of relief. Patterson produced a Apache war whoop and cried out in an affected English accent, 'Jolly good show, old bean!'; the Corporal put his thumbs up for the umpteenth time; and LAC Gunter appeared from the rear to bestow one of his shy smiles.

Across the airfield, the drivers of the fire engine and ambulance shook their heads in disappointment and switched off the motors in their vehicles.

Taxiing towards the nearest hangar, I was waved to a hardstanding and, after clearing the engines in a manner befitting an experienced heavy-boiler pilot, with LAC Gunter's assistance, I shut down and the huge airscrews tottered to a clanking standstill.

In an atmosphere of utter tranquillity, I threw off my straps and, after commenting on the vagaries of undercarriages and microswitches, found my way through the roof, down the ladder and on to the tarmac.

There I was met by Flight Lieutenant Gunn, the Corporal, LAC Gunter and five other airmen, all standing in line. Behind them were three young WAAFs, looking suitably shy and demure – and an Alsatian, which was relieving itself against one of the aircraft's landing wheels.

Excepting the dog, whose expression of bliss was for other reasons, they were all regarding me with what was clearly hero-worshipping admiration and, to my surprise and embarrassment, began to clap.

'Very well done, sir!' The Corporal had his thumbs up again. 'We knew you could do it.'

I made a not-too-successful effort to control my astonishment. 'You mean we had all this mob in the back? Eight of you?'

The Corporal nodded a trifle uncertainly, half expecting a storm to break about his ears.

I found myself gaping but slightly amused. 'The dog, too?'

An anonymous voice came from somewhere in the group. 'Don't worry, sir. He's thinking of joining up.'

After a series of minor adjustments, I made two further trips in the Albemarle that day, accompanied by Patterson, Corporal Jackman and LAC Gunter – but without the passengers and the Alsatian.

On both flights, I am happy to report that the Albemarle kept its single red light entirely to itself and behaved in an exemplary manner. I even remembered to lower 20 degrees of flap before each take-off.

Chapter 6

A Nasty Experience

A few days after my minor adventure with the Albemarle, there was a rather disturbing incident.

In order to increase my knowledge of our P.47, I resolved to do rather more than just fly it around the country or engage myself on fairly innocuous tasks of one sort or another. Instead, I would fly the aircraft hard at altitude and put it through its paces in a serious way.

I had been told that with its enormous engine and exhaust-driven supercharger, our aircraft would perform pretty well at 30,000 feet and above, but I had never thus far tested it at height or under anything like operational conditions; nor indeed had I ever tested myself in the aircraft on any such occasion.

Towards the end of March, I had flown our P.47C about a dozen times and had more or less acquainted myself with the mass of switches and unfamiliar devices that surrounded me in that massive cockpit. I was by no means comfortable in the aircraft, but the massive Pratt & Whitney engine was always smooth and reliable; and although I didn't know much about the supercharging arrangements, except that that magic device, rather strangely, was situated in the back of the fuselage and entirely remote from the engine, everything had seemed to work pretty well thus far, so that my ignorance most certainly amounted to bliss.

I remember the day exactly – 21 March, which was a Tuesday.

I had flown a Stinson L5 down to Warmwell and back in the morning, and because the afternoon was fine and dry, took off in the P.47 shortly after 2 p.m., climbing off in a southerly direction.

A little out into the Channel, I was at 20,000 feet before turning in a wide arc on to a northerly heading, so that when I looked down and recognised Salisbury far below, I was at 30,000 feet and still climbing, though at a much slower rate.

Some 5,000 feet beneath the slightly darkening blue of the heavens, there was a large, thin patch of broken white stratus cloud; otherwise there was little to be seen in the vast, cold, surrounding expanse of space. With the engine running smoothly and with nothing obviously amiss, I was relaxed and in good heart, if a little bored. I would go as far as 35,000, I decided.

I was at a little over 34,000 feet when I happened to glance below and observe a minute group of aircraft in finger-four formation, moving like insects across the top of a white patch of stratus at possibly 25,000 feet. As they were small and obviously fighters, I was instantly reminded of the autumn of 1940 and that I was witnessing, yet again, a small formation of German Me.109s over the southern counties of England, running for home.

It was like a light being switched on. Suddenly, it was 1940 all over again. I was thousands of feet above the enemy, they had not yet seen me, and I was in a prime position to attack. This was the moment! On a sudden impulse, I turned my P.47 on its back and fell like a stone in their direction.

Later, when I had time to think about it, events came back to my mind in flashes as they occurred. I briefly recall being at 32,000 feet and noticing 330 miles per hour on my airspeed indicator. Then, with the enemy directly below, I was over the vertical with the rising scream of the slipstream in my ears, shrill and almost frightening.

Intoxicated by the excitement of the chase and likely interception, I do not recall being at full or even half throttle, only that the speed of my aircraft was rising rapidly and that I was clinging on to the control column with both hands.

But all seemed well, if more than a little unreal – for a time. In seconds, however, things began to happen. First, the aircraft started to buffet and shudder horribly. Then the nose began to rise and fall, forcing me to hang on to the quivering control column even more firmly than before. I thought of re-trimming, fore and aft, but some inner impulse prevented me from so doing, which in the event turned out to be a godsend.

Finally, when I felt the aircraft running away with me and becoming beyond my control, concern rapidly turned into panic. By this time, I could barely move the control column and when, with all my strength, I attempted to pull back and raise the nose, all I succeeded in doing was to push my aircraft further into its now almost vertical dive. At which stage, I felt the P.47 to be completely unmanageable and that, even at a height of something well over 20,000 feet, I was facing disaster.

At this point, and to a quite extraordinary degree, I suddenly experienced a feeling of utter tranquillity. Faced, as seemed inevitable, by an ugly death, I began to think clearly and logically. I had to do something – but what? The speed of my aircraft was so great that I could not even think of opening the hood, far less baling out. Was this some structural failure, or what? I had no idea. And, incredible as it may seem, for some moments, I just sat there thinking.

Then, as so frequently happens and without any conscious thought, I chose the right solution – by very simply doing nothing but hanging on, grimly. A fleeting thought had no doubt crossed my mind: as my P.47 was rapidly entering a zone of increasing air pressure and higher temperatures, perhaps nature would come to my rescue.

Which, thank the Lord, it did. As I was passing through about 20,000 feet, the buffeting, shaking and cavorting gradually ceased and I found myself in an aircraft still descending vertically but only under the influence of the force of gravity. Although I do not remember doing so, at some point during the dive I had apparently closed the throttle.

Profoundly thankful and limp with emotion, after carefully dragging up the nose of my aircraft and assuming level flight, I flew around in circles for quite a time, recovering my composure. It had been an ugly minute or two, the more concerning as I had not known what on earth was happening to me, or why. Fairly used to the stresses of combat, somehow I felt the strain of involving myself in an incident of this nature even more acutely. It had been a very unpleasant experience and one I hoped would never be repeated.

When I had recovered sufficiently to see exactly where I was, I found myself at 18,000 feet and a little north of Andover. Turning south for home and passing close to Boscombe Down, I decided in an instant to land there in order that I might discuss my experience with some resident expert who might be able to explain what exactly had happened. Having flown Hurricanes as a member of No. 249 Squadron from Boscombe during the early part of the Battle of Britain, I was well aware that the Aircraft and Armament Experimental Establishment was accommodated there and felt sure that there would be someone available to provide the reassuring explanation I so desperately needed.

It was a decision that quickly bore fruit. Having landed and taxied to the First World War wooden huts that housed the Flying Wing headquarters of A&AEE, I was directed by the Flying Wing adjutant towards the 'A' Squadron hangar, where the single- and twin-engined fighters were tested. There I was courteously received, given a strong cup of sweet tea, and treated to an hour-long dissertation on flying at extreme altitudes and speeds and the possible hazards involved.

Somewhat to my surprise, the P.47 and its high-speed high-altitude difficulties were apparently well known to my hosts. Indeed, the General commanding the 8th USAAF, the celebrated 'Jimmy' Doolittle, had already been asking for his UK-based P.47 units to be replaced by those flying P.51s (Mustangs), as the Thunderbolts were experiencing more than a few unsuccessful interceptions over Germany as a result of their pilots running into difficulties similar to my own.

It was then explained to me that the speed of our latest fighters was becoming very much affected by the speed of sound, which at sea level was about 760 miles per hour, reducing quite significantly at height, where the temperature would always be very much lower.

Below the speed of sound, an aircraft 'slid' through the air, but at the speed of sound and above, it 'ripped' through the air like a tearing bullet, causing major shock waves, which resulted in noise, heat and, above all, a vast increase in drag. Moreover, even at speeds below the speed of sound, various curved surfaces on the aircraft had the effect of accelerating the local airstream to sonic level, causing lesser shock waves to occur, which brought about the buffeting, shaking and changes of trim I had only too plainly experienced in my P.47.

The airspeed indicators, even on our present high-speed piston-engined fighters, were, I was well aware, becoming almost redundant, as they were pressure instruments, calibrated to read correctly at ground level, but grossly under-reading at most other heights. Although the indicators were necessary at lower speeds and for landing and instrument flying, future high-speed fighters – the new jet fighters included – would also be obliged to employ Machmeters, which would display to the pilot the speed of his aircraft as compared to the speed of sound at the particular temperature and height at which he was flying.

The term Machmeter I had come across before, but much of the other information about sonic flight, the so-called sound barrier and other related information, plus their possible effects on the aircraft I was flying and likely to fly, were, even in early 1944, new, interesting and not a little disturbing. I was glad I had dropped in at Boscombe Down and decided it had been one of the most useful hours I had ever spent.

Perhaps it is of no significance, but I note from my logbook that I did not fly for three days thereafter. Was I really that much affected? On reflection, I just might have been.

On 27 April 1944, about a month later, Squadron Leader Anthony Martindale, a senior test pilot at the RAE (Royal Aeroplane Establishment) Farnborough, took off in a lightened Mark II Spitfire, to investigate the reactions of his aircraft when flying at very high speed at extreme altitude. It was agreed that he would dive the Spitfire at full power from 40,000 feet and that the aircraft's performance would also be monitored by test instruments carried in and around his cockpit.

When descending almost vertically towards 30,000 feet, he soon achieved the very high speed and was subjected to the same buffeting, shaking and very heavy stick forces I had experienced in the 100th Fighter Wing's P.47, as well as the almost uncontrollable steepening of the dive.

Worse was to follow. At 27,000 feet, there was a loud explosion and the Spitfire's airscrew disintegrated and flew off into space, dragging with it the reduction gear, which formed the front part of the Merlin engine. Greatly lightened, the aircraft then subjected Martindale to a violet 11g change of direction, which blacked him out completely, the cockpit of his aircraft, meanwhile, being covered in oil and filled with smoke.

Regaining consciousness and deciding not to bale out, after realising he could still control the Spitfire, with great skill and bravery he finally made a dead-stick landing on Farnborough airfield, some 20 miles away. The test instruments proved conclusively that a critical Mach number of more than .91 had been achieved and that his aircraft had flown at a speed of 620 miles per hour. This was, and remains to this day, the highest speed ever recorded by a conventional piston-engined fighter.

Some weeks later, Martindale was invited to fly another Mark 11 Spitfire, suitably fitted out with test instruments, to confirm the performance figures he had achieved on his first spectacular flight, as they were considered to be most unusual. With great courage, and I suspect not a little apprehension, he agreed to do so.

Initially, the flight proceeded much as before, the Spitfire climbing to 40,000 feet before he put it into a steep dive under full power. Once again, he experienced the same symptoms – shaking, buffeting, heavy stick forces and a steepening dive that became increasingly uncontrollable. And, once more, at about 27,000 feet, catastrophe! Only this time the airscrew remained firmly in place, but the supercharger apparently disintegrated and the Merlin engine caught fire.

Without an engine and at the time above cloud, the pilot was unable to land back on Farnborough airfield and was obliged to crash land at Whitmore Common in Surrey. The Spitfire was heavily damaged and Martindale suffered from a badly injured back.

But, as before, thanks to his enormous courage and skill, the test instruments were preserved and told a similar story: the Spitfire had flown at the highest critical Mach number ever and had achieved a speed that, for a conventional piston-engined aircraft, has never been surpassed.

These and many other similar test flights were, of course, carried out without my knowledge during that spring and summer of 1944. In fact, over the following months and years the terms 'sonic flight' and 'sound barrier' became increasingly in common use and many valuable pilots and aircraft were killed or damaged in pursuit of the new Holy Grail of supersonic flight.

But, at the time, as a young fighter pilot, I was neither immediately involved nor more than marginally concerned, although I soon became aware that both the American P.38 (Lightings) and P.47 (Thunderbolts) were considered to be low down the list when discussing critical Mach numbers, with the P.51 (Mustangs) only marginally better. However, as the 9th USAAF was a tactical not a strategic force, the engagements in which pilots of the 100th Fighter Wing were expected to be involved were not usually above 25,000 feet and critical Mach numbers were unlikely to be regarded as a major factor or talking point.

That unpleasant flight in the P.47, however, was to remain with me for a long time. For many years, in fact.

Surprisingly perhaps, and despite the fact that the fighting did not start until several months thereafter, I have for many years always associated the first several weeks of April 1944 with 'the Invasion of Europe', or what we used to call 'the Second Front'.

Possibly it was because I had time on my hands and did a fair amount of travelling around the south-western counties of England, by road in my old Morris 10, and by air in the 100th Fighter Wing's Stinson L5 and Spitfire, a very dodgy Hawker Typhoon, plus a Percival Proctor, Airspeed Oxford and several other light aircraft.

The weather, I recall, was pretty good and in my many idle, gazing moments during my frequent trips, I was able to see just a fraction of the massive array of men, ships and material being gathered, prepared and stored for the coming assault on the northern coastline of Europe.

On the main and even the minor roads of Hampshire, Wiltshire and Dorset, I now and then found myself sandwiched between scores of grinning men in the army uniforms of Britain, Canada, the United States and several other nations – the faces of happy, noisy soldiers riding in lorries and loaded trucks, always heading, it seemed, for undisclosed destinations.

Meanwhile, hundreds of tanks, large and small, and every sort of vehicle known to man lurched and rumbled along the highways and lanes of southern England, tearing up the tarmac and deeply rutting the fields and every square yard of common land with their steel tracks and heavy-duty wheels.

And as, with wide and enquiring eyes, I flew for miles along the south coast, I saw a score or more harbours and jetties below me, crammed to overflowing with vessels of every type and size – naval destroyers, landing craft, torpedo boats and even smaller unidentifiable vessels – many of them parked five or six rows deep, camouflaged, tethered and waiting: in all a truly staggering display of military strength. And all this, I knew, would be only a minor part of an irresistible, unbeatable Allied attacking force.

On the wireless, in the many six-page broadsheets, and even in that provocative and often scandalous tabloid the *Daily Mirror*, in addition to the scantily clad 'Jane', we received constant news of the progress of the war and those who controlled our lives in government and the military, whilst the glossy magazines – *Illustrated London News*, *Tatler*, *Sketch* and *Picture Post* – were full of portraits of brave men and beautiful young ladies who would otherwise be debutantes, with endless pictures of aircraft, ships, squadrons and regiments.

It was constantly hinted that 'the Invasion' could never be more than a day or so away and we were all kept well informed about the named commanders of our invading forces, their characters and achievements.

The Force Commander during what was to be christened 'Operation Overlord' was to be the American General Dwight D. Eisenhower. With little experience as a general, he had, apparently, the virtuous quality of being able 'to get on with people'. Interested in but not exactly impressed by his bland, slightly Teutonic features,

I was given to understand that he came from the small prairie town of Abilene in Kansas and, as late as the early 1940s, had merely been a lieutenant colonel in the United States Army.

I was to see him briefly on our airfield of Lashenden, in Kent, a month or so later, when he had just been flown over the beachhead areas in a converted Mustang, and again on several occasions in Washington DC, when, as the retiring President of the United States, he handed over to the newly elected President, John F. Kennedy, in 1960–61.

His deputy and second in overall command, Air Chief Marshal Sir Arthur Tedder, was, however, well known to me. I had met him first in the breathless heat of the late summer of 1941, when, as the designated Air Force Commander in the Middle East, he had visited 249 Squadron at Takali airfield in Malta, at which time, poor man, he was obliged to endure a long and passionate sermon from me, as acting Squadron Commander, on the inadequacy of the Hurricane as a fighter, and my strident assertion that we needed Spitfires immediately if the security of the island was to be assured.

A small, insignificant figure in his forage cap, nondescript khaki shirt and crumpled slacks, he hardly said a word during my lengthy discourse, but simply listened, smoking his pipe (I seldom saw him without a pipe), before eventually shaking my hand and, with a shy smile, quietly departing. As the relieving Spitfires did not turn up until six months later, my threat of imminent disaster was clearly not sufficiently convincing.

Tedder's appointment turned out to be an enormous plus, as he and Eisenhower 'got on' together famously and were often able to 'oil the works', so to speak, when difficult operational and personal decisions arose later, when several of their more vocal lesser commanders began to argue and disagree.

Not unexpectedly, the British General Bernard Montgomery was to command the Allied armies during Overlord, an appointment received with acclamation by the British but with some suspicion by the Americans, who usually resented any of their armed forces being commanded by a British senior officer, no matter how distinguished.

Although I knew a great deal about 'Monty' as a result of his enormous successes at El Alamein and North Africa during and after my own fairly undistinguished service in Malta and Egypt, prior to 1944 I had never met him personally. I only encountered him at RAF Staff College shortly after the war, and even had him attend lectures of mine at the School of Air Support at RAF Old Sarum in 1945.

A slight, Cromwellian figure, he had a high, penetrating voice, an acerbic manner and a self-opinionated demeanour I always found embarrassing. Articulate and successful he may have been, but he often irritated me personally and, during the period of the invasion and after, he certainly irritated many of his American colleagues from time to time.

It was also revealed that during Overlord, all naval and seaborne forces would be commanded by Admiral Ramsay, another British officer, and the air forces by Air Chief Marshal Sir Trafford Leigh-Mallory.

Despite serving briefly in several aircraft carriers and other vessels during the war, I knew little of Admiral Ramsay, except that he was said to be 'a very good man'. However, the Air Marshal I knew well, having served under him in Fighter Command during and after the Battle of Britain. He was a stiff but likeable, courteous man, and although it may be thought presumptuous of me to say so, I got on well with him – to such an extent, in fact, that it was suggested at one time that I might become his personal assistant. However, with the blindness of youth and having just been made a flight commander in one of the best ever RAF fighter squadrons at the age of barely 20, I had, perhaps stupidly, scoffed at the idea.

It was always my view that the Air Marshal, though able, was not a dynamic leader. He tended always to act, but only cautiously and on advice, and my experience was that he sometimes listened too readily to poor advice coming from the wrong people.

I saw him several times, but only from a distance when he toured American units in my local area, and he seemed a popular figure. However, not all of his senior colleagues in the RAF were so charitably minded and, after some high-level disagreements during the post-invasion fighting, he was moved sideways and appointed to command the Allied Air Forces of South East Asia Command in October 1944. Very sadly, a month or so later, he and his wife were killed when the Avro York aircraft taking them to the Far East crashed in bad weather near Grenoble, in the French Alps.

On about 5 April, there was noise and activity on the airfield at Ibsley as a large clutch of P.47s flew in and landed, a long line of them parading round the perimeter track like huge, plump, cackling partridges.

But strangely, not for long. Within a day or so they had gone, giving way to another group of twin-engined P.38s. Within days these also had left. Clearly, something was afoot.

Within a day or so, all was revealed. On 10 April, I and others received information that the 100th Fighter Wing headquarters, with four fighter groups from various distant airfields, would be moving, forthwith, to the Biggin Hill Sector of Kent, to a group of 'advanced landing grounds', whose names I had never heard of.

On 12 April, therefore, my logbook reveals that I flew an Oxford with five passengers to an airfield called Lashenden, in Kent. What surprised me almost as much as the name and position of the airfield itself is that I transported five passengers. I never remember an Oxford carrying that many!

Chapter 7
Back to Biggin Hill

I was delighted to learn that I would soon be moving to Kent, as I regarded that area as my home ground, having flown Mark 12 Spitfires with 41 Squadron from RAF Hawkinge (roughly Folkstone), and from Biggin Hill itself, for several months in early 1943.

There was, however, another reason that excited me: during my stay at Biggin Hill I had briefly met a young lady WAAF.

To those unfamiliar with this wooded and very appealing area of the Kentish countryside in southern England, the RAF station at Biggin Hill, affectionately known as 'Biggin on the Bump' and famous for its part in the Battle of Britain, was located about 25 miles south of London and some 40 miles from the English Channel. The airfield normally accommodated two or three squadrons of RAF fighters, so that between 50 and 70 aircraft would fly from there, usually en masse, two or three times daily during the hours of daylight, with just the occasional periods of night activity.

Within the Biggin Hill Sector as a whole, there were at least a further twelve Satellite and Advanced Landings Grounds, all of which came under the control of the Biggin Hill Sector Operations Centre, so that by June 1944, the number of RAF and USAAF fighters deployed in the area amounted to considerably more than 1,000.

A total of about 1,500–2,000 officers, NCOs and other ranks lived on the airfield at Biggin Hill, including around 250 who worked in the operations centre, the Sector's interception and controlling authority. In June 1944 this occupied a large converted mansion in nearby Bromley.

The Sector area itself incorporated much of the southern counties of Kent and East Sussex. The Biggin Hill Sector was flanked to the north by those of RAF stations Hornchurch and North Weald, whose operational areas included the Thames Estuary, Essex and Suffolk; and to the west by that of RAF Tangmere, covering the counties of West Sussex and Hampshire.

Outward-looking long-distance radars were sited, usually on cliffs, at about 50-mile intervals along the southern and eastern coastline, with medium-range and low-level radars, plus height finders, placed at strategic positions in between. These radars, in total, provided a vast overlapping picture of the air situation, which was infinitely wide, was about 240 miles in depth, and extended from ground level to 40,000 feet and higher. However, were intruding enemy aircraft or guided bombs to succeed in crossing the coast of Britain without being observed or detected, they would then be tracked internally by the Observer Corps, who, it was hoped, would produce all that was necessary to bring about successful engagements.

Although primarily built as a system for defending the United Kingdom, these various outward-looking coastal radars, together with the Control and Reporting system generally, had enormous offensive-action potential, as a sector controller, sitting at his dais in Bromley, could 'see' 100 miles and beyond into Continental Europe, and provide early-warning information for any friendly aircraft flying over hostile territory, besides being able to offer any such additional assistance necessary to bring about an effective attack on selected targets, or thwart a damaging enemy response.

At the operations centre, in a series of large, well-equipped rooms, mostly built above ground but often referred to rather disparagingly as 'down the hole', the Control and Reporting staff worked round the clock, controlling not only the various Air Force and Army units defending London but, in addition, all Allied fighters operating offensively over the Continent.

Working on a three-shift basis, the majority of those so employed (other than the controllers and other specialist officers and NCOs) were young women aircraft plotters of the Women's Auxiliary Air Force, who had earlier been recruited under the misleading and slightly mysterious title of Clerks SD (Special Duties). Mostly aged between 20 and 22, these young women spent much of their

working lives pushing their individual pile of markers, indicating
the position, height and direction of their allotted aircraft, around
a vast table map of the south of England, Channel coasts and a substantial part of northern Europe.

In so doing, they were usually the first to be aware of any airborne combat activity and were sometimes horror-stricken observers when, watching helplessly, they witnessed boyfriends and other
loved ones in the squadrons being shot down and killed or drowned
lingeringly in the freezing waters of the English Channel. Small
wonder that the job of aircraft plotter was always demanding, and
occasionally, nothing less than heartbreaking.

Apart from the more numerous airwomen plotters, there were,
as I now recall, about 15 WAAF officers using the officers' mess at
Biggin Hill, about half of whom were employed 'down the hole'.
The smiling faces of most of them I remember even now, but the
faces and the names of two were especially important to me at the
time: those of Flight Officer Eileen Hampton, the principal 'Ops B'
officer, and Section Officer Cynthia Oglethorpe, one of her junior
colleagues.

Flight Officer Eileen Hampton performed a key job, sitting on
the Sector controller's right hand in the underground operations
room and passing on his instructions to the squadrons and other
vital members of the defence organisation. She was an attractive
dark-haired girl, and I hoped she would be still around. And, happily, she was – to play an important part in this story, as I shall later
describe.

The 9th USAAF was primarily created to provide close air support
to the US 3rd Army during, and after, its landing in Europe. This,
to me, and indeed to anyone who had flown RAF fighter aircraft
during the early part of the war, meant continuous engagements at
medium and low altitudes, probably from a maximum of 25,000 feet
down to ground level.

Controlled, initially no doubt, from the Sector Operations Centre
at Biggin Hill, the aircraft of the 100th Fighter Wing would almost
certainly find themselves involved in countless 'area domination

missions', designed to protect medium bombers operating possibly 100 miles ahead of the main battle area. They would also be obliged to fly 'interdiction sorties' by the score, against bridges, supply trains, railway sidings and junctions, ammunition dumps, defensive strong points and, of course, hard- and soft-skinned vehicles of every kind. All day and every day. Endlessly.

I saw it all again in my mind's eye: the defending enemy tracer rising in soaring streaks of white, the brown flowering bursts of the larger ack-ack shells, the glowing balls of light ack-ack, ascending with deceptive stealth in clutches of five, lethal lumps of metal that followed one around as though magnetically attracted. And from time to time – though possibly not too often now, the Luftwaffe being greatly depleted – large but ragged formations of enemy fighters, 190s and 109s, diving, tilting and surging in one's direction, all of them spitting venom.

Yes, it would be a brutal, bloody business. And yes, there would be casualties by the score. I had experienced many similar engagements myself and seen all too many colleagues and friends shot down and killed when flying alongside me. And I thought immediately of the wretched P.51s, which, with their exposed, under-slung radiators, would be the ones likely to be more frequently damaged than the air-cooled, radial-engined P.47s.

Towards the end of the second week in April, the Mustangs programmed to join the Wing had not yet shown up, and I had only recently heard that the medium bombers likely to be employed would be twin-engined American B-26s (Martin Marauders) and A-26s (Douglas Invaders). Thus far I had not yet come across either type of aircraft, but no doubt I soon would.

And, as I gave the matter further thought, a major point: where, as a non-American headquarters 'wallah', did I fit in? I would always choose to be in the air, needless to say, but what precisely would I be doing during the fighting over the beachheads, and after? Clearly, I would have to discuss my position with Colonel Sanders, and also with the senior operations officer, Jim Haun (with his pipe, of course).

Whilst I would always be keen to see what was going on, I

couldn't honestly say that I was enthusiastic about being involved in the nasty low-level fighting that was likely to take place; nor, on the other hand, did I feel unduly apprehensive. With three years of combat behind me already, all I would be faced with was yet another dollop of operational flying in rather unpleasant circumstances – pretty routine stuff, in fact. But I would just have to see, wouldn't I?

Bound for our new airfield in Kent, I finally left the Ibsley area, with three other headquarters members, on 14 April – by car.

In my 1936 Morris 10, I drove off happily, loaded well below the Plimsoll line with a mass of kit, a 4-inch-thick rubber mattress I had recently acquired from a local US source (and still use regularly almost 70 years later), plus three fairly hefty American companions, whose considerable combined weight forced my ancient car to sag on its tired suspension like a old mule contemplating collapse.

My father had paid £47 10s. for the vehicle in 1937, and I loved it like a brother. It had a sunshine roof and automatic jacks, which the driver could operate by jiggling a lever without even removing himself from the driver's seat. It also carried 7 gallons of fuel, did about 30 miles to the gallon and, down a steep hill with a good following wind, could whip up a breathtaking 45 miles per hour.

Labouring in first gear up many of the steeper inclines en route, it took me almost five hours to travel the 100 or so miles to our new airfield at Lashenden. Once there we stayed only a moment or two to survey the wide expanse of meadow which had recently been bulldozed clear of hedges, ditches and trees and strengthened underfoot with a 'pierced steel planking' mesh, before moving on to look for our new living accommodation a mile or so further into the countryside.

We found it, eventually: a fairly rustic farmhouse-type building, sitting sturdily in a minor lane and in front of a large garden and field, in which were sited an untidy group of farm buildings and an industrial greenhouse of considerable size. Wide-eyed, we entered the house to 'case the joint' and enable each of us to select his individual corner in which to bed down.*

Though not exactly exotic, our new front parlour/bedroom was decently if roughly decorated, and even in its bare, unfurnished state, enticingly friendly. Moreover, I noted with relief that there was an adjacent lavatory, whose immediate proximity I found deeply comforting.

As I stood there, considering, I noted that my nearest companions were Alvin Hill and his office colleague, Major Bodenheim, each of whom was looking silently in my direction with an unsaid question in his eyes: would I care to join them? And I recall smiling and without a word, agreeing – with the result that we were to remain a group of three for the next nine months.

Then, almost as we stood there, a large formation of P.51s arrived, banking and circling in their sections of four, the familiar metallic roar of their Rolls-Royce Merlin engines music to my ears. As I watched them fly into the distance and sink towards their Staplehurst base several miles away, I was reminded of a whirling flock of starlings searching for places to roost on a darkening summer evening.

For the rest of the day I watched the headquarters staff settle in. Mobile cabins, looking like small railway carriages, were driven into the garden and local field; there were trucks and vehicles everywhere; and within the farmhouse, tempers were frayed and voices raised occasionally as 50 or more officers and NCOs selected their new private areas and office space, and sorted out their cabinets, files and personal belongings. It was wearying work. Fighting, clearly, was much easier than this!

My new room-mate, Al Hill, after a meeting with Colonel Sanders, returned to report that 'the Old Man' had decided that the big industrial greenhouse should be the new officers' mess hall. No kidding! The hothouse was to be our mess hall. We were all going to eat our steaks and steaming chow in temperatures of 120 degrees

* The 'rustic farmhouse' is now a handsome, double-fronted private home on Water Lane, Headcorn, whose delightful young owners were totally unaware of its wartime history when I visited them in October 2011.

Fahrenheit plus – or a lot more than that, if the summer turned out
to be unseasonably hot. The head man was out of his tiny mind,
Al protested: the guy was just plain loco! And something had to be
done about it.

But, although much was discussed and there were many long
faces, nothing was done about it: 'Tex' Sanders had his way and for
at least half the time we were in Kent, we ate our substantial midday
meals with perspiration running in rivers down our necks. And
that was not to be the only lunatic decision inflicted on us by our
unpredictable commanding officer.

Our interest was refocused during the next few days when the
100th Fighter Wing assembled more than 300 P.51s and P.47s on
the four local ALGs (Advanced Landing Grounds) – Staplehurst,
Lashenden, Headcorn and High Halden. We also learned that, further afield, the new airfields of Ashford, Kingsnorth and Wood-
church accommodated additional British and American aircraft, and
that on another group of landing grounds in the area of Dungeness,
the new Hawker Tempests were deployed, with other units of the
RAF. The whole area, in short, was awash with fighters. It seemed
there would scarcely be room for anyone to taxi, far less fly.

Vastly encouraged by the sight of the P.51s landing on nearby
Staplehurst, and learning that the unit was the 363 Fighter Group,
the following morning I was on the telephone speaking to the
squadron commander of one of the three fighter squadrons within
the group.

Having given details of myself and my appointment, and my
duties within the Wing, I asked if I might visit him and have a flight
in one of his aircraft.

The young officer to whom I spoke was courteous but a little
reserved – I later suspected that, having newly arrived from America,
he didn't know too much about squadron leaders in the RAF or,
indeed, about the RAF itself. Had I any experience of flying fighter
aircraft, he enquired cautiously, or any knowledge of air fighting?
He wasn't trying to put me off, he added, but he didn't want to jeop-
ardize the safety of even one of his very valuable aircraft.

I remember being ever so slightly nettled by his remarks but I managed to rustle up a smile before explaining that I had been flying in combat over Britain, Europe and the Middle East for almost four years, that I was fairly familiar with about a dozen different types of front-line fighters, and that I could be guaranteed not to break or even bend one of his precious P.51s.

I suspect that my reply rather took the wind out of my listener's sails, as, after the briefest of silences, he replied, 'OK, Squadron Leader, point made. Come across as soon as you like and we'll give you a ride.'

Having driven across to the airfield at Staplehurst, I was greeted by a tall, pleasant young man who, when he shook my hand, said, 'Sorry about my earlier remarks. We Americans tend to forget that you guys have been in the war for quite some time.' Then waving an arm, 'To prove how much I trust you, I'm letting you fly my own personal bird, OK? And as I don't know what you use in terms of equipment, I suggest you take my parachute and flying hat in case yours are different. And, of course, providing they fit.'

As we walked across to his aircraft, I asked, 'Is this a P.51B or C?'

My companion answered, 'B? C? Same difference. All the Cs have the new 85-gallon fuel tank behind the pilot's seat. But as most of the later Bs had it fitted retrospectively, the two aircraft are virtually the same now.

'However, I believe they also altered the supercharger on the Cs' later engines, to give a little more power on take-off, but the improvement is not obvious. Otherwise, nothing much has changed. Long-range drop tanks and armament, for example – you probably know, we carry four .5 machine guns on these.

'One thing you do have to watch, though: fully loaded, the bird is a bit unstable to start with, so you have to use most of the fuel in the back before it's comfortable to fly in cloud and you can think about fighting. But as you'll only be airborne for a short time, just flying around locally shouldn't be a problem.'

The aircraft to which my companion led me was in a dark green camouflage and stood with its hood hinged into two pieces, the roof folded sideways and the left-hand side folded downwards.

Climbing in, I sat down, the parachute in the small of my back already in place, and fingered the flying helmet and face mask I had been loaned, immediately becoming aware that everything American was ever so slightly different – the restraining straps, the Mae West, parachute and dinghy, the face mask and oxygen arrangements, pretty well everything. Ah, well! Strange people, strange ways!

To my new acquaintance, who was bending over to give advice, I said, 'I imagine, like the P.47s, you have an inertia starter on this. We don't on our fighters. And you employ a 24-volt electrical system. Again, we differ in the RAF, as we use a 12-volt external trolley-ack which turns the engine over directly, so that we manage without all this inertia stuff.'

My companion, apparently unimpressed, merely nodded before talking about some of the switches and other controls around the cockpit, and touching on the starting procedure. So, after responding with a few understanding nods, I fitted on my helmet, goggles and mask, checked that I was properly tied down and then went into action.

When initially confronted by this, my first P.51, I had immediately been impressed by its sleek lines and well-fitting cowlings and finish. Smaller than the P.47, it was obviously bigger and heavier than the Spitfire, and, as I was shortly to discover, had some quite distinctive characteristics.

The engine, one of the 60-series Packard-built Rolls-Royce Merlins – with which I was thoroughly familiar – unlike the British-built version had a Bendix carburettor, which produced a quite different warm-up sound: a series of staccato 'burps', interspersed with brief periods of silence, all of which gradually disappeared as working temperatures were reached.

The cockpit, too, seemed more orderly to my British eye, with the instruments – complete with their coloured lines showing working and emergency limits – sensibly deployed, although I still missed the RAF's standard six-instrument 'blind flying' group. And as I taxied away, pressing hard on the hydraulic footbrakes, I was immediately aware of their effectiveness, and also of the wide and rugged undercarriage of the P.51 as I crunched and rattled around the PSP perimeter track to the point of take-off.

The take-off run seemed longer than that of a Spit, the aircraft noticeably heavier. In the air, though, it was a joy, the engine smooth and seemingly better mounted than in a Spitfire, and displaying a rock-steady, automatically controlled coolant temperature of 115 degrees, which was a good deal higher than I was used to when flying behind a Merlin in a Spit. Furthermore, all the flying controls were capable of being trimmed – even the ailerons, which came as something of a surprise. Throughout, however, I was conscious of carrying a considerable load, which of course, I was – the weight of about 300 gallons of fuel, as compared with that of 100 or so in a Spitfire.

No, this was certainly no light, fast-climbing interceptor fighter, but, with its smooth laminar-flow wing, one suited to high speed, both on the level and in a dive. For the same throttle opening – my mind, even then, was constantly converting inches of boost into pounds per square inch – I felt it might be a trifle faster than a Mark 9 Spitfire but not quite so nippy. But, yes, I liked it enormously – except for the hood, that is. Dead keen always to see any enemy behind me, I had the feeling that the P.51's hood might make all the difference between life and death. On the credit side, however, when compared with the Wing's P.47C and its miserable belly band, it was a relief to be tied down securely with a proper shoulder harness.

And it was particularly helpful that I flew that aircraft when I did, as the very next day, the Wing's bright new P.51B (or was it a C?) arrived on our airstrip at Lashenden.

The Wing having arrived in Kent and been able to settle down for a day or two, I thought it necessary to introduce Colonel Sanders, and a few officers likely to be controlling his squadrons when in action, to the RAF Control and Reporting system in general, and the Biggin Hill Sector Operations Centre in particular. When I suggested this to him, he listened to me intently before nodding his agreement without a murmur.

So, in two soft-topped recon vehicles, accommodating the Colonel, myself and four others, we set off the following morning by road.

I remember it being a fine, sunny day and as we wound our way through the pleasant country roads of Kent, our conversation, almost to suit the occasion, became both light-hearted and instructive.

As we drove through the small town of Westerham and were passing the statue of General James Wolfe, I spoke of his famous victory at Quebec in 1759, which resulted in Canada remaining part of the British Empire. To which remark, and somewhat to my surprise as I only said it to needle my American fellow passengers, Tex Sanders remarked loudly, 'Yeah! Damn fine soldier! Pity he had to kill himself, though.'

Which prompted someone to comment, not too seriously, 'Hey, Colonel, I thought you didn't think much of British generals.'

This slightly offensive remark elicited the unsmiling response from Sanders, 'Wolfe was successful and I'll always give credit to a guy who's a winner, OK? No matter who he is or where he comes from.'

And later still, another voice. 'And doesn't Prime Minister Churchill live somewhere round here?'

To which I heard my own reply, 'Only when he gives himself a rest from running the war and wants to do a little amateur bricklaying.'

Which so confused my companions that nothing more was said for quite some time.

After arriving at Biggin Hill and wishing to show off a place I remembered so well, I shepherded my small group into the large and comfortable officers' mess.

Sadly, my good intentions fell flat. It being around lunchtime and the anteroom seething with officers, old and young, male and female, our little group in brown uniforms was lost in a sea of blue. Pushing my way to the hole in the wall that led to the newly improved bar, I ordered drinks for my companions and stood back, taking in the scene. I noted immediately and with some concern that the Colonel was beetle-browed and silent. I had hoped to see the station commander, whom I had never before met but whose name apparently was Hallings-Pott, but it appeared he was not around.

Then, as there seemed to be no other officer present who was sufficiently elevated to interest my senior, I suggested that we stayed for lunch, a proposal which Sanders immediately vetoed with the remark, 'To hell with that! We came to do business, not to eat. So let's go!'

A little stung by Tex's insensitivity, I simply shrugged, rolled my eyes, and led my group away – seething inwardly.

The 6-mile journey to the operations room in Bromley was endured in a painful silence. Throughout, I had a horrible feeling of impending disaster, as the Colonel, clearly boot-faced and in one of his least cooperative moods, appeared ripe for anything.

As we entered the modern SOC building, long since christened 'the gin palace', my apprehensions blossomed. Despite my warning the previous day of our approximate arrival time, my senior's name, rank and appointment together with the reason for our visit, there was no one to welcome us or, indeed, show any sign that we even existed.

Within its hushed interior, although the Operations Centre was obviously fully manned, there seemed to be an unusual placidity about the place. Around the massive plotting-table map, about eight young, shirt-sleeved WAAFs, with bland, expressionless faces, were moving their wands and chequerboard pieces around the board with practised ease, whilst several small groups of NCOs and others conversed quietly in the near distance, now and then introducing an occasional gesture or restrained laugh. All around were tall blackboards extending from floor to ceiling, vast dark panels on which were written the names and call signs of a score of fighter squadrons and the details, positions, missions and situations of a hundred aircraft.

Above all, I became aware of an all-pervading atmosphere of complete disciplined control. Nothing rushed, nothing hurried, every instruction and situation quietly considered and then developed and acted upon in an environment of absolute tranquillity. An admirable set-up: most impressive.

Thoroughly familiar with the design of Fighter Command Sector Operations Centres and what went on there, I soon found myself raising my gaze and studying the chief controller's position on the gallery above the plotting table. The Ops B desk would be on his immediate right hand, with some six or more other specialist officers and NCOs occupying positions further afield.

Observing that the controller was a comparatively junior officer and the Ops B a young section officer I had never seen before, I felt slightly let down. The young lady I was interested in was obviously not around either, perhaps because she was resting after night duty or because she was a member of another watch. Clearly, there was little important happening at the moment, which accounted for everyone being in so relaxed a mood. *Quel dommage!* First a bloody-minded colonel on my hands, and now this – just my rotten luck!

Disappointment focusing my mind, I suddenly decided on a course of action. Finding a spare room, I invited my glowering group to seat themselves whilst I tried to find a responsible officer able and willing to provide the information I had previously requested and for which we had all made a 40-mile journey – and I been denied a good lunch!

After a few minutes' search, I was directed towards an office in the Control and Reporting section, in which two non-flying occupants were facing each other over a big desk, one a comparatively elderly wing commander and the other a younger flight lieutenant. As they looked up in my direction, neither seemed much impressed by my arrival.

Controlling myself sufficiently to address them courteously, I introduced myself and explained my role as liaison officer. I then described why I was there, and with whom.

After that I added, with quiet vehemence, 'I'm afraid the RAF is not covering itself with glory. A senior officer of the 9th USAAF, who commands almost 300 fighters in the Biggin Hill Sector and who has come here especially to learn something about RAF methods and what the Sector can do to help his newly arrived squadrons in battle, has been totally and very rudely ignored. Not only has it embarrassed me but it has deeply offended my American friends.'

I went on, addressing the Wing Commander, 'What we have to do now, sir, is for you to meet my colonel and his group, and take as long as is necessary to explain to them everything they wish to know about what happens around here. If you do that to their complete satisfaction, it is just possible that they will leave Biggin Hill without kicking up a thumping great fuss. If they're not happy, and they do, I will support them absolutely, because I think they have been very shabbily treated. I hope I've made myself clear, sir.'

My speech clearly having an effect, the two officers, after exchanging slightly shamefaced glances, rose slowly to their feet.

The Wing Commander asked, 'Who is this chap again? And where is he now?'

I said, 'If you will follow me, sir, I will take you to them.'

And after that, I am pleased to say, everything went swimmingly.

The Wing Commander and his sidekick conducted my group around every part of the Operations Centre and talked to the Colonel separately for more than an hour, explaining every aspect of the control system and every detail of what the radars were, where they were sited and how they operated. As I followed the group around and listened intently on the periphery, I was quietly pleased. Well done!

And even Tex Sanders was impressed. I know that because, as we left the building, he winked slyly in my direction.

'That was OK, Ginger! Not too bad at all' was his final remark.

Chapter 8
Prelude to Invasion

For the remainder of May and into June and July, for the 100th Fighter Wing order emerged slowly out of chaos. Those of us on the headquarters staff settled into our new farmhouse accommodation, and the two adjacent airfields of Staplehurst and Lashenden were soon filled with about 150 P.51s of the 354th and 363rd Groups. A little further afield, there was a similar number of P.47s of the 358th and 362nd Groups deployed on the nearby landing grounds of Headcorn and High Halden.

The small collection of aircraft flown by us, the several flying members of the headquarters staff, were lodged and serviced in a small rectangular area, some 200 yards by 50, on the south-western end of Lashenden airfield.

Over a period of several weeks, the British Percival Proctor, Airspeed Oxford and Mark 5 Spitfire, which had given such yeoman service throughout the previous four months, were replaced by another Stinson L.5, a new P.47D, a twin-engined Cessna UC-78 and a four-passenger Fairchild C61. With the AT6 (Harvard) already on 'the line' and, of course, our recently arrived P.51, our small group became entirely American, and would later be supplemented by a C-53 (Dakota) and a Noorduyn Norseman, the latter a large single-engined Canadian aircraft.

As these new aircraft arrived, one by one, I felt like a child being presented with a new box of toys, and was suitably delighted. Although no fewer than seven of the headquarters staff were aircrew, 'Tex' Sanders and three of the others, because they were usually otherwise engaged, flew only rarely. Of the rest, Lieutenant Colonel Jim Haun flew the P.47 occasionally but concentrated mainly on the twin-engined aircraft, the doctor, Major Robert

Patterson, the lighter, non-operational types. leaving me to fly the P.51 and pretty well everything else that was flyable.That meant I had that splendid aircraft almost to myself, and left me to fly pretty well everything else that was flyable as and when I wished, which was a huge bonus and an absolute joy.

Much else was happening. With the invasion date clearly immi-nent but as yet unknown, preparation instructions rained down on the Wing like confetti.

With every expectation of being dunked in the water when reaching the enemy coast, every item of transport, and indeed most other pieces of equipment, large and small, had to be minutely waterproofed – a giant, almost mind-boggling task which, because it came so late in the day, had everyone reeling.

On a more personal level, I suddenly found myself presented with a new RAF uniform termed a 'battledress', which consisted of a short bum-freezer jacket, made in a coarse material, which was to be tied inelegantly around my waist. Beneath that were baggy trousers that came up to the chest, the whole ill-fitting affair being impregnated with some vile-smelling chemical which apparently would provide protection in the event of gas being employed by the enemy.

I was also suddenly provided with an American-type steel helmet and plastic inner, a .300 carbine and clips of ammunition, and a 'Wild West' .38 revolver, complete with bullets, all amounting to so considerable a weight that I began to regard the business of protect-ing my life as more a penalty than a benefit – one that became more apparent when I was obliged to safeguard the wretched stuff and cart it around for months to come.

Moreover, I already possessed a massive .45 revolver, given to me in 1940 by the RAF, a weapon I wore for just a single day, after which, because of the gun itself and its heavy holster and ammu-nition hanging around my middle, my uniform became so badly marked and creased that I left the whole caboodle at my parents' home in Northwick Park, on the north side of London, and never either used it or saw it again. No, I never was a gun-toting type of person!

In fact, I seldom wore the battledress either that year, much preferring my own airforce-blue tunic and slacks or a light brown American windcheater jacket, which had shoulder straps on which I wore a major's gold-leaf insignia. This, with my blue RAF uniform trousers, must have made me look very odd indeed, but I found this highly unauthorised rig-out far more comfortable when flying and I was never much concerned about my appearance – nor, indeed, did any of my American colleagues seem to mind.

I was delighted with our new P.51 and had flown it immediately it arrived, feeling utterly at home and taking it to the coastal range to test its battery of four .5-inch machine guns.

Our new P.47D I flew less often. Ours did not have the new tear-drop hood but carried the formidable armament of eight .5-inch machine guns. The battery of .5s I liked a lot. Quite unlike the .303 Browning guns in most of our early RAF fighters (which I had long since regarded scornfully as 'peashooters'), they were big enough to cause real damage. Moreover, they 'chattered' rather than 'thumped', as did the 20mm Hispano cannons in our Spitfires, Typhoons and Tempests.

Deciding that I would be more than comfortable using the P.47s on interdiction sorties against soft-skinned transports and trains, I was aware that they would be pretty useless, even so, against tanks and heavily armoured vehicles. On balance, therefore, I still felt I would be happier going to war in a P.51, despite its exposed radiator, which would be so vulnerable when engaged on low-level attacks.

However, there remained a problem: I still felt I needed formal approval for tacking myself on to any of the Wing's P.51 units, perhaps being regarded as a 'smart-Alec foreign intruder' rather than an experienced help.

The two other new aircraft I was to fly regularly in the months ahead were the Cessna C-78 and the Fairchild C-61, or Argus, as it was known in the RAF.

The Cessna Bobcat, which had something of a questionable past and qualified for one or two rather unflattering names, I found completely trouble free and extremely pleasant to fly. With its two 245-horsepower Jacobs radial engines, it carried two pilots and, at a squeeze, three additional passengers. Cruising around at about 150 miles per hour (on the clock), it was a very comfortable replacement for the Oxford, and I found it a most useful short-range load carrier. It was so comfortable, in fact, that I don't ever recall carrying a parachute, which, for a fighter boy like me, went somewhat against the grain.

The Fairchild, too, was a smallish, high-wing, four-seater communications aircraft. However, with its not overly powerful 165-horsepower Warner Scarab radial engine, I always felt that with three burly companions aboard, I was flying an aircraft that tended to totter rather than canter around the course. And, without parachutes or other items of rescue equipment, I never found the frequent journeys I made in the aircraft, fully loaded and across 90 miles of a very cold English Channel, experiences I found particularly appealing.

Then, a fortnight or more before the actual invasion date (which, needless to say, had not then been revealed to us), word came down from on high that every aircraft involved in Operation Overlord had to be painted with black and white recognition stripes across wings, body and tail.

Chaos immediately! Oceans of paint suddenly appeared and there was a sudden orgy of painting and spraying. The cry went up. What were they doing to us? Whatever next?

Anxious to discuss my involvement during the invasion fighting shortly to take place, I walked across the garden to Colonel Sanders' mobile caravan/office, to find him busily engaged in constructing something or other – the man was never idle.

Looking in my direction and without a smile, he growled, 'OK, Ginger. So what's on your mind?'

I took a deep breath. 'Two things, sir. I've flown the P.51 on several occasions recently and, more and more, I dislike the hood, mainly because I find I can't see very much to the rear. And, of course, the present hood can't be opened during take-off and landing, which is most important, and only partially opens during taxiing.

'Which all adds up to the fact that it is just plain wrong for a fighter aircraft and, in my view, could be a fatal design fault. So I have it in mind to fly down to Ford and talk to some friends of mine who fly the RAF's Mark 3 Mustangs, which have incorporated the new Malcolm bubble hood, designed by a chap in the A&AEE at Boscombe Down. Depending on what I see and how it measures up in the air, I would like your permission to have one installed in our own P.51 – provided I can find the company that manufactures and, presumably, fits it.'

I saw the Colonel silently thinking about my proposal, before giving a brief nod. 'OK, and what's your second point?'

'Well, that's all about me. We shall certainly invade in the coming days or weeks and the Wing's aircraft will be involved with some pretty nasty low-level fighting. I would like to fly with the P.51s from time to time, either from here at Lashenden or from Staplehurst, but, as I am part of your headquarters staff and I would be flying your aircraft, I feel I would need your permission to do so.'

I saw a thin smile pass across my senior's face. 'Looks like you're aimin' to get yourself killed.'

'I would be trying very hard not to.' I think I returned his smile, but I'm not absolutely sure of that. After which, I waited.

Then, after few seconds, 'I wouldn't want to stop you getting involved, Ginger, but I think you would be wrong to fly on more than a very occasional trip. Fighting is a rough, tough old business and to do the job properly, as you are sufficiently experienced to know, would require you spending a fair amount of time among the squadron members you choose to fly with. In short, it would almost be a full-time job and you already have a full-time job here, with me. You wouldn't be able to do both – not properly, that is.'

Then, turning away and speaking over his shoulder, 'But I'll leave it to you. My only advice is don't get yourself knocked off doing some damn silly thing because you think you have to.'

Then, turning again in my direction, 'And about the new hood: OK, go ahead and do whatever you feel is necessary.'

A little surprised that his consent would be so easily obtained, I thanked him, before saluting and leaving.

Outside, and standing in the garden for a moment or two, I

remember smiling to myself and considering our brief conversation. What a complete surprise! Such a civil and unemotional exchange of views – not a single 'biblical' expletive or expression. What on earth had come over the coarse and abrasive man I had sometimes encountered in the past?

The next day, I flew the P.51 down to Ford, near Arundel, on the south coast. I was aware that two RAF fighter squadrons were deployed there, No. 19 Squadron and No. 316 (Polish) Squadron. Both flew the newish Mark 3 Mustang (P.51).

One of the flight commanders in 19 Squadron, a young man who had served under me at Kirton-in-Lindsay, was more than keen to show me, his late Chief Flying Instructor, over his personal Mustang, and explain the better qualities of the Malcolm hood. And, as I sat in the cockpit of his aircraft, the advantages were immediately obvious.

First, the hood was much larger than that of the average Spitfire; also it slid to and fro very easily and afforded a much better view to the rear than that of almost any other fighter I had ever flown. There was also lots of space around my head, which was a blessing as, being a tall person, I had frequently experienced trouble in that area when fully kitted out for combat.

No, this was a splendid change for the better and I would certainly opt for one on the Wing's own P.51s. The questions to be asked, therefore, were: who made the hood, where was the manufacturer located, and how should I go about ordering one, as, clearly, I would not be able to do so through RAF channels?

As we sat in my young companion's office later, discussing the merits of his splendid aircraft, I was told of the number of sorties his squadron had recently undertaken, escorting B17s (Fortresses) of the 8th USAAF all the way to Berlin and back, involving flights of four-and-a-half hours' duration and at heights of between 25,000 and 30,000 feet.

Against an enemy who was perhaps less formidable than in earlier years, they had enjoyed a fair amount of success, his Mustangs performing more than adequately. The only criticism of their new Malcolm hood was that in the bright sunlight of the cloud-less heights, the considerable area of clear perspex had caused some pilots to complain of glare and heat when the searing strength of the sun had been focused on their heads and bodies. However, when compared with the disadvantages associated with the original hood, this, in his view, was a minor criticism that could be discounted.

When asked to identify the manufacturer of the hood, my flight commander friend immediately named the Martin Baker Aircraft Company and said that it had an assembly point on White Waltham airfield, near Maidenhead in Berkshire, smilingly adding that if I were a sensible sort of chap, I should visit the airfield immediately to investigate.

Which, with a light heart, I determined to do. I completely overlooked the fact that Wing Commander 'Bert' Hughes, my good CTO friend from Kirton-in-Lindsay, had recently moved down to Ford and that I might have renewed my happy association with him; unfortunately, in the excitement of the moment, I forgot, and I didn't. With the Malcolm hood on my mind, I only remembered Bert on my way back to Lashenden. A sad omission, alas.

The next day, I flew down to White Waltham in the P.51.

On the grass airfield, there was a row of hangars on what I judged to be the northern side, surrounded by sundry other small buildings. As I circled the landing ground, nothing much seemed to be happening and I landed without either RT instructions or a green Aldis light.

Taxiing unguided towards the hangars, I stopped on a convenient strip of tarmac, threw off my straps ... and waited.

Expecting to be greeted by some official person, I was disappointed; no one approached and there seemed to be a rather unusual Sunday atmosphere abroad. I remember thinking: Adolf Hitler with a bomb or two in his pocket would have a field day round here, no doubt being able to walk about the whole site absolutely unhindered. Clearly, security was not considered a major factor at White Waltham.

After climbing down and with my hands in my pockets, I strolled towards the open doors of one of the hangars. Inside, there were aircraft, a mass of equipment and benches, and a score of workmen busily engaged in assembling, or working on, what appeared to be a wide variety of aircraft parts. I was clearly in sight and observed by a few who casually looked up in my direction, but no one appeared to take more than a passing interest in my being there.

I had been standing, surveying the scene with interest, for a good five minutes, when I was approached by a tall man in a dark business suit and wearing a pair of thick-lensed horn-rimmed glasses, who, I deduced quite wrongly, was the local bean-counter (accountant) or office manager.

With a friendly smile, he asked me if he could be of any assistance, a euphemism which I immediately interpreted as 'What the heck are you doing, you silly blighter, trespassing on out-of-bounds territory?'

I replied, in an equally friendly manner and waving an arm, that I was the chap flying the P.51 over there, and that I was anxious, if I possibly could, to arrange for the provision and fitting of a Malcolm hood to my aircraft. I then went on to explain that although I was the person who mostly flew the aircraft, this particular P.51 really belonged to the Commanding General of about 300 fighters of the 100th Fighter Wing of the 9th USAAF, and that I was merely acting on his behalf – a slight exaggeration of rank on my part.

The tall gentleman smiled tolerantly in my direction and went on to point out that his company did not deal with individual requests but only with either the British Ministry of Supply or any one of the several US Army Air Force authorities. In any case, their order book for the Malcolm hood was more than full at the moment and they were, even now, behind on no fewer than 150 urgent orders. Moreover, if by some miracle my order were to be accepted, my request would simply be added to the very long list of orders at present in hand. My companion gave a weary smile and shook his head. No, it would be quite impossible, he was afraid. He was sorry, but rules were rules, and there it was.

As we continued to exchange pleasantries, my smiling companion gave his name as Mr Darley and, after a pause of several minutes for reflection, suggested that I might wish to join him in a cup of tea in his office, an offer which immediately caused me to think that he might have some arcane solution in mind.

The possible, and all too simple solution, took a few minutes for him to formulate and develop.

I was first questioned about what precisely I did as RAF liaison officer and the type of aircraft I normally flew. Then when I spoke of the various types used in the Wing communications squadron, after a brief exchange of meaningful stares, the solution was explained to me in simple terms.

If I could see my way clear to give him, Mr Darley, a few flying lessons, he would look seriously into the business of transferring my request for a Malcolm hood from last on the list to something much nearer the top. Provided, of course, that I could give him a convincing explanation as to who would pay for the new hood and the work of replacing the existing one.

Surprised and delighted by such a rapid change of circumstances, I replied loftily that the President of the United States would no doubt feel prepared to foot the bill, although, naturally, he would not at present be aware of the fact, and that it might well take a week or two to convince him of his obligation to do so.

We then, with broad smiles on our faces, shook hands on the deal, deciding also that I should wait until my new friend had finagled his side of the arrangement, after which I would sort out an aircraft in which to provide the flying lessons. However, I felt bound to point out that if the invasion of Europe intervened, I might have to devote myself to the greater task of defeating the Luftwaffe and winning the war. Mr Darley, to his credit, nodded gravely and accepted my proviso with a straight face.

On my way back to Lashenden that day, I decided not to tell 'Tex' Sanders of our cunning plan, but to wait until it was all under way before surprising him.

And I did not have to wait very long.

*

About five days later, I was sitting in my farmhouse bedroom when the telephone rang. It was Sergeant Carter from 'the line'.

'Hey, Squadron Leader!' came his loud southern voice. 'We got two English guys here, lookin' like Laurel and Hardy, who say they've come to fit a new hood to our P.51. What's cookin'? Do you know anything about it?'

I was already on my feet. 'Don't say even a word to anyone! I'm on my way up to you now.'

The two 'English guys' did indeed look like Laurel and Hardy, one large and fat, the other sorrowfully thin. Both wore rat-catcher's caps and were heavily into coffee and ring doughnuts.

I asked, 'You have the new hood with you?'

The fat one, between bites, said that they had. 'In the van there.' He nodded in the direction of a small 30cwt vehicle.

'Splendid! And how long will it take to fit?'

'Usually about a day. Provided there are no snags.'

'Snags! I take it you chaps have done this sort of job before?' I grinned at them with cheerful pessimism, well aware I was letting them loose on the Wing's (and 'Tex' Sanders') one and only P.51 and that the Colonel, thus far, was blissfully unaware of what was happening.

The two workmen stopped chewing for a moment, exchanged pitying glances, but did not deign to reply.

Deciding to leave them to it, I added, 'Right, then, I shall be away for several hours. But I will come back later and check that everything is going according to plan. OK? And, don't for Pete's sake, and my future's, muck it up, whatever you do.'

I left, not entirely reassured, with each of them chewing and drinking and staring into space.

I returned in the late afternoon, to find the new hood fitted and the two workmen gathering their tools and preparing to leave. Inspecting it from a distance, I thanked the two for what was obviously a successful job, before climbing into the cockpit and examining their new creation more closely. Yes, the new hood was a splendid improvement. If I was going to war in the near future, I couldn't do better than fight the enemy in this.

★

But, surprising as it may seem, I never did fly into battle under my newly acquired Malcolm hood. Two days later, I received another excited call from Sergeant Carter.

'Hey, Squadron Leader! Guess what? A brand-noo P.51D arrived with us this morning. Six guns, a cut-away back end and the latest tear-drop hood. You'll be carried away, I reckon. Shame, though, about all the work fitting on that noo hood. And before you'd even had a chance to try it out.'

But I knew the Malcolm hood affair did not end there. I still had to fulfil my part of the bargain I had struck with Mr Darley.

And, in fact, I did, as I note from my logbook that I flew across to White Waltham on two occasions and gave him several one-hour instructional flights in the Percival Proctor and the Stinson C78. Whether or not he enjoyed them I don't know, as I have no memory of the flights themselves or what he achieved. All I do remember is that the invasion of Europe started several weeks later and my happy association with that helpful gentleman ended, to become nothing more than a pleasant memory.

Chapter 9

Kings, Commanders and Colleagues

In the run-up to the invasion of Europe on 6 June 1944 – a date we knew nothing about until the event actually took place – our headquarters unit on the outskirts of Lashenden airfield fairly seethed with activity. For weeks we were thigh deep in generals and senior officers of various nationalities and colourful uniforms, some coming to instruct and inform, some to show themselves and encourage, some merely to improve their minds.

Meanwhile, our 'flyboys' in the P.51s and the P.47s just went about their daily business, roaming over the Continent of Europe, escorting, attacking, destroying and intercepting, but also getting themselves shot at, damaged, and now and then killed.

I was aware – although others had probably not thought about it – that the fighters of the 100th Wing would continue to fly from their British bases and not themselves be landing in Continental territory until days, or even weeks, *after* the initial beachhead assaults had taken place. And, indeed, not until the Germans had been cleared from their coastal airfields, and additional advanced landing grounds created, the local countryside having been bulldozed and flattened into usable, steel-meshed strips of open ground. I also felt pretty confident that I myself would be landing in Europe, with the fighters, but certainly not before.

Amid prospects of this and other exciting events to come, the announcement was made one morning by my room-mate, Lieutenant Colonel Hill, who normally dealt with such matters, that King Peter of Yugoslavia would be one of our first important guests.

In slightly awed tones, my room-mate added that our royal visitor would be arriving the following day, accompanied by a handful of generals and other supporting minions, it being planned that he would tour the two P.51 Groups, stationed at Lashenden, before taking lunch as the guest of Tex Sanders in the 100th Wing's greenhouse dining hall.

It was then explained to us that best uniforms would be worn, there would be a special menu for lunch, and a formal seating plan at the top table would be arranged.

When I asked if I would be required to attend, I was informed that the Old Man had especially demanded my presence, that I could be expected to be introduced to the King, and that I would be seated near the top table to prompt him if any problem arose.

I recall a rather light-hearted conversation taking place at this point in which I explained to Al Hill and others that, although I had never met him before, I knew a fair amount about the young King, most of it gleaned recently from information in the London editions of the glossy society magazines.

I knew, for example, that the King had been exiled in 1941, that he was three years younger than me – which made him either 19 or just 20 – and that he had been betrothed to a very attractive young lady, Princess Alexandra of Greece. However, I couldn't, at the time, remember whether or not they had recently married, so I would be unable to advise Colonel Sanders on this particular point.

There followed a discussion on the possibility, for example, of it becoming an act of *lèse-majesté* to serve the King Hungarian goulash, mashed potatoes and sweetcorn for lunch and not Yugoslav goat or camel burgers and French fries. And, if the temperature in the greenhouse even approached the expected 100 degrees Fahrenheit, would the ice cream served as a sweet appear as little more than a small white pool on King Peter's plate?

Finally, I observed Al Hill raise his closed eyes to heaven and mutter, 'I just hope to God the Old Man behaves himself and doesn't say anything likely to cause a war.'

In the event, the visit turned out to be comparatively uneventful. We had all scrubbed up well and the King and his entourage turned up at our farmhouse site more or less on time. We privileged few selected to meet him stood in line around our mess hall, waiting with interest to be introduced.

Walking forward and greeting His Majesty with a cheerful 'Hi-ya, King Peter,' the Old Man, clearly carried away by the occasion, appeared in excellent voice and, after shaking hands and waving his arms about a little more than was necessary, led his visitors in our direction.

The young King, slight in build, white-faced and looking not a day over 16 years of age, followed nervously and silently a step or two to the rear.

Following closely in his wake was the new General, commanding the 19th TAC, a tall, elegant officer, looking like a military version of the actor Gary Cooper. Then, after him, another American general, totally unknown to me, and several well-dressed hangers-on. I was told later that the Gary Cooper look-a-like was Major General Otto P. Weyland (or 'Opie' Weyland, as he later became familiarly referred to).

Having filed in and around the dining table, several of us found ourselves on the wrong side, so to speak, so that having been introduced to the King, we were not able to shake hands but merely obliged to grin and nod, or, in my case, produce a minor bow.

Then, having all been seated, it soon became clear that Tex Sanders was intent on enjoying himself, his conversation becoming loud and uninhibited. I glanced towards Al Hill's face, to find it wearing an expression I can only describe as starkly apprehensive.

And his expectations were well founded, as within moments, the worst happened. In a strident voice full of bonhomie, our gallant Colonel cried, 'Say, King Peter, where's that lovely gal you married recently? You should have brought her along today to eat chow with us.' Then, shaking his head fondly, he added, 'Yessiree! Mighty nice babe ya got there!'

Silence. Absolute silence! Then, with the King wide-eyed and looking as though he had just been kicked on the shin, I exchanged glances with my room-mate, and saw him shrinking in his seat and trying quietly to slide under the table. As were several others.

*

And still the visitors came, most of whom I met and made note of, but some, because I flew almost every day, I didn't.

Among the first, I remember, was the Commanding General of the 9th USAAF, Lieutenant General Lewis H. Brereton, whom I describe in my rather nondescript diary as 'a small, brisk, unsmiling man', adding that he was introduced to only a small group of senior officers and that I was not given the opportunity to meet him.

Our next visitor was the celebrated Marshal of the Royal Air Force, Hugh, Lord Trenchard – the so-called father of the RAF, or 'Boom', as he was more familiarly and affectionately known. A most impressive man, physically – about 6 feet 5 inches tall and built like the proverbial barn – with bushy eyebrows, moustache and enormous charm, he always smelt powerfully of pipe tobacco, lighting and puffing his pipe whenever the opportunity presented itself and as though wishing to cause it an injury.

I had first met him in 1940 at RAF North Weald during the Battle of Britain, and later on several occasions, most memorably when, in the spring of 1943, he had spent many hours with us at RAF Hawkinge, during the time I commanded No. 41 Squadron, flying Mark 12 Spitfires.

As he sat talking with us on that visit, he must have been well into his seventies, and I became aware for the first time that marshals of the RAF, with other officers of similar rank in the Royal Navy and Army, never, in fact, retire, but are always retained in a non-executive capacity (and, of course, on half-pay) for the purpose of advising, encouraging and generally improving morale among us lesser mortals.

For me he was indeed a great morale-raiser and he certainly impressed the American officers to whom he was introduced when he met them on Lashenden airfield that week before D-Day 1944.

But not everyone was so impressed. I learnt many years later that he and a formidable contemporary, Air Chief Marshal Sir Hugh Dowding, of RAF Fighter Command, never saw eye to eye on the employment and effectiveness of air power, and seldom thought fit to disguise their feelings.

A frequent visitor, too, during those several pre-invasion weeks, was Major General 'Opie' Weyland, the commanding officer of the 19th TAC who had accompanied King Peter. Succeeding Major General Elwood Quesada, the new TAC commander was a tall, fair-haired, handsome officer, quiet and agreeable in attitude and demeanour, and certainly better disposed towards Colonel 'Tex' Sanders, who obviously admired and worked well with him. As he usually accompanied most of the more important visitors to Wing headquarters and the two fighter groups based on Lashenden airfield, I saw him frequently and met him several times.

Indeed, on one occasion I recall sitting on the steps of 'Tex' Sanders' office trailer and him asking my opinion of some tactical aspects of the recent fighting. Naturally, I replied in my usual forthright way, but I doubt that my remarks much altered the course of the war!

Among many other names I associate with Lashenden and the immediate pre-invasion period, there are three that remain especially in mind – Patton, Eisenhower and Bickell.

Lieutenant General George Patton, the Commander of the US 3rd Army, was a 'blood and guts' personality, very well known in both the American and British armed forces. During various command appointments between 1940 and 1942, he had gained something of a tempestuous and unsavoury reputation, having struck an allegedly malingering soldier during the Mediterranean campaign. Later, and somewhat controversially, he was reprimanded publicly for this transgression by Eisenhower, the Supreme Commander in Europe.

Patton was quite tall though slightly built, with fair, close-cropped hair and very pale eyes, giving him the appearance of an albino. Although impeccably dressed when I first encountered him, he was seldom seen without wearing the white plastic inner lining to his steel helmet, two prominently displayed pearl-handled six-shooters on his hips and trousers so tight that they verged on the indecent.

Within our Wing headquarters enclave, he addressed a mixed gathering of officers and men, but, purposely choosing to remain on the periphery of the meeting, I did not hear exactly what he said. My room-mate Colonel Hill reported, however, that his expressions throughout were unpleasantly coarse and racial in content, which, I was given to understand, was usually the case.

I thought the man's performance that day tasteless rather than inspiring. My verdict, apparently, was widely shared with other American colleagues and later confirmed when I was given the opportunity to read transcripts of several of his so-called rousing speeches.

I did not see him again during the 3rd Army's six-month advance across France and beyond, but during my regular daily briefings, I became aware of his unhelpful comments and criticisms of other leaders. Throughout, I felt him to be a man of unbridled ambition, an irritant to many of his high-ranking colleagues, even his seniors, and not in any way a team player.

He was to lead the 3rd Army through France and well into Germany, after which he transferred to the 15th US Army. However, before he could take up his new appointment, he was involved in a road accident in December 1945 and died in hospital at the comparatively young age of sixty.

Although I possess a photograph of General Eisenhower, the Supreme Allied Commander, smoking a relaxing cigarette after stepping out of a converted P.51 fighter, I do not recall precisely the date on which the picture was taken of this quite unusual incident. The General had just been flown over the beachhead areas and is shown being accompanied by Major General Elwood Quesada, the late commander of 19th TAC, together with Lieutenant Colonel George Bickell, one of Lashenden's group commanders. The inclusion of Quesada raises an interesting point. Why was he in the picture at all, as he had relinquished control of 19th TAC some weeks before?

What is clear enough, however, is that the aircraft was a P.51B of either the 354th or 355th Fighter Group, converted to seat a second aircrew member when the rear tank of about 80 imperial gallons was removed, the aircraft being flown on that particular occasion by George Bickell.

What is less clear is when it was flown, the presumption being that it was some time shortly after D-Day, 6 June, as Eisenhower was still in Britain and he would hardly have wished to be flown over the favoured beachhead areas at a time when the landing sites were still so secret and certainly not known to the enemy.

George Bickell, one of the two P.51 Group commanders at Lashenden, though a minor figure in this story, was a pleasant and successful little man, who was highly regarded by 'Tex' Sanders and very much a friend of Alvin Hill, my room-mate. I also came to know him well myself and arranged several times to fly with one of his squadrons, although, sadly and for various reasons, not with much success.

Those pre-invasion months of April and May were also a period when my relationships with my American colleagues developed, about half a dozen forming a growing group of close companions.

Although I at first regarded the glittering-eyed, irascible Colonel Sanders as a slightly ridiculous poseur, I later discovered that his macho exterior concealed a man who was able, serious and really quite sensitive, and who, when we became better acquainted, became a friend and ally despite being my senior and unit commander.

Similarly, I increasingly developed close and friendly ties with Lieutenant Colonel Alvin Martin Hill, who ran Sanders' private office with quiet efficiency. Al Hill was 40 years of age and came from a farming family in Omaha, Nebraska, a town and state renowned, apparently, for their insignificance and, I was informed, only rescued from total obscurity by the fact that the late showman William Cody – 'Buffalo Bill' – owned a ranch in the area.

Al was a well-built, good-looking man with firm facial features suggesting rugged bravery, strength and determination, an appearance completely at odds with the fact that he was a quiet, gentle chap who was not at all daring and adventurous and that, strangest of all, he had chosen to be an officer in the USAAF, as he was not aircrew, plainly did not enjoy flying and almost always sat tense and white-knuckled whenever obliged to be in the air.

Al, however, was possessed of a thousand virtues in that he was a splendid administrator and was quiet and helpful in every way. A married man, he was, moreover, totally faithful to his attractive wife, Gartha, with whom he remained constantly and lovingly in touch. Unhappily denied children, as far as I was aware he never strayed from the straight and narrow path of absolute fidelity.

In short, Al Hill was the most decent of men and became a long-standing friend, not only during my time with the 9th USAAF but for the rest of his life and, indeed, for most of mine.

Major Bodenheim (or 'Bodey', as he was called – he never deigned to share his first name with me), the third member of our tiny dormitory, was a non-flying administrator who worked closely with Alvin Hill. Although he was similar to Hill in some respects, 'Bodey' was, however, an altogether different animal. Described by his more senior room-mate as coming from an affluent Los Angeles family, he kept very much to himself, so that in the ten months we lived cheek by jowl, I learned almost nothing of his private life, not even if he was married.

Small, in his mid-thirties, scrupulously neat and organised, he always seemed to have a half-smile on his face when he appeared forever to be weighing me up and glinting in my direction through rimless pince-nez. However, although he was quiet and comfortable to live with, I always felt that he was handling me with kid gloves, together with just the tiniest element of awe, so that we were never sufficiently close to enjoy an easy companionship.

There was, moreover, another slightly darker side to Bodey's character, as, like Top Sergeant Smedley, he would occasionally quietly disappear for several days and come back with a puffed face, split lip or a black eye, suggesting a drunken brawl in which he had come off second best. Which always amused and slightly saddened me, as I felt he had neither the size nor the stature to get involved in any bout of fisticuffs.

And it set me thinking at the time: why did so many normal, rational American males apparently drink for the sole purpose of getting drunk, and then feel obliged to lash out and fight? Yes, Yanks were pretty funny people all right!

Our small dormitory was surrounded by about 15 other officers in bedrooms of their own, a few of whom were rather special and worthy of comment, as they became closest to our small group of three, particularly as they spent much of each off-duty evening 'shooting the breeze', to use the current term, whilst sitting on or reclining next to my bed.

One of these was the tall and eager surgeon, Captain (later Major) Robert A. Patterson, the second-string doctor who, as I have described, had recently flown a brand-new Mark 8 Spitfire almost by mistake. In the run-up to the invasion date, because Patterson was such an enthusiastic pilot, we flew together a great deal – mainly in the Stinson and Fairchild – and our association blossomed from a pleasant companionship at first into a lasting friendship.

It also soon became obvious to me that my new friend had many strings to his bow, as he was very bright, if a little overpowering and noisy, and a very down-to-earth practical person.

That he was an able surgeon I never harboured doubts, although he had few opportunities in those early days to demonstrate his prowess. In short, I soon concluded that he was a most impressive young man and was likely to go far in whatever work he chose to undertake, either in or beyond the US Army Air Force.

About his private life, however, he chose to remain reticent. I became aware – I don't know how or by what means – that he was married and had fathered several children, although he never spoke about his family in my presence and seldom appeared to receive or send any form of correspondence.

However, it is worth adding that he was certainly not averse to the ladies and always demonstrated a rough if compelling brand of charm in female company. Indeed, in later years when I knew him better, I was introduced to several 'permanent' partners with whom he appeared to be on very intimate terms. In short, the large and dynamic Major Robert A. Patterson was, in every way, a very formidable sort of chap.

Patterson's immediate senior was also an important member of our circle, but the Irish doctor Lieutenant Colonel Frederick Loughran was an altogether different kind of person. A glowering, muttering Irish Fenian, Freddie was formerly a general practitioner in Boston, Massachusetts. Although by no means incapable as the Senior Medical Officer, he was at heart a policy man and not a nuts-and-bolts person, so that having a smart and able assistant like Patterson in the offing, he was happy to let him 'run the shop', so to speak.

To me, however, Freddie Loughran was always the 'officer in charge of grease traps'. Which requires a little explanation.

Freddie, it seemed to me, had two obsessions in life. One was his intense dislike of his commanding officer, Colonel 'Tex' Sanders – but, coming from the north, he had the good sense to keep his feelings to himself. The other was his preoccupation with the efficiency of the Wing's sanitation and drainage system – or, more precisely, the manner in which the cholera-causing mountain of excreta produced by thousands of healthy males doing what nature intended them to do at least once every twenty-four hours was properly dealt with. All this, plus the never-ending effort of disposing of this most unpleasant mountain of brown mud being produced every day of every week of every month.

In the days ahead, when events decreed that water closets were rarely available, invariably a mass of holes or ditches were dug in the earth, resulting in each one of us – often in full view of the world at large – sitting with his bum spread uncomfortably over a pole, doing his 'business', in close proximity to Freddie Loughran's grease traps – the quite primitive means by which the horrible stuff was trapped, covered, neutralised and disposed off, significantly reducing the ghastly smell and making life almost bearable again. All in the noble fight against cholera.

In the weeks and months ahead, the embarrassment of 'going to the loo' in the battle area was often more of a personal problem for me than the efforts of the entire German nation trying to write me off, so that the name of Colonel Loughran (and his grease traps) was to remain uppermost in my mind for many years to come.

Probably the most frequent evening visitor to our bedroom 'gossip centre' was Lieutenant Colonel Jim Haun, the head of A3, the Wing's Operations Section.

Described by 'Tex' Sanders as 'that slow ol' southern boy', Haun, with his pungent, ever-present pipe and rakishly worn service dress hat, was 31 years of age, an able and experienced pilot of 'the slower

Portrait of the author
with sword.

Portrait of Flight Officer Eileen
Hampton in Ghent, Belgium,
May 1944.

My first P.47C. Also termed a Razorback.

A P.47D over the coast of Cornwall with St Michael's Mount in the distance.

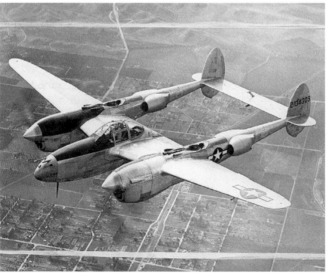

A late model P.38L, similar to that flown by me and used in the 100th Fighter Wing in the reconnaissance role.

My first P.51D, which I flew constantly and greatly admired.

The Albermarle caused such excitement and then heartache when its wheels refused to lock down.

I used the Cessna UC-71 (Bobcat) a great deal for light communication purposes.

My first P.51B, taxiing out on its dispersal of Sommerfeld Wire Mesh track on the ALG at Staplehurst.

I encountered the enormous Northrop P.61 Black Widow night fighters on the airfield at Cherbourg – the original streamlined bricks!

The Noorduyn UC-64 Norseman, or what I termed a 'flying furniture van'. It was the Wing's Norseman that suffered an engine failure on take-off, killing one member of the crew and badly injuring the pilot and several other members of the 100th Wing communications flight. It was also in the Norseman that the celebrated band leader Glenn Miller was lost.

King Peter of Yugoslavia on his visit to Lashenden airfield and the 100th Fighter Wing headquarters in May 1944. Seen with, from left to right: General Weyland of 19th TAC, Lt. Col. Bickell, General Royce and Colonel Sanders.

Marshal of the RAF Sir Hugh Trenchard with Generals Royce and Weyland, together with Colonel Sanders and Lt. Col. Bickell, during their tour of the 100th Fighter Wing airfields and units in May 1944.

General Patton of the US 3rd Army in the foreground with General Weyland and Lt. Col. Bickell, during General Patton's visit to the units of the 100th Fighter Wing.

General (later President) Eisenhower smoking a cigarette, accompanied by his pilot General Quesada and Lt. Col. Bickell, walking away from their modified two-seater P.51, having just flown over the invasion beaches on 4th July 1944. The P.51 was converted into a two-seater by removing the rear fuel tank in the fuselage.

A V1 pilotless flying bomb (doodlebug) within feet of diving into the ground. Two seconds later it probably destroyed a whole row of buildings and killed at least 20 people.

A doodlebug passing over the camera at night and at less than 400 feet. At RAF Biggin Hill I watched at least 20 of these fearsome weapons pass immediately over my head during one four-hour period in June 1944.

A downed doodlebug being examined by the Army.

A line up of P.51Bs at
Lashenden, wearing their
new invasion stripes.

George Bickell's P.51
at Lashenden wearing
its 100 gallon long-range
tanks.

A P.51B at Staplehurst, fitted
with the new Malcom Hood
and wearing its long-range
tanks which, later in the
year, were used as napalm
firebombs.

The much-decorated
P.51D, belonging to
Lt. Col. Eaglestone, on the
Continent. Like my P.51D,
it was fitted with the new
tear-drop canopy.

A P.47 from High Halden, 'loaded for bear', with invasion stripes, eight .5 machine guns, a long-range tank and two 250-pound bombs.

Been there, done that! The remains of a Kent oast house having been in the path of an unfriendly P.47 that experienced problems directly after taking-off from Headcorn.

The P.47 engine 'wot did it'! The wrecked aircraft, less its engine, which had to make an emergency landing on its way to Headcorn.

stuff', and a teller of tall stories, most of them about the 'mountain folk' in his home state of Tennessee.

Pickling us all in a fog of blue pipe smoke, he would tell us long and amusing tales of how, in his youth, he had sold bibles to the isolated 'hillbilly' farmers living in the foothills of the Great Smokey Mountains, descendants of the early English, Irish and Scottish settlers in America, who over the years had scratched the barest of existences from the soil and remained much as they were in the late eighteenth century, being shut off from the modern world by vast distances, ancient habits and traditions, and, not least of all, poverty.

He also related tales of the occasions when, forced to stay overnight in the primitive huts of his farmer hosts, he was obliged to 'bundle up', nine to a bed, struggling to sleep among family members of all ages and both sexes, and lay awake for hours, scratching endlessly, having been savaged by man-eating fleas hopping about like gazelles in the most unwholesome of blankets.

There were sad anecdotes, too, of the American Civil War in the 1850s, when young farm boys from Tennessee went off singing to fight for the south and never to return. And even further back, stories of the late 1700s, of isolated raids by 'them thievin' red varmints', who set fire to their rustic homes and drove off their livestock.

His vivid word pictures of early colonial America were amusingly corroborated by cartoons in the then very popular *Esquire* magazine, showing ancient Mountain Men, with their long beards, corncob pipes, bare feet and tall black hats, manufacturing their illicit 'moonshine' brews in the forest edges, surrounded by ragged children, chickens, gaunt family pets and rooting hogs. All these wonderfully evocative tales and pictures added greatly to my education and to the knowledge of at least some of my American colleagues.

An important other in our immediate circle was Captain Ray Firestein. Jewish to his bootstraps, 'Fireball' was one of the nicest men ever. With his bright blue eyes and more flashing white teeth than I had ever seen in a human mouth, he was quite unlike the typical olive-skinned, brown-eyed member of the Jewish diaspora. Moreover, he possessed a rare sense of fun altogether in keeping with his wide-toothed grin and happy attitude to life – his leg was pulled unmercifully, but nothing seemed to offend or upset him.

As he appeared to drift constantly in the wake of Patterson the doctor, I always assumed that he was either a junior doctor himself or perhaps a member of some allied profession. All I remember is that he was seldom out of sight, a constant visitor to my bedroom, and always the butt of some joke or victim of an incident in which he was the inevitable 'fall guy'.

Whatever, or whoever he was, Captain Raymond Firestein was one of nature's gentlemen and someone guaranteed to raise morale just by being around. Sixty-five years and more later, even the memory of him can still bring a smile to my face.

Chapter 10
Two Special WAAF Officers

During those hectic summer months, I was able to spend some time with my rather special WAAF officer lady friends, Flight Officer Eileen Hampton and Section Officer Cynthia Oglethorpe. As every day is a working day in war, there are no weekends, so I have no clear idea of when exactly these trivial events occurred, except that they all took place about mid-May 1944.

I decided to invite Flight Officer Hampton and her friend Section Officer Oglethorpe, both of the Sector Operations Centre, to Lashenden, to see how we 'poor wretched flying types existed' and also attend a formal evening social function arranged by the fighter group based on the airfield.

I then tackled Patterson, whom I saw as a helper and ally. Would he assist me in entertaining my two lady guests at the social function and also on an improving walk in the countryside the following day?

Patterson eyed me with interest. The two ladies in question he had met briefly before at Biggin Hill, he recalled. Yes, he would be happy to help me out at the Lashenden party and also on the 'improving walk', at which time he would probably be able to produce a little 'giggle juice', which would add to the pleasure of the occasion.

Sensing trouble ahead, I pointed out that the improving walk was intended to be a pleasant stroll in the sun followed by afternoon tea in some wild-flowered pasture, not a rowdy booze-up. Furthermore, the object of the exercise was for me to impress one lady in particular, in whose direction I was making sheep's eyes, so that he was in no way to cramp my style. OK?

An agreement being reached, I then went off to arrange (not

without some difficulty, I might add), suitable overnight accommodation in Headcorn for my two Biggin Hill guests.

The day started off well enough. The two young ladies arrived
at about lunchtime, laughing and smiling and clearly in a relaxed
state of mind.

I introduced them to their accommodation and, after allowing
them half an hour to 'freshen up', took them in my car the mile or
so to the airfield. There I met Patterson and together we showed
them round our aircraft, allowing them to sit in the small but comfortable Fairchild four-seater. After that, amid much light-hearted
banter, I recall we fed our guests coffee and doughnuts, which they
seemed to enjoy.

Everything at that point seemed to be going swimmingly: even
the weather was cooperating, the sun 'cracking the flags', to quote
an often used northern quip. Super! Aware that the social function
was to start at 6.30 p.m., we then led them back to Headcorn village
before leaving to allow them to prepare themselves for the evening.

The social event, I recall, was in the garden of one of the group
commanders, about 400 yards from our own Wing Communications
Flight parking area. It started off in the usual way, drinks being circulated and small conversational groups gathering amid laughter
and fighter-pilot gesticulations. I found myself discussing a possible
planned attack by a small group of about four or five P.51s – me
included – against a coastal seaplane base in southern France, which
(I thought privately) was nothing more than a ridiculous adventure,
as it promised the probable loss of friendly aircraft for little gain, my
pragmatic mind speculating sombrely, moreover, that it was to be
an event highly unlikely to shorten the war.

Throughout, I was conscious of my two female guests listening quietly and attentively to our conversation, of the tall figure
of Patterson towering above everyone, and of 'Tex' Sanders and a
group of my friends and acquaintances from Wing headquarters
who were surrounding him laughing and talking happily.

We all began to move forward in a broad, slow-moving queue,
presumably to be introduced formally to our hosts. I had Flight
Officer Eileen Hampton, my own particular lady guest, beside me.

'Tex' Sanders was somewhere ahead, accompanied by Patterson escorting my second Biggin Hill friend, Section Officer Cynthia 'Ogie' Oglethorpe. Little did I know that within moments an incident would occur that I can still, after an interval of more than sixty years, not believe.

In conversation, I glanced up to witness a brief commotion taking place a little ahead of me. And saw a pair of feet, in the air, and at head level!

With everyone around me, I was quite stunned by this strange phenomenon. *Feet,* where *heads* could normally be expected! Followed by a thud, and people looking down at the ground.

Stunned by this phenomenon, I moved forward through the people around me. What on earth was going on?

As a circle of silent, motionless figures parted, I looked down to observe the Old Man – Colonel 'Tex' Sanders – lying flat on his back, looking up at the sky with a dazed, bemused look on his face.

As I halted in surprise, a falsetto voice shrilled in my ear. 'Jesus! Did you see that? That English broad put an armlock on the Colonel and then threw him over her shoulder like a sack of apples! She must be as strong as a spooked steer!'

Then other voices. 'What happened? Anyone see what happened? Did he say something to her?' Followed by what I interpreted as an embarrassed ripple of laughter, as figures bent down to pick up the Old Man to dust him off amid several solicitous enquiries as to whether or not he was hurt.

I then heard another somewhat amused voice asking, 'Hey! Did you fall over somethin', Colonel, or were you just hit by the moonshine they're serving?'

But we all knew he had not tripped over anything and it had nothing whatsoever to do with the liquor.

I remember standing there feeling very uncertain – uncertain and embarrassed. For a guest of mine, a slight and attractive young English lady to boot, had just assaulted and floored the Commander of the 100th Fighter Wing, a very senior officer of the 9th USAAF. My God! Should I help him to his feet and apologise? Or, because he was probably a good deal more embarrassed than I was, should I do nothing and drift into the background, pretending that I had not witnessed my guest's extraordinary performance?

Chicken-heartedly, I chose the latter course of action and gently pushed the arm of my own lady friend towards the outer circle of the now gabbling crush, looking all the time for Patterson and Oglethorpe.

But Patterson and Oglethorpe had clearly come to the same conclusion and had wisely decided to make themselves scarce. Which they did so successfully that I did not see either of them until the following day.

Though I was temporarily unhappy about the incident, the rest of the evening, surprisingly, proved to be a step forward in my relationship with Flight Officer Hampton. Manoeuvring us towards the edge of the crowd, which by this time appeared to be engaged in discussing weightier matters, I found my car and quietly drove off in the direction of Headcorn. There my guest and I exchanged slightly self-conscious giggles before alighting slowly amid audible sighs of relief. What an embarrassing thing to have happened! And more to the point, remembering the look of shock and amazement on Tex Sanders' face, what, for me, might be the eventual repercussions?

With the resilience of youth, however, I felt that things could only improve – and they did. Hand in hand and with quiet smiles, we left the car and set off on an evening walk that took us into deserted country byways for what seemed to be an age, only retracing our steps to Flight Officer Hampton's village lodgings when we were enveloped in the silent blackness of an unlit wartime night. There, in the darkness of her room, with the blackout curtains left undrawn, we talked for hours on matters important for us but, because they were for us alone, not to be repeated for others to read about.

I remember leaving around midnight, quietly content. If the weather was fine tomorrow, the day could be very productive indeed.

Although the following day was bright and clear, I did not see my two WAAF officer friends until early afternoon, as one of them insisted on attending morning church service.

After driving out to Headcorn in my Morris 10 to pick them up, we met a smiling Patterson, carrying a bulging parachute bag, which he lifted into the boot of my car. When I asked what he was carrying, he merely smiled more widely and explained that his bag contained a couple of bottles of 'giggle juice' and Fireball's radio.

Having decided on an afternoon walk in the countryside – it was a balmy, sunny day – I drove about five miles to an area in which I knew there to be an old Kent oast house surrounded by meadows rich in lush green grass and early summer wildflowers. It is perhaps worth mentioning that unlike today, in wartime Britain there were very few mineral fertilisers available and farmers were obliged to rotate their crops regularly, so that about one-fifth of the country-side was left fallow each year, resulting in vast areas of pasture and colourful flowers being allowed to proliferate.

We stopped the car, selected our meadow, and settled down on the several blankets we had brought, the girls almost self-consciously removing their service caps and tunics to present Patterson and me with two sets of eye-catching shirt-enclosed bosoms. Yes, life was certainly worth living!

And as we all lay on our backs with eyes closed, savouring the sun, we talked endlessly about trivial things, laughed at each other's harmless jokes, and vastly enjoyed an ambience in which there was seemingly no war, no stress or hurt, no flying accidents or death, no responsibilities or anything else, in fact. I believe that, sensing that we were all submerged in an atmosphere unusually warm and gentle and loving, I actually prayed that I might later be blessed with memories of that very special afternoon.

As surprising as it may seem, Cynthia Oglethorpe's embarrassing demolition of Tex Sanders the previous evening was never mentioned, other than by me when first we met earlier that afternoon. In response to my obvious query as to what caused her to act so violently, she merely shrugged and said that Tex had made several rather unpleasant personal remarks to her, to which, had a much younger person made them, she would probably have responded with a laugh and a suitable riposte. But the Colonel, in her opinion, was just 'a dirty old man' and should have known better. Moreover, if he ever tried it on her in the future, she would probably flatten him again in much the same way.

A little surprised and dismayed by her remarks, I remember commiserating with her rather half-heartedly, adding, however, that if she intended to set about any future American commanding officer of mine, she should warn me beforehand so that I could take a few days' leave before and after the event.

And Tex Sanders 'a dirty old man'? I was most surprised. She was surely mistaken, as he had never struck me as being that sort of person. Coarse and rude sometimes, yes, but never 'dirty' in an indecent way.

My brief and fairly sombre talk with friend 'Ogie' differed greatly in tone from the light-hearted conversation I had with Patterson about the contents of his bag.

Having extracted the two bottles of his 'giggle juice', it was only after being pressed that the doctor explained that the 'clear stuff' in the bigger bottle was pure medical alcohol. Responding to our squeals of surprise, he went on to describe the liquid as being much purer and far less dangerous than the most refined tipple of vodka, and likely to be a positive joy for us to consume, especially when mixed with the contents of his second bottle, which was filled with the concentrated juice of a thousand plump Californian lemons.

Then, pouring quantities of each liquid into four paper cups he had produced like rabbits out of hat, he invited us to sample his drink, after which, he assured us, the rest of the afternoon would slip by almost unnoticed and life take on a distinctly more roseate hue.

The first cupful he handed round to each of us we sampled cautiously. The second tasted much better, but the third went down easily, brought a smile to each of our faces, and made even the dreary chamber music we were listening to on Fireball's radio – also produced by Patterson from his bulging parachute bag – more appealing.

Fireball's radio, poor thing – alas, it was to have an all too short life.

It had not been obtained without a struggle, the doctor informed us. His friend Fireball loved that radio like a brother and could barely let it out of his sight. Made back home in the 'good ol' US of A', it was Fireball's link with civilisation, he stoutly alleged. Moreover, it was apparently the only man-sized, long-range radio in the fighter Wing headquarters and was probably vital to the success of the forthcoming invasion. In short, in terms of communication it was absolutely priceless and had to be preserved and protected at all costs.

But Patterson, it appeared, had fought back gallantly, explaining that their much-valued colleague, the Squadron Leader, so highly regarded throughout the headquarters, was planning to entertain several important lady guests and it would help enormously if there was a little improving music on the side, so to speak. It would be greatly appreciated, therefore, if he, Fireball, would be sufficiently magnanimous to bend his quite understandable private rule and allow his radio to be loaned for this one very special occasion.

Deploying this and other powerful arguments, Patterson's persuading eventually carried the day and he came away with Fireball's much-loved radio in his parachute bag. And it certainly made its contribution to the success of our afternoon, as the sun, the muted music, the quiet mellowness of the occasion, but primarily Patterson's booze, lulled me, if not my companions, into a blissful slumber, which lasted until the early evening.

At which time, aware that one of our two guests had to be back at Biggin Hill in time for the late-night shift, we languidly got to our feet, dressed, collected our belongings and made our way back to the car. There, with stifled yawns, we packed the boot and, after climbing in sleepily, set off back towards the village of Headcorn.

After I had driven possibly a mile down a deserted byroad, a female voice interrupted my silent languor. 'I don't want to create an unnecessary fuss, but where's the radio?'

Without saying a word, I applied the brakes, came to a stop and closed my eyes. Dear God, I knew exactly where the radio was, because I had left it on the roof of the car!

After turning round and driving back, sure enough, the radio was there – in the middle of the road. Climbing out, Patterson picked it up and, holding it dramatically to an ear, shook it. Whereupon, I honestly believe we all winced, for it sounded as if he was shaking a half-empty box of nails.

Climbing back into his seat, he grinned in my direction. 'Am I going to explain this to Fireball or are you? After all, you're the captain of this ship!'

I honestly have no recollection of how, or by what means, my two WAAF officer guests made the 30-mile journey back to Biggin Hill that evening. It may be that I drove them myself in my own car – I just don't remember. What I do recall, all too clearly, however, was the conversation I had with Flight Officer Hampton before we parted that night.

After each of us had exchanged trite observations about how pleasant her two-day visit had been, I took a deep breath and told her of what I had in mind.

I said, 'Look, I'm planning to take a few days' leave, and I was wondering if you would like to come away with me?'

I saw two eyebrows rise in surprise. 'Go away with you? It sounds exciting but I really don't see how I can. The invasion is just a day or so away and as senior "Ops B" officer at Biggin, I have to be around when the whistle blows.'

But I persisted. 'Sweetie, the invasion has been "just a day or so away" for the last nine months, hasn't it? And surely, with about four million other service chaps lining up to invade, they're not likely to miss just the two of us, are they? Added to which, I haven't taken leave for ages and I suspect you haven't either. So, why can't we both take a day or two off, for heaven's sake?'

I saw her undecided, after which she asked, 'All right then. Where are you thinking of going, when are you likely to leave, and of course, for how long? And also how do we get there, bearing in mind that petrol is rationed and there are so few places in which to stay these days?'

Sensing that she was at tipping point, I went on excitedly, 'Look, if we made up our mind to go, we could resolve all these matters one by one. As to where we might go, I have no plan exactly, except that I would head for the south-west and aim for somewhere on the coast. Remember, I was abroad for more than a year and my parents saved my 6-gallons-a-month ration of petrol, so that I have enough for about a 900-mile journey. Also, I'm very good at transferring fuel by sucking it through a tube to fill empty 5-gallon drums, so I have a few tricks up my sleeve to show you if necessary. No, all you have to worry about is remembering to bring your nightie, a change of knickers, your toothbrush and, of course, your ration card. The rest you can leave to me.'

As I saw her shaking her head and smiling in a resigned way, I knew she had made up her mind but had a further important question to ask. And it came, precisely as I had expected.

'So, as we might be away for several nights, what sleeping arrangements have you in mind?'

Smiling, I had my answer well prepared. 'Sweetie, that would always be left for you to decide.'

Cynthia Olglethorpe was a 23-year-old when she was involved in her rather unusual fracase with Colonel 'Tex' Sanders on Lashenden airfield in May 1944. At the time, I knew her fairly well though not intimately. However, I was informed that she was the only daughter of a well-established family of solicitors living in Sussex.

Many years later, when serving in the British Embassy, Washington DC, I had occasion to pass through Georgia, and learnt, to my considerable surprise, that the name of Oglethorpe was very well respected in that state and that a university had been named after a forebear of hers, James Edward Oglethorpe.

On investigation, I discovered that he was described as a 'soldier and philanthropist' who had lived between the years 1696 and 1784. A Jacobite by inclination and named after the Stuart claimant to the British throne involved in the abortive rising of 1715, although tainted by his political beliefs the young Oglethorpe became a Member of Parliament in 1722, and in 1732 led a small group of eminent gentlemen, commissioned by George II, to set up a new state in colonial America, subsequently referred to as Georgia.

Returning to England, James Edward Oglethorpe, by this time a distinguished soldier, took part in the 'Bonnie Prince Charlie' insurrection at Culloden, Scotland, in 1745, before retiring from the public scene and living quietly in north-east London. Although he and his wife did not have children, two of his brothers did, and it was from one of these that my combative friend Cynthia was descended.

It is curious that Tex Sanders, who was always immensely proud of his southern roots, should have been dumped on his back at a party by a young English lady who herself had strong connections with a forebear who was instrumental in the formation of the State of Georgia.

As my flying logbook indicates that I normally flew at least once every day, the gap in my flying between 23 and 27 May 1944 suggests that this was the period during which my much favoured companion, Flight Officer Eileen Hampton, travelled west with me on our brief holiday together.

I well recall driving my venerable Morris 10 to Biggin Hill and stopping outside the WAAF officers' living accommodation in what had previously been the large station commander's married quarters.

Within moments, the front door opened and she approached at a run. Almost diving into my car, she arrived breathless and clearly on edge.

Grinning in her direction I said, 'You're not in uniform! It's the first time I have ever seen you in civilian clothes and you look so different.'

'Which is exactly why I don't want to be seen, so let's get out of here as soon as possible.' And as I started up and began to drive away, 'Anyway, how different? Better or worse?'

'Just different. With your summer outfit, silk stockings and high heels. And your hair just that bit non-regulation. Otherwise, just as beautiful, of course, and much the same.' I gave her an encouraging smile.

Five minutes later, we were well clear of RAF Biggin Hill and on our way to the west at a breathtaking 30 miles per hour. Facing each other, we laughed delightedly in each other's faces, like kids with their buckets and spades on their way to the seaside. Yes, life was fun! Life was absolutely super!

Some three hours later, we had the airfield of Boscombe Down to our left, and shortly afterwards, the ancient pile of Stonehenge to our right. Then, a mile or so beyond the small town of Amesbury, we stopped at a somewhat seedy café for a comfort break, a cup of tea and a tired sandwich.

Off again and still in good heart, we suddenly found the urge to sing as we positively thundered westwards at our steady speed of 35 miles an hour, my car clearly feeling the strain, as I was forced into first gear several times when climbing even some moderate hills en route. Finally, well into our drive, my companion asked rather plaintively, 'Do we know where we are and where it is we are going?'

I replied a mite testily, 'I don't know exactly, the government having removed every signpost between Land's End and John O'Groats, but we'll continue along this road for another hour or so and then look around for a place to stay.' More for something to say than anything else, I added with a smile, 'My bum's getting a little sore and I'm sure yours is, too.'

At something after 5.00 p.m., when we had been driving for around six hours since leaving Biggin, I noticed a roadside 'Bed and Breakfast' sign attached to an arrow pointing to a village in the near distance. Breathing a quiet prayer of relief, I turned off the road and headed in that direction.

The signposted house was large, grey and fairly ancient, suggesting that it might at one time have been a vicarage. Not exactly welcoming, it looked good enough for me, however, so that I stopped the car with a sigh and, leaving my silent companion looking tired but rather relieved, set off in search of mine host.

The rather buxom middle-aged lady who greeted me at the door was neat, bright and cheerful. She had only one room, she admitted regretfully, and if my lady friend and I were not sleeping partners, the best she could offer as a second bed was a mattress, blankets and pillows on a full-sized billiard table.

When, astonished, I laughed openly at her suggestion, she laughed with me and added that other visitors had used the table before and found it quite comfortable if rather less bouncy that the normal bed.

When, grinning widely, I reported the situation to my weary companion in the car, she was horrified and said that we must move on and find somewhere else.

Having been driving for almost a full day, I was not in the mood for further travel and disagreed. I said firmly, 'Sweetie, I vote for staying here. Don't forget I've been in the car for several hours longer than you, and I'm plain sick of driving.'

'Even so,' my partner protested, 'I just couldn't sleep in a comfortable bed knowing full well that you were tossing about on a rock-hard billiard table. No, I think you should go back and tell the woman that we've had second thoughts and have to move on.'

'But I can't do that,' I protested, 'after her efforts to please and all the chat and laughter we had talking about it.'

'In that case, if you can't face her, let's find a public telephone and you can speak to her over the phone. I'm sure her name and address will be in the book.'

'But I don't know her name or address!'

'Then you'll just have to find out, won't you?'

Which, a mile away and fifteen minutes later, I succeeded in doing – passing on our decision in an uncertain, jokey voice and with a very pink face.

We must have been well into Somerset at the time because we came across Exeter within about an hour or so.

Skirting the cathedral city to the south, we continued westward on the A30, running alongside Dartmoor to our left, for what seemed to be an age, before passing through a town I recognised as Okehampton. Finally, when I was feeling so tired that I was beginning to lose the will to live, we went through the equally small town of Launceston – whose identity was revealed only when I happened to read the name carved in concrete on a public lavatory.

A mile or so beyond Launceston, we struck oil. To our right, we came across a large double-fronted white house situated in a sizeable garden in which the familiar 'Bed and Breakfast' sign was prominently displayed. Muttering, 'Thank God for small mercies!' I stopped the car and tottered stiffly up a small concrete path towards the main outside door.

The middle-aged housewife who greeted me was in a long white housecoat but, unlike the previous landlady, she didn't laugh a lot. However, she cheered me up immediately by saying that she had two 'nice rooms' available and could produce an evening meal if we so wished.

So, collecting our bags and my very weary partner, I returned to the house to find it reassuringly clean, roomy, and full of light and our two bedrooms a positive joy. I recall sinking with a sigh into one of the softest mattresses ever and blessing the young woman in the next room, whose insistence had resulted in my not having to sleep on a billiard table.

We ate well that evening, I recall, and later, both slept like logs – for most of the night anyway.

The following morning was bright and clear. We each had porridge, a shell egg each with toast for breakfast, with tea and lots of milk and honey available if required, our new landlady explaining that one of the benefits of living in the country was that eggs, milk, a chicken or two, most garden vegetables and even a few slices of illicit pork were always available now and then, despite the most stringent of rationing regimes. Furthermore, she added with a straight face and a sly wink, 'seeing as 'ow you wuz both Air Force', she wouldn't be asking for our ration cards.

I remember my companion and I exchanging comfortable smiles of surprise and appreciation – Christmas had certainly arrived early this year.

Although we set off in the highest of spirits and though I recall facing my partner with a grin and saying, 'Not long now!', the next stage of our journey seemed to take an age.

As we toiled interminably around the narrow lanes and high hedges of Cornwall, I sensed that my companion was rapidly losing interest in our once so anticipated adventure. So much so that she finally bleated wearily, 'I do hope you've finally decided where it is we're going, because it would help if I knew too!'

Which prompted what I thought would be an encouraging reply. 'Point number one: we are here in Cornwall mainly because a distant forebear of mine was apparently Mayor of the Cornish town of Bodmin, about a hundred years ago. Point number two: we are heading for the town of St Austell, for no other reason than it's on the coast and to me it has always sounded rather a pleasant and interesting place in which to stay.'

My explanation was greeted with a sideways glance and absolute silence.

Arriving eventually at St Austell at about 5.00 p.m., I successfully located the hotel I had previously been told about. It was pleasantly old, full of beams and nicely creaky, clearly very comfortable, had suitable single-room accommodation for each of us, and also offered the prospect of decent meals. Super! It appeared that we were dead lucky.

After we had settled in for an hour or so, and as I stood alone at the bar sampling a welcome drink, I found myself surrounded by a noisy group of people whose faces I recognised immediately. I was also suddenly confronted by Flight Officer Hampton, whose face wore a look that was distinctly glum.

As I began to tell her excitedly that our immediate companions in the hotel were the actors Tom Walls and Ralph Lynn, and that the noisy crowd of 'lovelies', technicians and hangers-on were all part of a film that was at present being made locally, I was suddenly silenced by the sombre look in her eyes.

She said quietly, 'I've just been on to Biggin Hill and they want me back immediately. It looks as though things are just about to start.'

I looked blankly in her direction. 'You mean they want you back now?' My voice had probably risen an octave.

'That's what I understand, yes.'

'Now? But we've just spent 12 hours in the car driving more than 300 miles. Are you really suggesting that we just turn round and do it all again?'

'I'm sorry, but it rather looks that way.'

I took a deep breath – probably several very deep breaths! 'Well, as it's getting on for 6.00 p.m, we'll just have to cancel the rooms and have a bite to eat here. After that, I'll have to find petrol from

somewhere in the town, as there won't be any all-night petrol stations open anywhere.' I looked at her hopefully. 'Are you really sure
this is what you want to do? Because it means another 12 hours of
purgatory in the car, and most of it at dead of night?'

To which I received merely a shrug of the shoulders and a silent
resigned nod.

I don't remember all that much about our journey home, except
that it was miserable beyond words – dark, raining, just a few pallid
gleams from my filtered headlights, nothing to eat or drink, and a
number of short but important comfort stops, during which I was
also able to snatch a few minutes' sleep.

Dawn came at about 4.00 a.m. and we finally reached Biggin Hill
around mid-morning to learn, to our weary disgust, that the invasion was now not likely to take place until later.

I drove back to Lashenden feeling so tired that when I was turning my car to park it against the wall of our farmhouse bedroom,
I had not the strength to fully turn the steering wheel, so that l
crunched into the bricks and quite badly damaged my offside wing.

As I sat there in thought for some minutes, I calculated that in
little more than 48 hours, I had spent about 21 of them in my car and
had driven close to 700 miles.

And for what? Just to impress one young WAAF officer, for Pete's
sake! Love? It was certainly a very powerful emotion, my goodness!

Chapter 11
D-Day Approaches

The next day, feeling rather jaded and not a little dejected by the events of the previous two days, I decided not to fly but to attend to my damaged car, which was standing forlornly against the outer wall of my ground-floor bedroom.

Driving round to the Wing headquarters' MT Section, about 75 yards away, I consulted the NCO in charge, a burly chap with a creased, well-worn face and an intimidating voice that articulated a brand of fractured American English I hardly recognised. However, he apparently had no difficulty in understanding me, so that when I suggested that he might be able to help in repairing the bent and scratched wing on my car, and perhaps change a well-worn tyre as well, he responded immediately with an elaborate gesture and 'Sure ting, my very good sir! Whatever the squadron leader wants, OK?'

Then, raising his voice to minor screech level (and American NCOs can really screech), he called out the names of two of his assistants.

Within half a minute, two Sumo-wrestler-type figures, draped in fatigues and crumpled hats, and so disreputable that they would have made even an Iraqi tribesman look well dressed, came into view and shambled towards us. The NCO howled a series of instructions in their direction, to which the two listened without a word. Then, with blank faces and after exchanging a couple of silent, glassy-eyed stares, they turned and followed me to my car.

As we walked the few yards to where my car was parked, I was prattling on about it possessing built-in jacks on all four wheels and saying that the spare wheel could be found behind the seat in the back. However, my words appeared to have little effect, as on reaching the vehicle and exchanging a word or two I did not hear, one of my Sumo companions unscrewed the wheel's nuts almost with his fingers, after which his mate stood alongside the off-side wing, and with his bare hands, *lifted* the car bodily into the air – as though it weighed no more than a bunch of keys. This enabled the first one to remove the wheel and slip into place what I took to be a wooden ammunition box beneath the brake drum to keep it in position.

Staggered by this quite amazing show of strength, I was further astonished when the weightlifter chap set about the damaged wing with a brute of a hide-faced hammer and walloped it into shape with a few massive blows that had me wincing in sympathy. Dear Lord! What were they doing to my precious car?

And that was not the end of my surprises, as within seconds, they had sanded off the damaged paint, daubed on a thick filler used for sealing cracks on aircraft wing leading edges, and covered it all with a gooey grey primer, all of which they smoothed off with amazing dexterity.

Then one of them set about replacing the tyre: he opened the boot, extracted the spare with just several fingers (I normally tottered about, holding the wheel tightly to my chest with two hands), and then banged the boot shut with such force that I swear the car's three remaining wheels jumped inches off the ground.

But it was not to end there. After a further display of naked strength during another lifting session when the spare wheel was fitted, it was pointed out to me that the tyre just removed had suffered a slow puncture: did I want it fixing, they asked?

Torn between caution and gratitude, I unwisely agreed, saying that would be helpful, and hastened to provide the two tyre levers I always carried in the back of my car, noting, with just a tiny spasm of apprehension, my two Sumo-wrestler helpers viewing them, and me, with what I can only describe as amused indifference.

As I watched open-mouthed, they attacked the offending tyre with my two rather puny implements, ripping off the outer cover from the wheel like navvies digging a hole in the ground, and I witnessed a sight I had never seen before (and will probably never see again): of tyre levers actually being bent when in use.

It was an unforgettable, almost frightening experience. I had never seen such a display of sheer naked strength. I thought sombrely: what if these two chaps turned their hands to robbing banks or molesting old ladies?

Finally, joined by the NCO in charge, and with his two helpers standing alongside in silence, I was told that I could drive my car away if I wished, but needed to return it when the priming paint had dried sufficiently to enable a top coat of black gloss to be applied. I recall glancing at my watch and shaking my head. The whole procedure had not taken them more than fifteen heart-stopping minutes. What a performance!

As I hesitated, one of my wrestler chums spoke up almost for the first time, mischief in his voice and eyes. 'You wanna have us give you a push?'

To which I responded (I think), with something of a smile, 'Thank you, kind sirs, but my car usually starts on its own. Furthermore, I don't think it would be equal to any push you are likely to give it. No, I'll leave it here and hope you'll have finished the painting by the time I get back.'

Walking then in the direction of our greenhouse mess hall and a welcome midday meal, I noted it was shortly before twelve o'clock – Americans tend to rise early and eat at most uncivilised hours – so that within minutes, I was tucking into a mound of 'chow' that would probably have kept a single British civilian feeling gorged for a week, reflecting on the extraordinary, if trivial, performance which had just been enacted in front of me.

It was so utterly American – so violently over the top. And even in my limited experience, there had been so many examples over the last several years of the brutal power, the shameful profligacy and the sometimes embarrassing inadequacies of 'Uncle Sam', in stark contrast to the many praiseworthy triumphs achieved by the United States nation as a whole.

Although I had spent more than a year in Malta and the Middle East in 1941 and early 1942, I knew very little about the Americans, apart from what I had learnt from flying one or two of their fighter air-craft, known later as the Tomahawk and Kittyhawk. In fact, it was only after the Battle of Alamein in late 1942 and Operation Torch – the invasion of North Africa from the west by a combined British and American task force in early 1943 – that I knew anything at all about the US Army.

However, friends and colleagues of mine serving in the Desert Air Force and the British 8th Army most certainly did, and much of what I was to hear later about the Americans came from them.

For more than two years the 8th Army had experienced mixed fortunes in North Africa, being vastly successful against the Italians in Cyrenaica, but frequently being forced to retreat and regroup when confronted by the Luftwaffe and Germany's celebrated 90th Division, so ably commanded at the time by Field Marshal Erwin Rommel. Indeed, it became something of a sick joke when the toing and froing up and down the Mediterranean coast came to be referred to among RAF and Army units alike as 'the Benghazi Handicap'.

All such jocular racing terms, however, stopped abruptly when in mid-1942, General Montgomery took charge of the 8th Army and brought about an altogether more professional attitude, in which meticulous planning and unrelenting pressure from the air and on the ground became overriding factors, with nothing less than total victory an absolute requirement. It was as a result of this changed frame of mind that the 8th Army, after several days of bitter fighting, swept aside the powerful and efficient German military machine, which, from the small desert town of El Alamein, was threatening Egypt, the Suez Canal and Middle Eastern oil.

There, in the sandy wilderness around El Alamein, the enemy was dealt a series of crushing blows, pursued over a distance of 1,500 miles to the borders of Tunisia, so that, within weeks, Montgomery's victorious divisions had joined up with the combined American and British forces closing on the key towns of Tunis and Bizerta

The 8th Army's success at El Alamein acted as an enormous fillip to morale throughout Britain, as this was the first major victory on land since 1939. In particular, both the Army and the RAF were so cock-a-hoop and confident in battle that they considered them-selves, like the Coldstream Guards, second to none. And with the pride, almost inevitably came a sizeable slice of hubris, as the British Army in general looked down almost contemptuously on their new American comrades.

Their rather condescending, slightly amused attitude towards 'the inexperienced Yanks' (about which I was told by friends and knew from my own experience) mirrored almost exactly the aver-age Briton's opinion of American forces in general, which, although around in large numbers, appeared to be making a lot of noise but doing very little to win the war. It was considered unreasonable, too, that Americans always insisted on doing things their own way, seldom listened to advice, were reluctant to take orders from any other than their own senior officers, and often created more than their share of operational blunders.

In short, even in 1944, the vast military power and industrial might of the USA, so evident in the months and years to come, had yet to be made obvious to a British nation which had already suffered massive war damage and loss of treasure, and was slightly resentful of America's role as a world leader.

There were, however, some important examples of American intransigence, one of which ought properly be mentioned here.

In January 1943, Mr Churchill had discussed with Lieutenant General Ira C. Eaker, the American Chief of Air Staff, the policy of long-range daylight bombing so fervently espoused by the American Air Force. It was said that the Prime Minister had pointed out that the RAF had tried daylight bombing over Germany in 1939 and 1940 but had suffered such severe casualties that they had turned to bombing at night. Might it not be prudent, he had suggested, for the USAAF to review its present policy and methods as, for the last six months of 1942, the 8th USAAF had deployed at least 500 four-engined bombers and 29,000 men throughout East Anglia, and had not yet dropped a single bomb?

General Eaker had, however, so earnestly pressed home his opin-ion in favour of the existing policy that Mr Churchill, somewhat reluctantly, withdrew his objections and the planned long-distance bombing attacks by the B17s (Flying Fortresses) and B24s (Liberators) began, the bombers being escorted at least part of the way into Germany by P.47 (Thunderbolt) fighters.

But by the autumn of 1943, the casualties among the bombers and the loss of aircrew (each aircraft carrying a crew of at least ten) had become unsustainable and the massive planned daylight assault on Germany had stuttered almost to a halt. Beyond the range of the escorting P.47s, the bombers, heavily armed as they were, could not adequately defend themselves and were being shot down like pigeons.

Fortunately (and some would say by the grace of God), sufficient P.51s (Mustangs), newly fitted with Rolls-Royce Merlin engines, were available as replacement escort fighters, and these, with their longer range and better performance at altitude, finally tipped the balance in favour of the bombers. The situation was eventually retrieved – just – but even the American generals were later to admit it was a close-run thing.

Young and inexperienced though I was, in the summer of 1944 I was not overly influenced by the shortcomings of my American colleagues, as I was all too aware of at least two industrial achievements which had influenced me profoundly over the years.

Since the commencement of the war in 1939, Britain's losses in merchant ships had been catastrophic, largely as a result of U-boat attacks, mines and enemy bombing. With the entry of the United States into the war in late 1941, agreement had quickly been reached to mass produce in America a type of cargo vessel based on a well-known British design. The vessel was planned to be between 11,000 and 14,000 tons, have a speed of 12 knots and a crew normally of about 40, and would be known eventually as a Liberty ship.

Having decided on a plan of action, among other American industrialists a certain William Kaiser set to work to produce, at a hitherto unheard-of speed, a mass of these ships to bridge the all-important gap. In the following four years, more than 2,700 cargo vessels were constructed, sometimes at a rate of one every 16 days – on one notable occasion, the hull of one ship taking no more than four days to build, following the keel being laid down. The vessels themselves were constructed of prefabricated parts, spot-welded instead of being riveted, and usually launched, almost literally, by sliding them sideways into a local river.

Understandably perhaps, a few Liberty vessels came apart at the seams and broke up, but most of those not sunk by enemy action survived the war, many eventually being bought by enterprising Greek businessmen – to their considerable advantage, needless to say.

The building of the wartime Liberty vessels was a classic example of the Americans' know-how and their energy and ability to mass produce almost anything. The design and construction of the P.51 (Mustang) fighter in 1940 provided another graphic illustration of the ingenuity and enormous production capacity of the United States as the Second World War progressed. During the last months of 1940, the prototype of what would later be known as the P.51 or Mustang was designed, built and flown in a matter of several weeks rather than two years, although it must be added that at least some of the important design data on the aircraft's unconventional wing had already been obtained from a number of other sources.

As a young flight commander in No. 249 Squadron, flying from RAF North Weald in the early months of 1941, I had heard about the new Mustang and been shown photographs of the prototype. I had also been told the remarkable story about the British Purchasing Commission, who, seeking to buy suitable aircraft for the RAF in 1939 and 1940, had invited the North American Aviation Company to undertake production of the then ageing P.40 fighter, designed and built by Curtiss, a rival manufacturer.

The invitation, not surprisingly, was promptly declined. However, in order to sweeten the pill, the North American directors offered to build an aircraft to their own design, which would incorporate all the features the British wished to name, within 120 days of any production agreement being concluded. Greatly astonished by the quite extraordinary proposal but not wishing to look a gift horse too much in the mouth, the Commission very quickly signed a contract for an initial order for 320 aircraft.

The North American Company then embarked on a work plan

that can only be described as frenzied, and resulted in the complete airframe of the first aircraft being built within 18 days of the time stipulated. However, because the Allison engine – which was the only American in-line power plant then available – was not quite ready, there was a delay of 20 days before the motor could be installed. In all, therefore, the first complete aircraft was available for flight after 122 days – only two days later than the time predicted.

These two outstanding examples of American enterprise, planning and drive have always impressed me greatly – the Liberty ship operation because it made a very significant contribution towards winning the war at sea, and the design and construction of the P.51 fighter because, although the aircraft had its initial teething problems, it became, with the British Spitfire, one of the two most effective and well-loved fighter aircraft of the Second World War.

Returning that May afternoon to the Wing headquarters' MT Section and my Sumo-wrestler chums, I picked up my car with its repaired tyre and now bright-new wing, and drove to the airfield. There, very conscious of the fact that I knew only a little about the technicalities of our new P.51D and that I could well be fighting for my life in it within days, I decided to consult my two senior 'line experts', Top Sergeants Smedley and Carter. Our subsequent discussion was protracted – and very revealing.

I started by explaining that my flying thus far in the P.51 had amounted to little more than a few exploratory excursions, but with the invasion likely to occur within days, I wished to test its qualities as a weapon of war. For example, I needed to know very much more about its fuel capacity and range, its guns, their rate of fire and harmonisation pattern, and also how much ammunition was available to me. I required to be informed, too, of the details and limitations of the engine and, bearing in mind my frightening experience some weeks before when the P.47 had run away with me, how this new P.51D was going to behave at altitude and at high speed.

As the result of which, withdrawing into a nearby hut and surrounded by pages of technical bumph, with my two line experts I pored over graphs and a catalogue of performance details and possible hazards, all associated with the splendid new aircraft standing quietly beside us.

Within minutes, I learnt that the fuel capacity of the P.51's two wing tanks was about 180 US gallons (imperial gallons were slightly larger), which was straightforward enough. However, a new rear tank, situated behind the pilot's seat in the 'D' model, had additional capacities varying between 65 and 100 gallons, depending on which piece of bumph I read; a 85-gallon tank was the final choice. The weight of this tank shifted the aircraft's centre of gravity a little too far to the rear, so that pilots were warned to carry out only gentle manoeuvres until the fuel in the rear tank was reduced to 25 gallons.

I was also interested to read that the considerable range of the P.51 could be further enhanced by the fitting of two jettisonable underwing tanks, each of 108 gallons' capacity, which had the effect of increasing the absolute range to over 2,000 miles and the radius of action to more than 750.

As this could result in flights of up to seven hours' duration in a cockpit that already had the unenviable reputation of either kippering its pilot into a wilting heap or freezing him almost to death, they were not figures I found particularly appealing. Still, with the 9th Air Force operating in a tactical role, perhaps I would never be called upon to experience such flights.

The complications that might arise from my getting involved in any active fighting during the invasion also came to the fore when we came to discussing the possibility of day-to-day combat and the business of rearming the P.51.

The effectiveness of its .5-inch machine gun I knew about all too well, in particular the ability of the hardened core of its explosive bullet to pierce even the incredibly tough armour plate installed in most fighter aircraft. An unpleasant incident involving a close friend of mine, Flying Officer Pat Lardner-Burke of No. 126 Squadron, had occurred in Malta, when he was nastily wounded by an Italian Maachi 202 firing .5-inch bullets from a range of less than 100 feet. It was an occasion I would never forget.

As he taxied slowly in at Ta Kali airfield, I could see that a bullet had penetrated the armour plate as though it were little more than a sheet of tin, passed then through the pilot's seat and, after striking Pat in the back and puncturing cleanly his left lung, continued by way of the dashboard and gravity fuel tank into the blackness of the Hurricane's Merlin engine, some 8 feet in front.

Poignantly, I can remember my stricken colleague's exact words when I was struggling to lift him out of the cockpit. 'For Christ's sake, don't shake me, Ginger! The bastards have just hit me in the back!'

I'm sure it was the memory of that traumatic occasion, together with the potency of the .5-inch machine gun, that prompted me to ask: should the invasion take place within the next several days, what would be the availability state of the P.51? And if not fully prepared for immediate combat, how long would it take to make it so?

Somewhat to my surprise, after a brief exchange of slightly worried glances between Smedley and Carter, there came the admission that neither the P.47 nor the P.51 was at present armed, though it would only take a day or two to raise the P.51 to full combat readiness.

There were, however, problems. Theirs, they added, was what they described as a 'communications outfit', not a fighter squadron, and if I had combat in mind on a regular basis, there would have to be some additional 'ordnance guys' employed on 'the line'. Either that or I would have to seek assistance from one of the fighter squadrons based at Lashenden, or even Staplehurst. There were only five of them keeping six or more different types of aircraft in the air, and that was already a full-time job. Moreover, there were not the facilities on 'the line' to store or safeguard thousands of rounds of ordnance; nor was there the manpower to make up endless belts of ammunition. No, Squadron Leader, sir! Fighting was definitely out as far as they were concerned, unless it happened only occasionally and they were given proper prior notice.

Recognising the strength of their argument, I said I would keep their opinions in mind. However, with the invasion likely within days, I wished to test the guns and also the P.51 to its full extent. For this very important reason, I would be glad if they could have the aircraft suitably armed and prepared as soon as possible.

I see from my logbook that I flew the P.51 several times on 30 and 31 May, having, I recall, discussed guns and their harmonisation with a doubtful and silent Smedley.

Apparently, our 'D' model mounted six guns – two more than the 'B' and 'C' versions – and carried a few extra rounds, bringing the total to 1,880 for all six guns, which I thought a bit odd at the time, as six into 1,880 didn't go. However, after doing a little mental arithmetic, I worked out that, based on a firing rate of about 800 rounds per minute, my P.51 would be able to fire a continuous burst of around 23 seconds – which was less than I had hoped for but much better than the 15 seconds of .303 we had in our Battle of Britain Spitfires and Hurricanes, and the 10 seconds of fire from the 20mm cannons used in most of our Spits.

As regards harmonisation, I insisted that the six guns on the P.51 be slightly realigned so that they provided the normal concentrated grouping at 200 yards and not the usual 250, arguing (almost sheepishly) that my shooting was so bad I couldn't 'hit a pig in a jigger', to quote a slightly raunchy description used in the back streets of Liverpool!

Having taken the P.51 down to the coastal firing range and made three passes at the ground targets there, I was pleasurably surprised when all six guns fired their quota of rounds without a single stoppage. As it was the first time I had ever fired a battery of six .5-inch machine guns, I thought I detected a slight increase in recoil effect compared with that of the battery of eight .303 Brownings employed in our older Battle of Britain aircraft. Otherwise, much was the same, in particular the most satisfying noise of a protracted burst – not exactly a metallic chatter but like the sound of coarse linen being violently ripped in two.

Then I climbed the P.51 steeply at full climbing power, through several thousand feet of cloud, before levelling off in clear air at 20,000 feet. Taking a deep breath and trimming the aircraft carefully into a slight dive, I increased the speed until the figure of 400 showed on the ASI, the P.51, to my utter relief, remaining rock solid as the true airspeed, I was able to calculate quickly, reached the formidable figure of 520 miles per hour.

And that really was the end of a successful day, though I did experience some 'snaking' (lateral wobbling) when later I encountered a zone of turbulent air, and needed to nurse a very light elevator when dropping down through a thick bank of cloud. Otherwise, the P.51 behaved excellently throughout. In any case, as my role was to support ground forces, I thought it unlikely I would ever be called upon to fight at anything much above 15,000 feet.

No, roll on the invasion! I was feeling in good heart. The P.51 was just about the best aircraft around in which to go to war – provided the Germans were considerate enough not to shoot at me too much from the ground. Because light flak I definitely did not like – not one little bit did I like being shot at sneakily and anonymously from the ground. Too many of my friends and colleagues had been lost that way, doing damn silly ground attacks against targets that were either dangerous and shot back or did not warrant being attacked anyway.

Chapter 12
The Invasion

The Allied invasion of northern Europe, with the code name Operation Overlord, took place on Tuesday, 6 June 1944.

Stationed on Lashenden airfield in Kent and flying an American P.51D fighter, I wish I was able to report that, full of enthusiasm, I flew madly into action, shot down at least a handful of Luftwaffe aircraft, and made a sizeable contribution to the success of the beachhead landings and the ultimate winning of the Second World War. Alas, I can make no such report.

In fact, I can't remember being more than mildly interested when news of the invasion was announced in the early-morning news bulletins. I, with millions of other servicemen, had watched the vast build-up of Allied forces in Britain over the previous 18 months, so that the invasion itself came as something of a welcome relief. We had all known for months that it was imminent, and were pretty confident the Allies would eventually win; but we also knew that many of us would not be immediately affected were a successful landing to be achieved.

Stationed in the delightful meadows of Kent, pilots of the 100th Fighter Wing had long been aware that they would simply continue to do what they had already been doing for weeks: fly operation-ally from bases in Britain until either suitable landing grounds on the Continent had been constructed, or existing ones cleared of the Germans and considered fit to use. All of which could take days, or even weeks.

Even so, it seems I was sufficiently keen to see what was taking place on the historic day of 6 June, as my logbook records that I flew the P.51 on two occasions. I have no recollection of the first flight I made in the morning, but the one in the afternoon I remember very well.

I well recall the P.51s, based at both Lashenden and Staplehurst, being airborne frequently that day, presumably engaged on their normal operational duties over France. The P.47s from Headcorn and High Halden were similarly employed, resulting in a mass of aircraft wheeling about dangerously at low level. I also remember that visibility was poor and that there was an abundance of low cloud, making identification difficult, as aircraft kept flitting in and out of the fringes of the murk. In short, it was by no means the best day for flying.

Having become airborne that day I wished to fly in the general direction of the invasion beachheads, but I had no idea where precisely the beachheads were. The actual plan of attack during Overlord had long been regarded as 'Top Secret' (when I learnt later that the precise positions of the five landing areas, together with the whereabouts of even minor military objectives, had been revealed to many junior Army officers, I was more than surprised) so that on D-Day itself, I personally knew very little of the overall invasion plan and even less about what was actually taking place. Moreover, I doubt that many of my American colleagues in the Fighter Wing were any better informed. It was also interesting to learn later that the Germans, very fortunately, were equally ignorant!

After staying well below cloud and passing out over the cliffs of Beachy Head, I flew on a heading of about 240 degrees in the general direction of Le Havre, which, I knew all too well, was around 80 miles distant. I had seen no aircraft thus far but there was a line of small ships beneath me, heading roughly in my direction. Having heard from someone or other that about 5,000 vessels, large and small, were expected to be in the invasion fleet, where were the other 4,995, I wondered?

I felt very buoyant. With a battery of six very potent .5-inch machine guns in my bright new P.51D, should I be lucky enough to meet any wandering Hun, I would really be able to give him what for, my goodness!

Within about 10 miles of Le Havre and still at 1,500 feet, to the west of me I saw a wide expanse of dark smoke sitting like a cloud above a large huddle of medium-sized ships, surrounded by a mass

of smaller craft, most of them flying tethered blimp balloons, presumably to ward off low-flying attackers.

Which immediately set me thinking: Were there any Huns
about? I was not being controlled by anyone, purely because I had
forgotten to request GCI (Ground Controlled Interception) assistance and had not been receiving any information of enemy aircraft
in my area. Silly me! It was remiss of me and I ought to have been
more organised.

Observing bright flashes of gunfire in the distance, I immediately decided against flying any closer, having in mind the very
unpleasant picture of battleships firing their 18-inch guns and massive naval 'bricks' whizzing around my ears. The thought so put
me off that I instinctively turned away and headed north. No point
in getting in the way of barrages of that sort and risk being shot to
pieces.

Turning for home, therefore, I retraced my path across the sullen
grey waters of the English Channel and landed back at Lashenden
after an uneventful flight of just over an hour. So much for the first
day of the invasion.

Having dismounted and stretched my legs, I spoke briefly to
several people, mentioning where I had been and what I had seen,
but I don't remember anyone being more than casually interested.
Which was understandable, I suppose, as Wing headquarters and
even the 100th Wing's 12 squadrons, amounting to around 300 aircraft, were not expecting to move into France, or wherever, for a
further month or so.

The news on the following day, 7 June, was very encouraging.
Major elements of the British, Canadian and American forces had
fought their way ashore at five beachheads in Normandy and had,
it seemed, consolidated their positions. There had been successful
mass landings of parachute and glider troops further inland. It was
also reported that there had been some hard fighting, resulting in
quite a few casualties, but things were going well.

My flying logbook records two flights I made that day in the P.51.
After the first, in the morning, about which I made no pencilled

comment, I well recall returning to our headquarters site about noon and walking in the direction of our controversial hothouse mess hall, hoping to find a decent cup of coffee. As I was passing Colonel Sanders' living quarters and office, the door of his mobile home opened and he appeared on the raised walkway platform, leading a visitor of general officer rank.

Observing me immediately, he called me across and introduced me as his RAF liaison officer, who normally flew his P.51 aircraft, and who had visited the beachhead area the previous day.

All three of us then talked briefly about my flight and I was informed that the visiting general was intending to fly to the American Omaha beachhead within the next hour or two, being transported in a piloted C-47 (Dakota) assigned to him.

Surprised, I immediately pointed out that as far as I knew, there was no landing strip on the Omaha beachhead. Furthermore, the fighting there was apparently still raging, the two factors together, in my opinion, making his journey impossible.

Appearing a little taken aback, the General hesitated; then he said he had been given other information that suggested that a landing might just be possible. Anyway, he would give it a try and just hope for the best.

I suppose it was the officer's devil-may-care attitude that brought about a sudden rush of blood to my head as, almost to my own surprise, I heard myself explaining that as it was my intention anyway to visit the beachhead areas later on, if he and Colonel Sanders agreed, I would be happy to escort the General's Dakota, flying the P.51. At which point, glances were exchanged, there were nods all round, and an agreement was reached that we would rendezvous 90 minutes later over Lashenden airfield, before crossing the Channel together.

Which is precisely what happened, our two aircraft heading out at about 2,000 feet, with me in the Mustang, describing figures of eight around the General's C-47.

The outward journey would take us about 40 minutes, I estimated, but time was no concern – with a full fuel load I could hang about for several hours. Moreover, bristling as I was with six .5s, woe betide any Hun who got in our way. Super! Although there was still a lot of low cloud about, things were gong well.

As we flew closer to the American Omaha beachhead the scene became nothing less than breathtaking: masses of ships, large and small; sharp-nosed boats of every kind; landing craft and barges by the score, many empty but some weighed down with cargo and vehicles, almost all of them flying their own private balloons. And overhead, surprisingly, aircraft: more than a dozen of them. All darkly camouflaged C-47s (Dakotas), flying in a wide circle – a slow deliberate parade. And after a time, tilting and turning towards a newly laid airstrip, parallel to the coastline and within yards of the water's edge.

Then ... singly ... they were dropping down ... down ... down ... to land silently on the runway ... stop ... turn left ... and then slowly taxi away.

Beyond, in every direction, there was an endless vista of leaden sea, with ordered lines of flat, pitching vessels butting into the surf and trailing their white, churned-up wakes to mark their progress.

Almost hypnotised by the sight of so compelling a picture below me, I flew around, two, three, four times, the prospect of an enemy attack from the air totally absent from my mind.

Until, on my fourth circuit and for reasons I could never later explain, I decided to land. On a small AVG (Advanced Landing Ground), later to be referred to as A-1, arguably the first to be constructed during the Allied invasion of Europe. What was I doing? Taking an unacceptable risk? As I was totally engrossed, the thought never crossed my mind.

Minutes later I had descended to 1,000 feet and joined the parade of about three Dakotas then in the circuit, two of them obligingly spreading out to let me in.

Not using my RT and not in contact with anyone, without a care in the world, I prepared for landing: downwind now ... wheels down ... turning left on to finals ... flaps extended. . . holding off ... and finally touching down. Crunching into the steel-meshed sand, I let my aircraft run to a stop.

Taxiing back carefully, I looked around with interest. The whole landing strip was about 100 yards wide. There were several C-47s moving around, enormous mounds of cargo and baggage everywhere in heaps, and lots of sand in the air, picked up by the revving airscrews of the C-47s.

I pulled to one side of the landing strip and, after a few seconds, having examined all my pressures and temperatures, shut down my engine and sat back.

Wow! After all the noise, there was silence – comparative silence, anyway.

About 100 yards to my left, I observed a man standing on a heap of baggage, waving his arms about like a policeman, screaming his head off and shaking a fist at aircrew clearly upsetting him, and blowing a whistle now and then.

For a time, I watched him with interest and amusement before deciding he was the chap in charge and the very least I could do was to tell him who I was and why I had landed. Climbing down from my cockpit, I strolled across to where he stood – still hurling abuse at someone and waving his arms – and shouted up at him when there came a convenient gap in his obscenities.

I screamed, 'Tell me, are you the movements officer or the chap in charge round here?'

The shouting and the waving continuing. I was ignored.

Raising my voice, I repeated my question, but it did no good – the shouting and the waving went on.

Then, when I had shrugged and was turning away, the angry man above me howled in my general direction.

'No, bud, I'm just standing in! The guy in charge is dead. A sniper got him this morning.' And, after a further bout of arm waving, 'He's under that sheeting there, OK?'

After glancing down in horror at the anonymous lump immediately to my left, I shouted back, 'A *sniper*? Where was he standing?'

My noisy companion turned towards me with wicked grin.

'Just about where you are now, bud! OK?' He turned away, and the waving and shouting started anew.

A sniper, for heaven's sake! Suddenly, the invasion took on a new meaning.

Ten minutes later I was back in the cockpit of my P.51, airborne and over the English Channel, heading for Beachy Head and Lashenden.

There being no one of importance about when I had landed, I did not report the sniper incident to anyone. In fact, I did not speak at all about my landing on the beachhead until about a week later, when I happened to mention it to Al Hill during one of our evening bedroom discussions.

Some days later Tex Sanders came to me on the telephone.

'Hey, Ginger! Al Hill's just told me that you landed on the Omaha beachhead when you escorted that general the other day. You didn't tell me about it.'

Replying with a trace of penitence in my voice, I answered, 'Colonel, I didn't plan to tell anyone. In fact, because it was such a non-event, I didn't consider it worth mentioning. I was only there for around 15 minutes and I left, as I was clearly getting in the way.'

'Well, you should have told me. Hell! You're probably the first guy in a fighter to land in France after D-Day.'

'Colonel, there have been quite a few guys in fighters landing in France after D-Day, the difference being they were probably shot down. Which doesn't make my landing there all that important, does it?'

Shortly after the sniper incident, I was obliged to deal with a somewhat unpleasant situation, which I found worrying, as until then my relationship with all my American colleagues had been nothing less than totally harmonious.

Lieutenant Colonel Harry A. French had joined the 100th Fighter Wing on or about 1 May 1944. To me his was just a new face that suddenly appeared. My friend Al Hill described him as the newly appointed Deputy Commander of the Wing and spoke of him warmly.

Apparently, he was from the south, a West Point regular officer, and about thirty years of age. I seem to remember him wearing pilot's wings, but I don't recall him being an active pilot – he certainly spent very little time on 'the line' among the several fighter aircraft the Wing possessed.

I always remember him as a 'brown' man: he wore a brown uniform, and had brown hair and brown rather soulful eyes. He also had what I call a 'brown' sense of humour, always dry and never requiring him to laugh openly.

He and I got on well enough at first, though in a restrained way. We were never exactly 'buddies', although our relationship warmed when he began to visit our communal bedroom and join in our sometimes ribald evening conversations. And it was on one such occasion that this rather telling incident arose.

I recall sitting on my bed quite comfortably when he arrived and sat down beside me. In a moment I realised he had been drinking and, though not drunk, was in what I would describe as a 'confidential' frame of mind.

After we had exchanged a few pleasantries, I was quite surprised and not a little embarrassed when he put an arm around my shoulders and gave me an affectionate squeeze.

Then, breathing an alcoholic whisper in my left ear, he said all too clearly, 'Ginger, I like you, I really do. I want you to know I think you're a great guy. All right? But d'you know what I think, Ginger? What really gets my goat? Well, I'll tell you. And it's nothing to do with you, you understand? Well . . . I hate the bloody British! I do! *I really hate the bastards!'*

A little taken aback by the remark and the manner in which it had been delivered, I tried to make light of his offensiveness by smiling and replying, 'Harry, if you like me, how on earth can you say you hate the British? Is it because we beat you up at Bunker Hill or tried to burn down the White House? What makes you so cross with us poor British?'

But Harry was not in the mood to be placated. Wagging an admonishing finger, he looked at me owlishly. 'Look! We held off a whole goddamn British army at Bunker Hill before retiring in good order, OK? As for the White House, that was nothing. No, my gripe is, for 300 years the bloody British have tried to colonise pretty well the whole world – Canada, Australia, New Zealand, Africa, the lot. All you have to do is look at a map. Business-wise they've got the whole place sewn up. Malaysia and India, the Middle East, South and East Africa, the West Indies, you name it. Why, we can't buy a decent chocolate bar in the States because the bloody British have cornered the market in West African cocoa beans. It's the same everywhere. No, the British Empire just has to go, and the quicker the better.'

Almost stung into retaliating, I had the good sense to hesitate. Aware that I was a bit shaky on my historical facts, I suddenly felt it necessary not to get involved in what was essentially a political argument. Instead, I decided I would try to reduce the tension and lighten the atmosphere – my friend Harry was a bit 'pixilated' and would probably regret what he had said the next day. So, with a jest and a few calming words, I let the matter rest. Harry then got to his feet and beat a slightly wobbly retreat to the door, and peace was restored.

Several days later and still a little upset by what had happened, I approached my room-mate, Bodenheim.

'Bodey? You probably heard Harry French telling me a few nights ago that he hated the British. Tell me frankly, do you hate the British?'

I was a little surprised and faintly concerned when Bodenheim hesitated before replying. Then, his eyes glinting at me through his pince-nez, he gave a not too convincing answer.

'Ginger, I come from a state that has all the sunshine and wine in the world, plus a million miles of sandy beaches. So frankly, we don't give the British very much thought.'

But I persisted. 'All right then, do you consider that, business-wise, we British have the whole world sewn up?'

On that, Bodenheim was clear and unequivocal. 'Oh absolutely! Of course you have. You guys have been at it for a long time and you're very good at what you do.' Then with a not unfriendly smile, 'But it'll all end soon, I believe, and I'm not sure if I'll be happy about it, or sad.'

All of which worried me more than a little. Not only that, my relationship with Harry French was never quite the same thereafter.

Which was a pity, as he was promoted within weeks, being confirmed officially as Deputy Commander of the 100th Wing in July
1944, before going on to command the 19th Tactical Air Command
the following December.

Chapter 13
Rockets and Doodlebugs

On 13 June 1944, a day that will always remain in my mind as unusual and rather special; having flown the Fairchild to Biggin Hill and back in the morning for some reason I do not recall, I drove my Morris 10 in the afternoon for several hours to Northwick Park, on the northern outskirts of London, to visit my parents, whose house had been damaged slightly in the recent bombing. Arriving there about 4 p.m., I stayed with them until late in the evening before setting off on my return journey to Kent just before darkness set in.

It took me quite a time to nose my way through London, and several hours more to 'feel' my way towards Maidstone in almost total blackness and, later still, meander blindly through the back roads of Kent before finally arriving at my farmhouse sleeping quarters in Headcorn.

Aware that it was then about 1.30 a.m. and that much of the campsite would already be sleeping, I quietly parked my car against the outer wall of my bedroom, and was in the act of gently closing the driving door of my Morris, when a hoarse, tremulous whisper, in an accent straight from the Texas badlands, came to me out of the darkness.

'Hey, izzat you, Squadron Leader? Jesus, God, I sure hope so!'

As I strained my eyes into the blackness, a tall, beanpole of a figure, stinking of fag ends, wearing a steel helmet and clasping a rifle in a visibly shaking hand, loomed out of the gloom and, standing next to me, breathed a thankful prayer of relief in my direction.

'Jesus! Am I glad to see you!'

Surprised, I exclaimed, 'It's almost two in the morning! Why on earth are you walking about at this hour? And why the gun and the soldier's outfit?'

A reply came in a frightened, squeaky voice.

'It's because I'm a goddamn sentry, that's why. And I'm shaking all to hell and back because I've bin scaring the shit out of myself for the past hour, waiting for my throat to be cut by some Kraut paratrooper. OK? And it's all because of what happened earlier on, when the Old Man suddenly ordered sentries be posted all around the headquarters site. OK? And I'm one of the goddamn sentries, right?' And as I watched the rifle begin to shake again almost uncontrollably, my companion muttered almost confidentially to himself, 'Jesus, God! And it should happen to me!'

I was immediately interested. 'So what was so special earlier on?'

'You don't know? It's been on the radio just about every minute since it happened. The bloody pop-pop thing: the flying bomb! Came right over the house. Very low down, going like hell and escorted by two of your British fighters.' Then, in a voice an octave higher, 'You mean you haven't heard? And the word is, not just one but thousands more later! It's sure spooked the Old Man, because he's bin goin' round telling everyone we're about to be invaded and has put special guards around the headquarters. Christ, that guy Schmelling* with a carving knife! That's all I need right now!'

The prospect of the Germans invading us being unlikely, I immediately dismissed the possibility from my mind. However, the flying bomb thing seemed real enough, as both the 9th Air Force and the RAF had been attacking the launch sites for weeks and the commencement of what were later referred to as 'diver' attacks was certainly more than likely.

However, as it was almost 2 a.m. and I was feeling pretty jaded, I thought that if my quaking sentry colleague could avoid having his throat cut in the next few hours, he and I could further discuss the subject in the morning.

So, after dismissing the still gibbering man with an encouraging message, I crept into my silent bedroom. I was feeling about for my pyjamas when Al Hill's whisper came out of the darkness.

---

* Max Schmelling, the former world heavyweight boxing champion, was said to be a German paratrooper.

'Hi, Ginger! Glad you're back. Have you heard the noos?'

'About the flying bomb, you mean? Yes, I have. Also, that the Colonel has posted sentries, as he's expecting a German parachute attack any moment.'

I sensed Al hesitate. 'Parachute attack? I don't think he ever mentioned anything about that, though he sure as hell has been running round like a headless chicken and has even been talking about us all digging foxholes for ourselves in the garden and actually sleeping in them. Apparently the official scoop is that there are masses of these so-called doodlebugs in the pipeline and that a lot of people are likely to get themselves killed. All of which has frightened the hell out of him.'

'Well, if Tex does have his mind set on foxholes in the garden, he ought to have his head examined' was my weary reply. 'People will be crippled, falling into them at dead of night, and, with the weather we have in his country, any foxhole will be inches deep in water in no time. As I see it, within days we'll probably all be dying from pneumonia, not from bomb blasts. No, our gallant commander – and not for the first time – is just plain nuts and I, for one, will not be digging any personal hole in the garden, now or later. However, with any luck, Tex'll eventually see sense and forget he ever issued such a damn silly order.'

I remember then flopping into bed with a sigh and sleeping soundly. I also recall the foxhole instruction being either overlooked or conveniently ignored in the days that followed.

In the days that followed, understandably the national news was devoted almost entirely to the fighting in Normandy and the devastating effect of the bombing brought about by the so-called doodlebugs or Vis, the vicious little weapons of destruction then surging in their hundreds across the counties of Kent and Sussex, one of the first of which had flown over the top of the 100th Wing headquarters house in Headcorn.

However, I also found my mind engaged on what were, for me, other more serious matters: first, my own miserable contribution to the war effort when measured against the sacrifices being made in France, and the casualties arising from the bombing in nearby London; and second my growing and affectionate relationship with Flight Officer Eileen Hampton, my 'Ops B' lady friend, employed 'down the hole' in the Biggin Hill Sector Operations Centre.

The initial beachhead successes of the Allied armies had apparently been consolidated, though with some difficulties and many casualties, the bocage of Normandy – the countryside with its tiny fields and tall trees – proving to be a most difficult area in which to fight and advance. Moreover, the aim of the British and Canadian Armies to take the key, pivotal town of Caen on the first day had not been achieved. This was mainly because of the fierce resistance by the German defenders and the town itself being made almost impossible to capture or bypass because of the massive Allied bombing, which had reduced the buildings to rubble, thereby creating inadvertently a barrier to our own forces and an unintended means of defence for the enemy.

Even so, the fighting in the main had gone well. Thousands of parachute and glider-borne troops had landed successfully during the night and early morning of 6 June, well beyond the beachheads themselves, and advances had already been made in a westerly direction in order to cut off the Cherbourg Peninsula and enable the several airfields in the area to be used by the Allied air forces. In short, the only major trouble spot initially was Caen – and to the discomfort of the Allies, would remain so for many days to come.

Meanwhile, the doodlebug threatened and it was hoped that the nature of the weapon, and the details of its construction, speed and potential for damage, would soon became more widely known. On 13 June, the first day of the 'diver' attacks, about 14 of the missiles were launched from the Pas de Calais area in France and not more than four (one of which was the one that had flown over Headcorn) actually reached the environs of London; the rest crashed prematurely into the Channel or the cliffs of Dover.

Within a day or two thereafter, exact details of the so-called aircraft became available: a wing span of about 18 feet, an overall length of 25 feet, an impulse duct or pulse jet engine (whatever that was) that sounded like a motor bike, and a massive warhead or bomb of about 2,000lb. The whole machine was capable of flying at about 400 miles per hour at heights between 500 and 2,000 feet. The statistics were frightening: it was clearly a fearsome weapon.

My P.51, I was aware, was one the fastest aircraft around. It was capable of about 425 miles per hour but that was true airspeed at emergency power and at about 20,000 feet, where the air was thinner and the drag less, not at ground level. At 1,000 feet I would be lucky to coax more than 375 from it straight and level and only a little more than 420 indicated in a slight dive.

Moreover, I would be lucky ever to achieve an overtaking speed of even 20 miles per hour, in which case, should I be fortunate enough see a doodlebug as far away as 2 miles (which was doubtful because of its camouflage), it would take me five minutes at least to catch it up and get in position to shoot it down, by which time the wretched thing, after crossing the Channel coast, could be over the greater London area.

The threat grew rapidly to alarming proportions. By 20 June, at least 200 divers a day were skimming over the rolling countryside of England, causing massive destruction and casualties by the hundred. The nation most certainly had a serious problem to contend with. Furthermore, the doodlebug was only Vengeance Weapon No. 1. Weapon No. 2, the unstoppable, lethal rocket (V2), was apparently being prepared further afield and was almost ready. The Germans were at bay but the future for Britain looked ominously bleak.

In order to seek further advice and possibly a little cooperation from friends, I decided to fly down to Newchurch in my P.51 and talk to my colleague Roly Beamont, who commanded the Newchurch Wing of Hawker Tempests.

In early 1943, Beamont had been in charge of No. 609 Squadron at Manston, at a time when I led 41 at nearby Hawkinge. I recalled that we in 41 were flying the Mark 12 Spitfires, which were marginally faster low down than the Typhoons of 609 – a fact which rather upset Roly when he had visited us at Hawkinge to fly one of our aircraft.

Landing at Newchurch, I found Beamont waiting for me. As I stepped down from my aircraft, he greeted me in a manner that was friendly but not effusive, leading me to sense that I was intruding on his territory and that I would get advice from him but not much else. However, he at once offered me a mug of tea and a comfortable chair while we discussed the diver problem in general and how I might fit in flying my P.51.

It immediately became plain that there was indeed a problem of organisation.

Roly explained that there were already too many freelance operators involved, flying a variety of aircraft and getting in each other's way. Moreover, some of the gunners – mainly trigger-happy Americans and undisciplined anti-aircraft batteries – were well nigh out of control, not only firing at flying bombs but also damaging, and even shooting down, a number of RAF fighters – his wing had already lost two Tempests. At least some of the time, he reported, his pilots spent more time dodging the flak than they did shooting at the divers.

Clearly the guns had to be restrained and moved to coastal areas alone, and specific zones established in which guns and fighters were permitted to operate. With agreement at Fighter Command, only RAF Tempests, Spitfire 14s and Mustang 3s would now be allowed to get involved in the V1 battle, American Thunderbolts and other comparatively slow aircraft being banned from the main attack area.

It had also been agreed that the guns would be allotted a 'Diver Zone', extending 10,000 yards into the Channel and 3,000 yards inland – the whole area being covered by about 1,200 light and heavy anti-aircraft guns from the British Army, the US Army and the RAF Regiment, many of them firing the newly introduced proximity-fused shells, which had been found to be doubly effective.

Finally, it was further intended to fly an additional 1,000 barrage balloons throughout the London area generally and in what was coming to be described as 'the V1 corridor', bringing the overall number to a remarkable 2,750.

With me almost blinking at the volume of resources being

deployed, Beamont and I then discussed the most important business of actually shooting the flying bombs down.

First, the divers were so difficult to pick up, flying as they did at up to 400 miles per hour against a background mosaic of green and brown, that it was absolutely necessary for the intercepting fighters to be controlled on to their targets. Ad hoc sightings were simply not good enough. Neither should attacks on the missile be attempted at ranges below 300 yards, despite more accurate shooting being likely at shorter distances; this was vital, as a 2,000lb bomb exploding in the air – which occasionally occurred – usually caused serious damage to the pursuing aircraft.

Furthermore, there was only about a four-minute window of opportunity for an interception to take place as, having crossed the coast unscathed, a V1 would have reached the outskirts of London or be within the barrage balloon area. This meant that it was very often necessary for a fighter to be travelling at more than 500 miles per hour, very close to the ground and over the lumps and bumps of a succession of hills, valleys and woods, requiring the full attention of the pilot and very accurate flying as well as shooting. Whilst the guns were certainly doing their valuable bit, it was clearly up to the fighters to shoulder most of the business of defending London and the southern counties.

Worryingly, too, these devastating flying bomb attacks were likely to continue for as long as it took for the invading Allied forces in France to overrun the launching sites around and beyond Calais. Even then, the defeat of the V1s was only half of the problem solved. The more lethal and upsetting V2 rockets were apparently already available, and as the launching pads for those were well into Germany, it would probably take weeks or even months before that particular threat could be eradicated.

Somewhat heartened by the knowledge that the RAF's Mustang 3 (and presumably my American P.51) were one of the several approved types of fighter considered capable of taking on a doodle-bug, I resolved to 'have a go' myself, no matter what Roly Beamont's arrangement with Fighter Command had been. I wouldn't be controlled on to the missiles, I knew; I would just have to make a visual interception, taking care, as I did so, to keep out of the way of any other intercepting fighters. It was a risk I well understood, but, I believed, an acceptable one. After all, I was part of the US 100th Fighter Wing, and not exactly subject to RAF Fighter Command restrictions – or so I very conveniently persuaded myself.

Between 30 June and 5 July, therefore, I made several attempts to shoot down a diver, but sadly with little success.

On my first flight, and not under the control of GCI (the Ground Control Interception system), I wandered around a little north of Dungeness at about 2,000 feet but soon discovered I was a little too close to the restricted gun zone. Mindful of the potency of 40mm Bofors shells fitted with proximity fuses, and suddenly observing a string of glowing red balls rise slowly and ominously in my direction – possibly as a means of warning me off – I beat a hasty and undignified retreat.

My second attempt showed signs of being rather more fruitful when, again at 2,000 feet, I caught sight of a flying bomb about 10 miles into Kent and heading for London. My target being about 1,000 feet below me, I turned towards it in a diving quarter attack and remember seeing more than 420 miles per hour on my airspeed indicator. Then, when I was encouraged to observe that I was gaining on my quarry, I was suddenly dismayed to notice another fighter, slightly lower, a little to my left and marginally ahead of me, which was clearly intent on attacking 'my' diver. Recognising at once that I was almost certainly intruding on a controlled interception, I pulled to one side, deeply disappointed but also relieved that I had not inadvertently baulked the other pilot and caused him to abort his attack.

My third effort could have been wholly successful had it not been for my lack of determination (or perhaps my lack of ruthlessness), coupled with a pang of conscience.

Having been fortunate enough again to intercept a doodlebug low down and some 5 or 6 miles into Kent, I followed it for some minutes at a speed of more than 450 miles per hour, until I was certain I was alone and, at about 250 yards' range, in a prime attacking position. Concentrating absolutely on my gunsight and my target, and controlling my speeding, bucking aircraft, I was about to open fire when I suddenly realised, to my dismay, that I was over a built-up area close to Sevenoaks, and that my success would probably result in the death of countless people directly below, who were helpless and fearful observers of the drama being enacted immediately above their heads. So, deciding in an instant, I once more pulled away into a climbing turn and left, knowing full well as I did so that the wretched thing would probably fly on for another 10 miles before diving into the ground and killing, perhaps, 20 other poor helpless souls.

Later, I was full of remorse. What sort of hero was I? But what action should I have taken? It had been so difficult to decide at the time and even now, it is a painful dilemma to recall.

But not all of my encounters with flying bombs were so remote. Some appeared almost to be attracted to my very presence.

Towards the end of June and a few days before we all left for the invasion beachheads and Normandy, I decided to take my new American friend Lieutenant Colonel Hill to meet my parents at their home in Northwick Park.

Having boarded the Metropolitan Line train at Baker Street, we were quietly but happily trundling along at a swaying, clattering 60 miles per hour between Finchley Road and Wembley Park stations, each of us, no doubt, with a vacant mind. I was seated on the left and facing forward, with my friend Hill opposite, and just gazing into space.

Suddenly I was jerked into action when, gazing around, I was presented with a very unpleasant sight, causing me to lean forward quickly and thump my companion sharply on the knee.

I said tensely, 'Don't look now, Al, but I think we're being followed!' He followed my gaze as I turned my head, and no explanation was required.

A doodlebug, at about 300 feet, was travelling almost parallel with our train but on a slightly converging course, its angular camouflaged shape sharply silhouetted against the darkening evening sky and its flaring exhaust seeming to accentuate its vast potential for evil.

We both watched in fascinated but horror-stricken silence, when about 100 yards in front of us and only a little to our left, the nose of the diver fell sharply and, after not more than three or four seconds, the 2,000lb flying bomb fell and exploded in a line of houses closely bordering the railway line. Instantly there was a bright flash and a chaos of whirling debris in the middle of a mushrooming cloud of thick black smoke as an entire line of buildings was violently blown into the air. The force of the blast was so fierce that even our speeding train rocked and wobbled alarmingly for several seconds.

Stunned absolutely by the sheer violence of the incident, we exchanged wide-eyed glances but surprisingly did not utter a single word. Meanwhile, the train continued to race ahead, so that within moments the accident site had been left behind and only a little later the brakes were being applied in order to bring the train to a stop at Wembley Park.

It took another ten minutes for us to reach our destination, and as we alighted, I remember saying quietly to my companion, 'Look, I'd rather you didn't say anything about what we have just seen to my parents. There's no point in upsetting people unnecessarily.'

To which Al, to his credit, silently nodded his agreement – and we never did.

And, in another example of the quite extraordinary way the human mind adjusts in order to cope with such ghastly happenings, a day or two later I had occasion to fly several passengers to Biggin Hill in our small four-seater Fairchild.

Taking advantage of my unexpected visit, I arranged to have dinner in the main officers' mess with my 'Ops B' lady friend, who happened not to be on duty at the time. A little later and hoping to be on our own for an hour or two, we decided to take our after-dinner coffee in the WAAF officers' quarters, situated immediately across the road from the main officers' mess building. I have no clear recollection of where exactly we parked ourselves, but I have in my mind's eye a small open paved area on which we reclined in garden chairs, talking quietly and drinking our coffee in a totally relaxed state of mind.

Until that moment, the day had been comparatively quiet, but the sheer bliss of an early summer's evening was broken when divers by the score suddenly began to soar over our heads, almost as though they had been programmed to do so.

We sat there, at first horrified and then increasingly less concerned, and watched helplessly as the noisy, evil-looking scorpions raced over our heads at heights of less than 400 feet – Biggin Hill airfield is 600 feet above sea level.

Reluctant almost to deny ourselves a free demonstration of perverted science in flying mode, rather than take cover we sat open-mouthed for more than an hour, as no fewer than 20 flying bombs passed either directly overhead or within 1,000 yards of where we were sitting, the noise of their pulse-jet motor-cycle engines strangely foreign to our ears, and the bright flaring tails to their dark bodies giving them the appearance of angry fizzing fireworks. But, we were both well aware, they were fireworks with a difference, as each, with a 2,000lb bomb enclosed in its slim metal interior, was capable of bringing death and destruction, not only to the two of us with coffee cups frozen to our fingers but to much of Biggin Hill as well.

Looking back, it seems almost beyond belief that we at Biggin, the services generally and later much of the nation, after first regarding the V1s as something of a nine days' wonder, actually began to take them for granted. By early July, only 17 days after the first one had exploded in London, they came to be regarded as just another bang being foisted upon us, another hazard to be borne, another horror to get used to. But this, surely, was what war was all about: merely a part of the painful business of fighting for one's life.

Although thus far I have referred to the V1 and V2 attacks on Britain in fairly mundane terms, had they occurred a year or so earlier they would probably have seriously affected the outcome of the Second World War. Although always regarded as very troubling and unpleasant, when the full extent of the so-called 'vengeance' attacks became known and assessed, it was realised that they might well have come close to succeeding in their mission to terrorise the British population into capitulation.

Between 13 June 1944 and 29 March 1945, a total of 9,251 V1s, or flying bombs, were plotted, of which 2,419 reached London.

The total destroyed was 4,261 – 1,971 by anti-aircraft fire, 1,979 by the Royal Air Force, 278 by balloons and 33 by the Royal Navy. The 2,419 which were dropped in the London boroughs killed 5,126 people, whilst outside London, a further 2,789 flying bombs caused another 350 deaths. In terms of casualties, therefore, the doodlebugs could well be regarded as being worse than the 1940 Blitz.

Later the V2 rocket, the other 'vengeance' weapon, also carried a 2,000lb warhead. However, it was perhaps more deadly than the V1, as it was unstoppable. Flying at about 3,000 miles per hour, it took just five minutes to fly from launch to impact. Moreover, it travelled too high and too fast to be tracked down, with the result that there was never time to issue a warning.

From September 1944 to March 1945, 1,115 V2 rockets were launched against Britain, killing 2,612 people in London and 212 civilians elsewhere. London received 517 rockets and 537 fell outside the capital, the remainder falling into the sea. The attacks only stopped when the rocket launching pads were overrun in 1945.

Although the flying bomb attacks were largely aimed at London and the south-east of England, the north did not go entirely unscathed. On 24 December 1944 – Christmas Eve – about 50 Heinkel 111 bombers carrying V1 divers attacked the north of England – largely Lancashire and Yorkshire – dropping the flying bombs they had been modified to carry. The weight of the attack fairly insubstantial and having little more than nuisance value, it nevertheless came as an unwelcome surprise to those in the north who had thus far watched comfortably from a distance their unfortunate neighbours in the south being bombed. But, like those in the London area, they quickly recovered their aplomb and apparently regarded the incident as little more than an unpleasant blip.

And on a more personal note, in December 1944, I happened to be waiting with a pile of luggage on the airfield at Antwerp, Belgium, when a V2 rocket, entirely unannounced, arrived with a whoosh and a scream, to explode within 1,000 yards of where I was sitting. Although I was in the open and actually looking in the direction of the rocket's landing, I never at any time saw it coming and certainly never saw it arrive. In a moment there was a huge flash and explosion, and bits of several aircraft and trees were suddenly whirling about in the air, the effect on me being nothing less than absolute surprise and utter, numbing shock.

Minutes later, however (and I was never told of any casualties), the airfield as a whole soon continued to operate as though nothing untoward had occurred. The aircraft I was waiting for arrived on time and I was quickly borne away, totally relieved that I had been spared, my feeling of complete vulnerability being coupled with amazement that human beings could so quickly adapt to the most violent and difficult of situations. In short, that the stoicism of most people in war is almost beyond comprehension.

Directly after that dramatic evening in June, there followed a most significant week. The 100th Fighter Wing – both the headquarters element and its four fighter groups – was ordered to move by stages to France, starting on 1 July 1944. And it was during the same brief period that I made a decision that would determine, absolutely, the shape of my own future.

Within hours the movement began. First the orgy of packing, lifting and storing – amid much excitement, arguing and laughter – followed by the crawl of a mass of vehicles, large and small, on to the local country roads, all heading for unknown rendezvous points and destinations.

Watching the exodus with interest and not a little sadness – I had enjoyed our brief sojourn in Kent – I drove out to Lashenden airfield and our aircraft on 'the line', knowing that the communications flight would be the last to move. In addition to myself, Jim Haun and Patterson, several other junior pilots in the headquarters had been co-opted to help out. I would fly the P.51, of course, the others the five or six other types of aircraft.

At that stage, strangely enough, I don't recall being informed of where exactly I would be heading or on which airfield in Normandy I would be landing. Such was the uncertainty in war: although the chiefs were usually properly informed, we Indians often knew little of the wider picture and official intentions, simply being told what to do and, thereafter, just carrying out instructions.

My flying logbook reveals that I flew the P.51 four times between 3 and 6 July, on whatever tasks I do not recall. However, Wednesday, 5 July remains especially imprinted on my mind.

Having watched most of my colleagues depart, despite flying at least once that day I found myself becoming somewhat restless and bored. My two room-mates, Hill and Bodenheim, had departed and both the greenhouse mess hall and our ground-floor bedroom I found empty and dispiriting. I recall going to my lonely couch rather early but not sleeping, my mind active. Eventually, and still wide awake, a little after midnight I rose and, throwing on a flying jacket, walked out into the night.

I saw immediately that the communications caravan was standing on its own in the open adjacent field like a sentinel, having been left, presumably, to preserve a few last links with Biggin Hill and beyond. I entered, expecting the various telephones to be manned, but there was no one around – or if there were, the incumbent was hiding.

Seating myself, I picked up the instrument connecting me to the Sector. I paused, knowing exactly what my next step was to be.

After I had gone through the motions of ringing, a female voice responded.

'Sector Controller!'

Recognising her voice, but not wishing to be overheard, I asked quietly, 'Would that be yourself?'

A short pause, and then a muted chuckle at the other end of the line. 'Why on earth are you up and about at this time of night?'

'Well, most of the others have already left for France and I'm only one of a few left behind to fly some of our aircraft.'

'And you're lonely and just wanted to have a chat, is that it?'

'Not quite. There's something I want to ask you.'

'And what would that be?'

'Well ... will you marry me?'

There was another pause – a long one!

Then, 'Are you really serious?'

'Of course I'm serious!'

'Yes, but why? And why now?'

'Well, to answer the first question, it's because I think we'd be good together. And the second, I shall be leaving in a day or two, and I thought that now would as good a time as any to ask. But you haven't answered me, I notice. So, again, will you?'

Another pause. 'Well, if you're really serious ... of course I will.'

I recall breathing a sigh of relief. 'That's fine! Then what I suggest is that I fly up to Biggin probably tomorrow, at which time we can have a chat about it, OK?'

'Goodness! I'm a bit lost for words. But whatever you say. In the meantime, am I allowed to say anything to the girls and perhaps one or two others?'

Suddenly, I felt a bit stranded and responded cautiously, 'Er ... no. I'd rather you didn't.'

'Why not?'

'Well, having had our chat later, you may decide to change your mind. After all, we really don't know each other that well, do we?'

'Very well. If that's what you want.'

The following day, I collected Patterson and invited him to join me on a final farewell party and evening out in London. I decided not to mention my marriage proposal, explaining merely that we would travel by car, first to Biggin Hill to pick up Miss Hampton and a section officer colleague (a small Irish girl named Pamela Webb), before driving into London and very seriously painting the town red.

Always a chap for a 'knees-up', Patterson immediately and very enthusiastically agreed to my suggestion, adding that he would bring with him a bottle or two of his very special 'medical alcohol giggle juice' to give a little zip to the occasion.

The day started well and improved with the passing of time, the giggle juice more than playing its part, so that by mid-afternoon all four of us were walking on air and feeling very little pain.

We ate at some expensive restaurant and went to a show somewhere, although being in such an advanced state of mellowness, I have no recollection of what the show was or the name of the theatre in which it was performed. What I do remember all too well, however, was that we finished up in the late evening at the very fashionable Embassy Club in the West End.

I distinctly recall the place being very small, the décor red and pink, and that we sat, huddled together like four chicks in a nest, in a secluded corner cubicle lit by tiny shaded lights and so very personal and private that we could barely see each other in the gloom.

Within feet of me, Patterson seemed huge and Section Officer Webb positively wee, as each of them, in full flow, told slightly inebriated stories: Anglo-Irish Pamela about having her family home in Ireland regularly burned down by the IRA when the rascals managed to get at the 'black stuff' and had nothing much else to do, and Patterson slightly glassy-eyed tales of his medical and flying experiences over the years and early life in far-away Illinois.

I recall, too, my favoured one being in a simple black and maroon dress I had never seen her wear before, dancing slowly and intimately with me on a tiny square so small that there was room for barely a dozen dancers, provided we didn't turn too quickly and knock each other over. All to the beat of a muffled drum and the soft notes of a piano accompanying the quiet lilting voice of Dom Marino Barreto, the celebrated Cuban entertainer (I think I have his name correct, although he's too old to argue about it now!), who smiled at us unendingly whilst constantly brushing a cowlick of black hair from an olive face fairly gleaming with perspiration.

On and on for hours, it seemed, the hands of our timepieces edging past the twelve of midnight, and then the smaller figures of one and two in the morning.

Later still, and arms around each other in the darkness, we looked up silently to watch pale wandering searchlight beams scan the heavens for the five or six invisible bombers passing overhead, the faint drone of their engines adding to the noise of detonations far and near as descending bombs whistled and thumped, and the 3.7-inch ack-ack guns sited in nearby Hyde Park barked in retaliation, their exploding shells sparkling and 'crumping' faintly but defiantly in the endless bowl of absolute blackness above.

Our car journey that night at 4 a.m., beneath a scattering of doo-dlebugs and other bombs (to which, in our blissful, alcoholic state, we paid not the slightest attention) ended at Biggin Hill, where our two lady companions climbed out and tottered wearily towards their beds, anxious to get in a few hours' kip before commencing their 8 a.m. stint of duty 'down the hole'.

For me, however, with the large, inert lump of Patterson snor-ing noisily at my side, there was a further drive of 25 miles to my own lonely bedroom, where, weary beyond belief, I did not have the strength to turn the steering wheel of my car sufficiently, caus-ing me again to crunch into my bedroom wall, damaging the same wing and the pristine paint job my Sumo-wrestler chums had worked so energetically to restore.

Not only that, but our carefree night of wine-induced jollity could well have ended much more seriously.

Shortly after my beloved and her friend had climbed into their Biggin Hill beds, a doodlebug apparently landed near by, the explo-sion bringing down much of their bedroom ceiling. However, drugged as they were by sleep, 'giggle juice' and (as I later suggested) the warm, comforting glow of my marriage proposal, neither of them heard the enormous detonation or even became aware of the quite sizeable chunks of plaster that must have rained down like confetti on their unconscious befuddled heads.

Three days later, during the morning of 6 July, I took off from Lashenden in Kent and flew my P.51 to the airfield A-2, in Normandy, France.

Chapter 14

Normandy

It was only late in the day of 5 July that I had learnt that my destination in Normandy the following day was the airfield A-2, near the small village of Criqueville.

Just inland from the Utah beachhead, the airfield was only the second to be prepared for the invading American fighter squadrons. Eventually, more than a hundred such airfields were used by the 9th USAAF in France, with about a similar number, prefixed by the letter 'B', being used by the Royal Air Force operating in the more northerly parts of France and Belgium.

Approaching from the sea and crossing the Utah beachhead – my previous very brief landing on the A-1 had been on the Omaha shoreline – I saw that the scene was very much the same: a mass of boats, large and small, many flying their own captive balloons, a slow-moving pall of drifting smoke and a chaos of unidentifiable objects in the water, lining the shore or crawling inland along the rural roads.

The A-2 airfield was only a few miles inland and after making several exploratory circuits, I landed without difficulty. I was surprised to see so few aircraft about; I had expected to see at least some P.51s of the 354th Fighter Group from Lashenden, as they had apparently left for France on 17 June. But, it seemed, they were otherwise employed at the time.

Looking about as I taxied in, I was relieved to be welcomed by at least several friendly faces and, after shutting down, I remember sitting back and relaxing with a sigh. I had been flying against a most active Luftwaffe for almost four years. This, surely, was a turning point.

Britain and her allies had successfully invaded in the face of stiff resistance, particularly on the two British beachheads of Gold and Juno and the American beachhead of Omaha, but the Luftwaffe had not been particularly in evidence. Not surprisingly perhaps, as I was merely a Johnny-come-lately, I had not thus far seen a single enemy aircraft, and here I was in France, a country over which for years I had shot at the enemy many times but where, all too often, I had been a German target. A country, too, I had always regarded as a hostile place, where to be forced down invariably meant captivity and umpteen months or years as a prisoner of war.

Now here I was, sitting calmly in France, very much in one piece and, it appeared, on the winning side. Not only that: I was flying a splendid aircraft in which, if I were attacked, I could more than adequately defend myself. Yes, the Divine Provider thus far had been very good to me. I was a lucky chap, all right!

Having dismounted and sorted myself out, a recon, with snub nose and camouflaged canvas top, bounced me uncomfortably along a series of tree-lined lanes and paths until I was deposited among a collection of canvas tents and marquees, sited amid a number of more permanent-looking caravan structures. This clearly was the new if temporary home of the 100th Fighter Wing headquarters.

After being greeted by Jim Haun, Patterson, my smiling countryman Squadron Leader Carr and several others, I was shown to my sleeping quarters – one corner of a large square tent. There I found myself one of three occupants; the beds and belongings of the absent Al Hill and Bodenheim were in two other corners. I was quite moved to see that someone had already erected a folding wooden contraption for me to sleep on, covered by my much-loved 4-inch sorbo mattress. Clearly, some kind soul had remembered to tie it into a roll before flying it across the Channel. I found myself shaking my head – such thoughtfulness was touching.

Later the same day, and accompanied by Carr and one or two others, I was driven in a jeep several miles into the heavily wooded bocage in order to acquaint myself with the area in which much of the Utah beachhead battle had occurred, and beyond which a mass of gliders and airborne troops had landed on the night of 6 June. Despite there being a gap of several weeks since the fighting had taken place, to see the effect of the battle was a sobering and unpleasant experience.

First, the countryside itself was so unlike Kent. Ragged, tree-lined and unkempt, it had none of the cultivated, ordered look so evident in the fields and farms of southern England. The winding minor roads and paths, too, were pot-holed, poorly maintained and bordered by occasional farmhouse buildings barely on the right side of being regarded as ruins. The whole area, whilst exhibiting a rugged beauty, gave evidence of extreme neglect and decay, brought about, I assumed, by the exigencies of war and the heavy hand of the German invaders.

Even the few members of the French peasantry we encountered, besides being dressed like scarecrows, seemed crushed by the poverty of their environment and their present way of life. If they were happy to see us they certainly gave no sign of their good spirits, either ignoring us completely or presenting glum and blank faces as we drove past with smiles and two-fingered victory salutes.

But the miserable aspect of the people and countryside was nothing compared with the devastation brought about by the recent fighting and the signs of the chaos that clearly followed.

We were confronted by the remains of possibly fifty gliders, scattered and pointing in all directions, the majority of them appearing to be reasonably whole but most of the others either damaged in part or completely wrecked, as the result of crashing into trees, banks or other obstructions, or having just been obliged to make landings in the dark or half-light in the smallest and most difficult of sites.

Leaning and in many cases crippled and broken, they made a pathetic sight, made more poignant when realisation dawned that the twenty or so well-trained, eager young men in each glider had all either perished or been critically injured. Such a terrible, horrible waste! I was greatly moved.*

This tragic picture of violence and death was, however, only

---

* Later, I saw photographs of scores of dead glider troops, laid out in lines beside their crippled gliders.

slightly more disturbing than that seen on the roads along which we were slowly progressing and in the nearby hedges and fields: an almost unending trail of burnt-out or immobilised tanks, armoured vehicles and trucks, mostly German, together with many small heaps of discarded weapons and personal equipment.

Possibly a week before there would also have been bodies – casualties by the dozen, dead and dying – which mercifully had been removed or dealt with by the time we arrived on our brief inspection tour.

One ghastly reminder of death, however, remained: the carcases of scores of animals, mainly cattle and horses, which had been killed in the fighting and left to rot, their bodies bloated, their legs pointing obscenely upwards into the air, as though posing for a macabre picture to be painted by some demented modern artist – and, the weather being warm, all amid a most unpleasant sweet stench of corruption that almost defied description.

After some minutes, sickened by the sight and reek of so much death, I think we were all relieved when our driver turned our vehicle about and headed back towards our newly created headquarters site, all of us silent and with me thanking God that I was an airman and did not have to face violence in its starkest, most upsetting form, as did the poor wretched Army chaps fighting for their lives on the ground.

Looking back now, I remember that week or so following the arrival of our headquarters contingent at Criqueville as a time of heat, dust, rumour and confusion, with confusion the most vivid memory.

Strangely perhaps, although I remember it as a period of setting up, organising and taking stock my logbook shows that not only did I fly the P.51 regularly throughout and beyond the battle area, but I also took the Cessna and Fairchild – packed to the 'gunnels' with passengers and equipment – back and forth to England, crossing and re-crossing the Channel several times.

In the latter part of June, the Germans had evacuated the Cherbourg Peninsula and American forces took over the area on about 2 July, thus freeing at least two airfields formerly used by the Luftwaffe. And it was to one of those airfields, close to the village of St Pierre Eglise and referred to as A-15 or Maupertus, that the 100th Fighter Wing headquarters moved on 15 July.

Flying in first the Fairchild, and later one of the Wing's P.47s and my much loved P.51, I found aircraft of the 363 Fighter Group from Staplehurst already in possession of the airfield and apparently quite at home. Of the several P.47 Fighter Groups in the Wing, formerly at Headcorn and High Halden and now somewhere in Normandy, there was not even a sign; they had just disappeared. Scores of big, fat Thunderbolt fighters had just plain vanished!

Yes, war was confusing, right enough, and the closer you were to the sharp end, the more confusing it became. In fact, everything was confusing. And uncomfortable. And hot. And thoroughly unsettling. Oh, for a nice static war in England where you didn't have to keep hopping about like demented fleas!

On the credit side, the headquarters element was accommodated in a splendid if elderly chateau, which delighted Tex Sanders, who had long craved for even minor splendour. I was happy, too, as it at least meant we had lavatories, which, although massive and ancient, were tolerably decent water closets, and thankfully, not the 'sitting on a pole over a hole' variety that invariably went with living in the field. And, once again, I found myself sharing a massive, high-ceilinged bedroom with my friends Hill and Bodenheim.

The building itself was impressive but, like most aged French buildings, was urgently in need of repair. The two French owners – an elderly seigneur and his lady – still lived on the premises and were frostily welcoming, no doubt believing – as, it appeared, did most of the French – that the Germans could well return.

On the negative side, however, having apparently previously housed some senior Luftwaffe personnel, the rambling overgrown gardens and grounds were riddled with protective minefields, all of them marked with skulls and stark notices saying 'Actung Minen!'. The mines themselves were the anti-personnel 'S' variety, which, we had been warned, were particularly vicious, as when trodden on or otherwise activated, the ghastly things would spring up to face level before exploding and scattering a mass of ball bearings in all directions, killing or mutilating any person or object within a 15-foot radius.

And, sad to say, one of the first unpleasant tasks of Colonel Loughran and his medical team was to go to the aid of several French villagers who had raided a local flour mill and been horribly wounded, having mistakenly (and very stupidly) attempted to find a useable path between the mines.

As I happened to be with Freddie Loughran when the request was made, I unwisely volunteered to accompany the small rescue team of the Colonel, Patterson and two NCO medical orderlies, the latter pair included in order to drive the ambulance and help with any stretcher bearing that was necessary.

On arriving at the scene of the accident, we were met by several voluble French villagers standing and gesticulating on the edge of a well-marked minefield. In the middle distance and between several small sacks of flour, two bodies were lying on the ground, neither of them showing any sign of life.

We recognised our problems immediately: how we were to get into and through the minefield without getting ourselves killed, how to communicate with the very excited French villagers – their French being quite different from mine – and, having reached the victims, exactly how to minister to them and get them out to safety.

These matters were discussed with difficulty and at length with our villager companions, until it was agreed that one of them, who allegedly knew the way, would (we hoped) lead us safely through the minefield; and that we would make just one trip to pick up both bodies on our two stretchers.

Which is more or less what happened, although carrying one end of the second stretcher, I experienced moments of sheer mind-numbing terror during several occasions when I thought we would blow ourselves up. There was, moreover, one horrible moment for me when as we struggled to lift the mutilated body of the younger of the two victims – a boy of about 13. As I looked down with sadness and concern on his apparently dead body, it suddenly showed apparent signs of life, a single eye wobbling obscenely like a ghastly white golf ball rolling about in a sea of blood.

I remember helping to load them both into the ambulance, after which I stood, weak-kneed, feeling quite sick and unable to move. Breathing deeply, it took me quite some time to recover my composure and be able to join the others, determining, meanwhile, never *ever* to volunteer for any similar rescue act again.

In our new chateau accommodation, and not for the first time, the 100th Wing headquarters element began to organise itself and get down to business.

One of the first activities of the day was a morning briefing, during which all staff officers gathered around a large wall map to hear details of the daily situation and the most recent positions of the various front lines.

Both my RAF intelligence officer colleague, Carr, and I made regular contributions, after which the commanding officer, Tex Sanders, usually said his piece, followed by other department heads who had something vital to add. Usually, the meetings were friendly, relaxed and informative, but occasionally criticism was levelled at someone or some department, resulting in long faces and, now and then, occasional sharp disagreements and arguments.

Although the war situation was proceeding favourably on the whole, there were occasional dark mutterings against 'the British' because of their slow progress around Caen, and Carr and I had to watch very carefully what we said in the discussions that inevitably followed. Moreover, even at our comparatively low level, he and I were all too aware of rumours of dissension among the ranks of both senior British and American commanders, as General Montgomery's strategy and methods, as well as his acerbic manner, were not to everyone's taste.

But, as events were to prove, the emollience of General Eisenhower, together with the able assistance of the quiet and effective Air Marshal Tedder, proved equal to the task of maintaining an acceptable measure of accord.

It was with these slightly worrying matters in mind, and aware that 450 RAF Lancasters and Halifaxes had, only a few days before, dropped over 2,000 tons of bombs on the town in a single 40 minute daylight raid, I decided to visit Caen and surroundings in my trusty P.51, to see for myself. In addition, I would also make a tour of the Channel Isles, which were still very much in German hands, having purposely been bypassed by the Americans.

Despite going into an active battle area, strangely I had little fear of being intercepted by enemy fighters – they, it seemed, had almost totally disappeared, although a few sizeable formations had apparently been encountered now and then much deeper into France. Clearly, they were being withdrawn or reserved for reasons that were not immediately obvious – or perhaps simply because of a shortage of fuel. Whatever the cause, remembering the Luftwaffe of old and its then very effective fighter force of Focke-Wulf 190s and Me.109s, I thought it very odd – almost sad in fact.

Arriving in the area of Caen and flying at about 8,000 feet (which would keep me above much of the nastier enemy low flak if they decided to shoot at me), I could see even from that height that the town, apart from the northern suburbs, was an almost unrecognisable mess, with devastated buildings and a thousand craters lip to lip, over which it had been difficult for the Allied ground troops (who had cheered their heads off at the time of bombing) to advance.

Looking down on the horror scene below, I was reminded of my father's stories about the massive shelling that took place before the British advance at Passchendaele in 1917. As a soldier himself, he remembered the action vividly. Following days of remorseless British shelling, the infantry were unable to advance across the thousands of shell holes created, and hundreds, even thousands of men, wounded and unable to swim, drowned in the mass of flooded craters.

I was, of course, well aware that the bomber boys were only acting according to a plan and doing what they were told to do, but it was all very well for them to drop their bangers and go home to tea, leaving the 'poor bloody infantry' and tank wallahs to fight their way through the chaos their bombs had created. Who would be in the Army, thought I?

Lt. Cols. Bickell and Eaglestone pose for a photograph beside a Lashenden P.51, which is fitted with the older type split canopy.

Pilots of the 382 Fighter Squadron at Staplehurst pose for their photo.

One of the hundreds of Waco gliders that took part in the invasion-day landings.

RAF Typhoons, which created such chaos in the German Army during the Falaise Gap fighting in August 1944. Here is one fitted with four cannons and eight 3in rockets with 60lb heads.

Maintenance on the Typhoons was often done under the most primitive and dangerous conditions.

A B.25 Mitchell bombs Caen, sometime in July 1944.

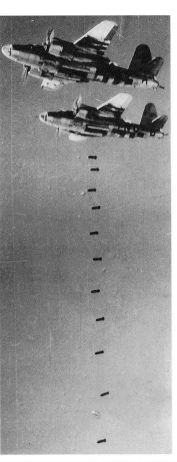

B.26 Marauders of the 9th USAAF bomb Caen during the month-long siege of the town.

Five-inch rockets being fitted to a P.47 during the latter part of the fighting in November 1944.

A French Morane-Saulnier aircraft. One of many French fighters I encountered when I was obliged to land at Villacoublay when searching for the missing 100th Fighter Wing headquarters in August 1944.

Flight Officer Eileen Hampton (far right) leads the first group of WAAFs sent to France to man the 24 Sector Operations centre, first in Amiens then in Ghent, Belgium. Here, in September 1944, they are embarking on an RAF C-47 (Dakota) at Lyneham.

A wedding photograph of Miss Hampton and me on 3rd June 1945.

The first pictures taken of Spitfire 3W-K, as it was when it landed at Rennes airfield in France in August 1944.

The same aircraft after having the camouflage paint removed some months later and the initials of the new owner (Wing Commander Marian Duryasz) painted on in 1945.

Mark 14 Spitfire of No 322 Squadron with its Dutch pilots. Flying Officers Jonker sitting on the wing and Burgwal holding the airscrew. Jonker flew Spitfire 3W-K into Rennes on 20th August.

The silver Spitfire with the armament removed and two Polish airmen, Sergeants Krzysztof Pawlik (left) and Józef Bieńkowski of No 317 Squadron, in attendance.

A group of high-ranking Polish officers in Germany in 1945 with the Wing Commander Marian Duryasz second from the right.

Another group of Polish officers with Squadron Leader Ludwig Martel standing on the left. Martel was the officer who finally disposed of the silver Spitfire.

The Channel Isles, on the other hand, presented an almost idyllic summer scene. As I wandered over all three main islands, inhabited I was aware by thousands of Germans, not a shot was fired in my direction despite my flying at less than 2,500 feet.

Looking up at me, what were they thinking, I wondered. Had they recognised the hopeless position they were in? Had they simply lost the will to react and fight?

Our way of life in the headquarters of the 100th Fighter Wing brought me into contact with new faces, new officer colleagues and several new departments I never knew existed, with responsibilities I had never heard of.

First, there was a very active, high-priced group, including a chap named Sade (a distant relative, he said, of that infamous libertine the Marquis de Sade), who spoke French fluently and whose primary duties, it appeared, were to interrogate indignant French collaborators claiming to be innocent, and to help to identify the mountain of goods the Germans had plundered as a result of their victories in battle.

These covered a wide spectrum of valuable prizes, from racehorses to old masters, fine wines to precious stones, furniture and pieces of art, to pretty well anything, in fact, of artistic merit or monetary value, the list being almost endless. All the Germans felt it necessary to do was plonk a written message on the bottle, picture, object or animal, indicating that this particular piece of merchandise was 'Reserved for the Use of the Wermacht', after which they considered it legally theirs. Anything so named, however, was fair game for my colleagues in the 'liberating department' – and the opportunities were vast.

The result was a constant stream of heavy trucks loaded down with 'liberated' items – endless cases of champagne, wines and other small, portable goods, for example – which began to pass in and through the precincts of our headquarters, and, on far too many occasions, find their way on to, or beside, my bed.

One memorable day, I arrived in my room to find umpteen bottles of Benedictine liquor, a similar amount of Calvados, two cases of champagne, three Lugers, a Mauser machine pistol (all the guns with ammunition), an expensive 16-bore shotgun and a .22 hunting rifle, besides numerous packs each of 200 cigarettes, and boxes of cigars – everything being the result of my being an accredited PX (Post Exchange) member, plus my share of a mound of swag obtained from a recently crippled enemy supply train.

As I was a non-smoker, someone who seldom drank and a person who had no interest whatever in guns, my problem, I realised at the time, was to get rid of the stuff without offending those who felt they were doing me a favour.

It was about this time, too, that on hearing that there was an officer in the area sporting a 'powerful British accent', I followed it to its source and found the speaker to be an old Battle of Britain colleague of mine, Squadron Leader Anthony ('Tony') Bartley, late of 92 Squadron, formerly based at Hawkinge. I recalled meeting him in London at an official luncheon at Simpson's and we exchanged news. I learned that he, like me, was a liaison officer with another 9th Air Force Fighter Wing, and he was on the trail of 'some local tack' to go with the horse he had just 'liberated' from the Germans.

I then smilingly watched him operate, not without a considerable measure of awe and admiration. A smooth, polished young man, Bartley spoke fluent French and was soon in communication with a very rough-looking French individual. I have not the slightest doubt that his negotiations proved to be successful, although I did not remain to see the final result of his endeavours.

I left almost immediately and I did not see him again. I heard much later, however, that he had first courted, and then married, the very attractive young actress Deborah Kerr, who, throughout the late autumn of 1944, as a member of an ENSA acting group, was entertaining British forces in France.

July slid by and August loomed, the first ten days of which proved to be a momentously successful time for the Allied forces, although for me, it was merely a period of passing interest, as events took me out of France for a number of days and away from much of the action that ensued. I remember it, too, for some unusual sporting activities.

Being an athletic type of person, I entered wholeheartedly into the many games held in the shadow of our rambling French chateau during off-duty hours and soon became a dab hand at volleyball, American football and, to a lesser extent, baseball (I could always raise my American colleagues to a fury when I explained that baseball was regarded in England as a 'cissy's' game called rounders, and usually played by schoolgirls).

I also found I could kick a football better then most but never did get the hang of delivering the long, twisting hand pass; and, although a reasonably good batsman in cricket, I found the baseball bat rather more difficult to handle successfully. Even so, whenever a game took place, there would always be lines of officers and others shouting encouragement whenever their 'Limey' squadron leader colleague moved up to the plate.

Soccer, however, was different. Very much different, my goodness!

The Mayor and Corporation of the local village, St Pierre Eglise, had challenged Wing headquarters to a game of soccer and with very few Americans familiar with the game (very many fewer in 1944 than now), I was immediately appointed organiser, coach, captain and general adviser.

Selecting a team was difficult, but I managed eventually to persuade ten other members of the headquarters staff to take part, some officers, some not. After that, I tried to explain the rudiments of the game, the various positions and, of course, the rules, being all too aware that my explanations were not being taken at all seriously by my grinning companions.

There came then the business of finding the kit, a problem swiftly resolved when an officer I had never seen before set off in a six-ton truck and within hours reappeared with a mountain of shirts, shorts, stockings, shin guards and football boots, everything brand spanking new. But as I examined the boots – virgin yellow leather, as stiff as boards and bristling with rows of lethal-looking studs – my heart sank. With the temperature in the high 80s and the ground rock hard, I had an immediate mental picture of blisters, pain and total disaster.

On the appointed day, my team trotted bravely on to the pitch – all wearing their hats, and one or two their gloves. Surprised, I pointed out that hats and gloves were not exactly *de rigueur*, but recognising that to an American a hat was at least important as his trousers, I was not surprised when no one took any notice.

We lined up, excited and waiting, each of my team uttering war cries and springing up and down in anticipation. After which, the whistle blew, to encouraging cheers from the crowds lining the touchlines.

With the kick-off, to the utter surprise of the French, who were clearly taking the whole business very seriously, every player in my team – other than the goalie and me – rushed in a solid phalanx in the direction of the bouncing ball, all screaming Indian war whoops. Then, having absolutely flattened about five of the French team who were not able to get out of the way in time, they began booting the ball about in every direction – other, that is, than towards the French goal.

When it happened to come to a player head high and, in attempting to head it, my player had his hat knocked off, he would immediately stop, return to replace the hat and then rush back to take part in the battle.

Watching, wide-eyed, I was immediately reminded of the circus act in which two teams of small dogs, all done up in coloured shirts, raced around, barking madly and leaping high in pursuit of several floating balloons.

It was chaos! The French team, picking themselves up meanwhile and nursing bruised and bleeding limbs, were utterly baffled. Screaming hysterically to my team to keep their positions, I was totally ignored. It was football gone mad!

By half time, most of my team were exhausted and, having removed the boots from their blistered feet, were tottering about either barefooted or in their stockings. And it was at this critical point that the French dealt the *coup de grâce*: they brought on the champagne.

Thereafter the game degenerated into farce. If the first half was comedy, the second was a fiasco, members of my team roaming about, flushed with wine and in owlish good spirits, most of them clutching half-empty champagne bottles and boots in their hands. Limp with shouting and laughter, I retired to the touchlines and collapsed, totally exhausted.

I have no memory of the score but it didn't really matter. Soccer! Dear Lord, soccer was never, ever, like this!

About 64 years later, I received a telephone call from a foreign-sounding gentleman – I believe he was Dutch – explaining that he had for months been scouring Europe and the United States, trying to find the RAF officer who had organised and led the 100th Fighter Wing football team in 1944.

The event had apparently gone down in French history as positively memorable, and the elders of the St Pierre Eglise area were arranging to celebrate the 65th anniversary of the 1944 invasion in the greatest way possible. Sounding ecstatic that he had finally found me, my Dutch informant explained that he would report back, after which I would shortly receive a gold-plated invitation to appear as guest of honour, prior to taking a leading part in the mammoth festivities that were being planned. Money, apparently, would not be an issue. My hosts would also be happy to send a private aircraft to ferry me from and to wherever I was living, I could stay as their guest as long as I wished, and I could be assured that I would be treated as magnificently as visiting royalty.

A month or so later, an invitation did indeed arrive with a pressing plea (in the most exquisite French) that I should make every effort to accept, as the event was of national, even international, significance.

Sadly, however, I was forced to decline, offering as excuses my advanced age and that I was already committed to other pressing engagements. Moreover, and though I might not have admitted it at the time, I probably suspected that my schoolboy French might not be equal to the occasion.

The very considerable event, therefore, took place without me. However, the good citizens of St Pierre Eglise in Normandy sent me a formidable pack of literature and photographs of the event, together with a splendid memorial plaque celebrating the occasion, all of which I shall treasure with pride – and not a little amusement.

Tuesday, 1 August, a warm day but overcast.

Dressing myself in the morning, I was suddenly confronted by my immediate senior, Jim Haun, who arrived with his hat rakishly askew and with his pipe working overtime.

'We've just been allotted a brand-noo C-53,' he explained. 'It's at present at Aldermaston in England and you and I are going across this morning to pick it up, OK? We'll use the Cessna (C-78) to get there, and Patterson and one of the line NCOs will come with us to bring the aircraft back.'

'What's a C-53?' I asked, pulling on my shirt.

'It's a C-47 (Dakota) with a difference and called a Skytrooper,' Jim explained. 'A sort of personnel carrier, seating up to 25 bodies. Otherwise, everything's much the same, OK? I also want to drop in to Heston on the way,' he went on, carefully neglecting to tell me why.

So, after collecting an all-too-willing Patterson and Sergeant Smith (Smitty Major), we took off, more or less on time.

After crossing the Channel without incident, we flew towards London, dropping down into the small, historic grass airfield at Heston on the western fringe of the city, marked, I always recall, by an enormous dark gasometer which rose and fell, silently but regularly, almost within the airfield circuit.

Sadly, the landing ground has long since disappeared to make way for housing estates and shops. Sadly too, because it was a friendly well-worn place which I was to use many times in the months ahead when I wished to make a quick trip by air into the London area.

We found the airfield of Aldermaston (a little to the west of Newbury), packed tight with 100 aircraft of different types, including our C-53.

My first memory of our new aircraft was of a steep climb from the rear-entry fuselage door to the cockpit and, having arrived, finding I could barely fit my 6-foot-3-inch frame into either of the two pilot's seats – the design of the aircraft being of the early 1930s, it did not possess the more modern tricycle undercarriage arrangement. Otherwise, though small up front, it was comfortable and friendly, with green leather everywhere and a mass of switches in the roof. The Americans did go in for electricity and switches, my goodness!

The two engines were 1,200-horsepower Pratt & Whitney R-1830 radials, which in later months I grew to love, as they could be throttled back to below 30 inches of boost and 1,800 revs, at which settings they would bumble along quite happily for hours on end. On start-up, the motors would shake themselves like spaniels shedding water, and come to life amid minor clouds of blue smoke, to the whining noise of their inertial 'whizzer' starters. And in all the many hours I flew alongside them, they never gave me a moment's trouble; all I had to do was to keep the various cockpit pointers 'in the green' and sit back.

Our particular aircraft did not have an automatic pilot (or if it did, I was never aware of it), so that I was always obliged to fly it manually. The controls were as heavy as lead after a fighter but not tiringly so, and I was soon to learn that in a C-53 nothing was done in a rush. There was no question of a vertical turn, an 'upward Charlie' or even a slow roll, for example.

Nicknamed the 'Gooney Bird', ours could accommodate 25 passengers sitting sideways on, most of them blissfully unaware that with me at the helm, had anything dropped off or misbehaved I would not have known what to do. Indeed, I always made a point of taking with me one or two NCOs of our communications flight. Although unqualified to fly the aircraft, they at least knew where all the switches were and which did what. Even the several radios were a mystery to me and usually left in the capable hands of the unflappable Sergeant Smith Senior.

Jim Haun sat in the captain's seat on my first introductory flight. In his element, and still wearing his hat at its usual rakish angle, he puffed at his pipe, kippering us all in a blue fog of Mackintosh-toffee smoke, complaining meanwhile about the absence of ashtrays.

After several landings, he allowed me to take the controls, showing me how to use the tail trimmer to gently 'wind' the aircraft off the ground, the stick forces being far too great, in his opinion. Also, I was instructed firmly not to 'rack the ol' crate around so much', as I was 'not in a fighter now'. It was all trivial, light-hearted stuff, and within an hour or so, I was thoroughly at home in the aircraft, having learnt to 'grease' it back on the runway on its main wheels rather than attempt to make the usual three-point landing.

Flying the C-53 back to A-15, our airfield at Cherbourg, I experienced a new thrill. It was fun being a transport pilot – different, anyway.

For the next several days Haun, Patterson and I, with a variety of helpers and passengers, flew around England, 'getting the hang of things', calling in at Heston several times, Burtonwood, in the north, and several other airfields of our choosing, until our joyriding came to an end when news was received that the Wing would be moving to the A-27 airfield at Rennes, some 120 miles to the south – a change of venue which requires me now to explain and describe the war situation, which had altered considerably during the few days we had been wandering around England.

During the month or so following the invasion on 7 June, as a comparatively junior officer I was not, of course, privy to the plans, conversations, disputes and jealousies that existed in the many command elements controlling the day-to-day fighting by the various Allied formations. I was, however, as the result of my experiences in the Middle East in 1941 and 1942, reasonably knowledgeable, for example, about the views and methods of the officer commanding the Allied ground forces, General Bernard Montgomery. This, plus my constant flying around the invasion area and meeting officers who were much better informed than I, together with my frequent daily intelligence briefings, enabled me to accumulate information and gain a pretty accurate knowledge of what was going on.

At the time of the 100th Wing's move to Rennes, the situation, as I saw it, was roughly as follows.

The invasion had gone well and the Germans, though resisting strongly in several areas, had not thrown their full weight against our beachhead forces, the Luftwaffe's involvement, strangely enough, being much less than expected. Our inability to capture Caen had been, as I have said, a major stumbling block and the use of strategic bombers from Bomber Command and the American 8th

Air Force in the invasion area had been a mixed blessing and caused some expensive and tragic problems of their own. The Allied tactical bomber and fighter forces had, on the other hand, done wonderfully well and the cooperation between Allied ground and air forces was improving almost daily.

In line with what I always knew to be Montgomery's mindset, it was always his intention and method, as in North Africa, to contain an initial enemy attack, build up his own forces to overwhelming strength, and then not only defeat the enemy but destroy him. To this end, the American 3rd Army, under the controversial General Patton, which had only recently landed in France, was redirected from moving westwards to conquer Brittany to face east and, with elements of the US 1st and 2nd Armies, head for the Seine and Paris. These forces, together with the British and Canadian Armies, when they had broken out from their distractions around Caen, would first destroy any German counter-attack before, together, proceeding eastwards. Until overwhelming force was achieved, however, and he was manifestly ready to go, it was unlikely that Monty would ever be distracted by political interference or even high-level disagreements.

Moreover, as a general policy, various strongly held towns and fortified areas held by the Germans would in future be bypassed and not assaulted, except from the air, the result being that the Channel Isles, the naval centres of Brest, Lorient and St Nazaire in Brittany, together with the Channel ports of Le Havre, Boulogne and Calais, were simply left to wither and surrender, which some of them did as late as the end of the German war in 1945.

The plan, therefore, was straightforward and simple, even if the implementation of it might take time.

Largely because I had cultivated a nasty summer cold during the early days of August, I decided not to fly but, on Patterson's recommendation, travel the 130-plus miles between Cherbourg and Rennes by ambulance. Wrapping myself in several of the dark blankets in the rear of the vehicle, I laid myself down, having resolved to take a welcome, recovering nap.

But what a hope! The ambulance rode like a steel-wheeled hand-cart, travelling over cobbles. Moreover, within an hour I was a mass of bites, having been assailed by much of the flea population of northern Europe. Rising from my couch, I shouted for the driver to stop, instructed the second medical orderly to take my place in the ambulance interior, and seated myself beside the driver, scratching and dripping. Our journey then proceeded in a silence broken only by my occasional snuffling, coughing and scratching. Patterson, by God, would have some explaining to do about the state of one of his precious ambulances!

Having driven about 50 miles, we drew up for a comfort break. Deep into the French countryside, we observed several minor crowds of bedraggled-looking scarecrow figures staring woodenly in our direction like ruminating cattle.

My driver, having seen similar groups earlier in the day, explained, 'They're prisoners, working on the land left behind by the Krauts. Mostly Russians, probably. Nowhere to go and probably starving. Still, they're probably better off than they were, poor guys.'

I remember thinking: Poor guys! What was this character saying? They should consider themselves fortunate, not having to move around in this lurching, flea-ridden monstrosity of an ambulance!

We moved on.

I was quite looking forward to reaching Rennes as Dornier Do 215 bombers I had shot at during the Battle of Britain had operated from there and it would be interesting to see their former base, and also be nearer the front line.

Arriving at my new home in Rennes, I found myself again accommodated in a tent and sharing it with Hill and Bodenheim, who, having arrived some time before me, had thoughtfully arranged to have my kit unpacked and bed set up. And as before, our domestic site was surrounded by unpleasant-looking minefields. Patterson, Freddie Loughran and a few other colleagues were clearly around, but our gallant commander, Tex Sanders, was missing. He was said to be searching for another chateau in which to bed down.

Having been driven in a jeep to inspect the nearby airfield, I saw that the runways were in a very poor state, breaking up in places and in some areas a mass of loose stones and gravel, suggesting a high rate of tyre wear on the P.51 and our other communications flight aircraft. I found this rather surprising, as the airfield had only been liberated a few days before by the 3rd Army, having before then been in constant use by the Luftwaffe.

Our disparate gaggle of about eight aircraft was parked in one corner of the airfield, whilst the remainder of the considerable area was occupied by the P.47s of 362 Fighter Group, formerly at Headcorn. The P.51s of the 363rd Fighter Group, with us at Staplehurst in England and Cherbourg (A-15), had just disappeared – where to I had no idea. There were heaped masses of equipment and baggage everywhere; and in the middle of the landing ground, scores of dumpy P.47s, still wearing their black and white invasion stripes, were interspersed with minor groups of grazing cattle.

I found myself wearily shaking my head. This was a chaotic situation. Units and aircraft kept turning up out of nowhere, and then just as quickly disappearing. Someone important probably knew what was happening and was issuing the orders, but I was certainly being kept in the dark. And I was a member of the so-called controlling headquarters staff, for heaven's sake!

During those early two weeks in August, when we in the 100th Fighter Wing headquarters were settling in at Rennes, 120 miles to the north and east the British and Canadian Armies had successfully broken out of their enclave around Caen and joined up with the American Armies, which had been similarly successful on their western flank.

Meanwhile, the US 3rd Army, with the turbulent Patton in command, was, as expected, striking north and east. And it was against this very considerable combined force that the German 7th Army, ordered by Hitler to fight to the death, launched its counter-attack on 7 August.

The savage and bloody engagement that followed over a period of about three weeks, later referred to as the Battle of the Falaise Gap, was one of the most decisive and significant engagements of the Second World War. The conflict resulted in a German defeat of almost cosmic proportions and the later admission of the German commander, General von Kluge, that, in their four much-vaunted panzer divisions, only 100 tanks finally survived out of a force of 2,500 tanks, armoured vehicles and guns, and that casualties amounted to more than 60,000 men. Furthermore, it was only because there was hesitation among the Allied hierarchy over the employment in the tactical battle of the strategic bombers of Bomber Command and the US 8th Air Force that the entire German counter-attacking army was not completely wiped out.

As intelligence filtered through to us in Rennes, the tremendous hour-to-hour successes of the RAF's rocket-carrying Typhoons became evident. I flew over the area several times in my P.51 and observed some of the mayhem as it happened: the fizzing white streamers of the rockets with their lethal 60lb heads as they lanced downwards into the lines of passive and impotent targets. A salvo of eight rockets from a single Typhoon was equivalent to a broadside from a naval 6-inch gun cruiser – indeed, each 60lb semi-armour-piercing head *was* a converted 6-inch naval shell. Then, if that was felt to be insufficient to cripple the toughest German Tiger tanks, the 'Tiffies' could employ rockets incorporating a solid 25lb head – a heavy lump of steel that would pierce even the thickest of armour.

As I flew around, watching it all happen, I felt genuine sympathy for the hapless German tank crews below: men of flesh and blood, constantly on the retreat, stunned by the sight and sound of the spine-chilling, screaming rockets, and cringing in the face of the havoc wrought on them from above. With nowhere to hide, no wonder that even the bravest of them sometimes deserted their tanks and vehicles and crouched, terrified, in the roadside ditches.

Then, within a week, with the obvious benefits of complete Allied air superiority still vividly in mind, I was to witness another sight almost as riveting but fortunately less disastrous: that of General Patton's 3rd Army, pushing hard for the supreme prize of being first in Paris, strung out and motionless along 30 miles of roads and lanes – hundreds of tanks and vehicles that had stuttered to a standstill, having outdistanced their supplies and fuel.

In its own way, it was a sight almost as chilling as that I had so recently witnessed at Falaise. Remembering the victorious German army columns of 1940, aided by Junkers 87 dive bombers laying waste to everything in their path, together with the vivid and tragic picture of refugees and elements of the French Army fleeing before them and jamming the roads, I thought how fortunate it was for General Patton that the Luftwaffe had been unable to operate against his troops with anything like the same potency.

Was the 3rd Army's rapid advance an impulsive error brought about by an over-zealous commander eager for military success and glory, or a calculated risk?

At my level and the facts unclear, it was difficult to decide.

Chapter 15
Enter the Spitfire

As this vital war scene was being enacted before my eyes, I experienced an almost overwhelming urge to be a part of the excitement and a feeling that somehow I might be able to join in the fighting. But how? The Allied plan demanded that the more lightly armed fighters of the 9th Air Force be otherwise employed. Moreover, the P.51s of both the 354th and the 363rd Fighter Groups had for the moment disappeared, and, as a lone aircraft, I couldn't just tack myself on to the Rennes-based P.47s.

So, disappointed and feeling more than a little guilty, I recorded in my logbook that in addition to the P.51, I flew the C-53 and C-78 several times, for unremembered reasons, and even the more lowly AT6 (Harvard).

But events were to change – dramatically – when, on about 18 August, a lone British Spitfire suddenly arrived on the scene.

It turned out to be a very unusual day.

Being driven in the communications flight jeep, I was heading for our aircraft on 'the line', intending again to take the P.51 towards the battle area up north. It was late morning and I was looking forward to an interesting day's flying and being part of an important piece of history. As I drew near, however, I was greatly surprised to see another fighter parked within yards of my intended mount – one I recognised immediately as a Spitfire.

A Spitfire, for heaven's sake! Where on earth had that come from and what might it be doing here? To encounter a Spitfire at least 100 miles south of its normal operating area, and in the American Sector, was about as strange as coming across a camel in Trafalgar Square. Instructing my driver to stop, I climbed out to inspect the new arrival.

It was a Mark 9b, the type we had used so successfully in the
Biggin Hill Wing in 1942–43. Not only that: it was pretty shabby,
with scratched panels and a pair of very part-worn tyres. On its side
it had the identification letters 3W-K, which indicated that it was
from an Allied squadron and not the RAF. Otherwise, there were
no other means of identification, a white band having been painted,
seemingly in haste, immediately in front of the tail unit, obscuring
the normal aircraft number. In short, it looked a very tired aircraft
indeed. No wonder it had been landed – possibly because of unserviceability – in out-of-the-way Rennes.

I turned to question Sergeant Smitty Junior. 'Tell me,' I asked,
'when did this thing arrive and did you see it land?'

Smitty waved an arm. 'It wuz when you wuz away, sir. Came
in from that direction, a-bangin' and a-poppin'. Then it landed and
taxied in, making a terrible noise. After that a guy got out, as mad
as a crate o' snakes, sayin' he didn't want no more of that "somethin'-somethin'" aircraft.' Smitty lowered his voice deferentially as
he uttered some very ungodly words. 'He was in your blue outfit
but he was sort of foreign-like. Didn't speak English too good. After
that he disappeared and after a long time, another bird, looking like
a greenhouse with wings, came and picked him up.'

I remember smiling. An Avro Anson, no doubt. 'And didn't he say
who he was or where he came from?'

'No, sir, he sure didn't. He just arrived, left it here, then disappeared. And didn't say nuthin' about comin' back to pick it up.'

Deciding to postpone my flight, I discussed the new aircraft with
Sergeants Smedley, Carter and Smith Senior, all of whom, I knew,
had worked on Spitfires when serving with the first American squadrons to appear in England. Was it worthwhile trying to discover the
nature of its problem and perhaps make it flyable? Meanwhile, we
might perhaps check the aircraft over and try to start the engine.

This we did, although it took some time, as the Americans only
employed 24-volt starter trolleys and the Spitfire incorporated a
12-volt electrical system. Moreover, on searching about in the cockpit, there were no parachute in place, no pilot's helmet, no map of
any kind and no servicing documents – although we were aware

that on an operational sortie, the last named papers would never normally be carried.

It having taken about two hours for my NCO companions to sort out all these various difficulties, I finally sat in the cockpit and had a go.

At first the engine just didn't want to cooperate. It coughed and it jerked and spat blue smoke at us until, seeing that we weren't about to give up, it finally decided to burst into life.

And there it was, the big four-bladed airscrew whacking away in front, the engine sounding like someone shaking a bag of spanners and the instrument panel wobbling like a demented jelly. Something very obviously being wrong, I made faces at the four NCOs watching me and shut the motor down.

After a long discussion and deciding that it might only be an ignition problem, I suggested they might investigate further and, not wishing to interfere with honest artisans, left them to it.

The following day, the Spitfire was still there, looking as lonely as ever, with Smedley reporting that they had had another look at the engine, successfully located and cured the problem, and checked it over. The trouble was, however, that with no documents in the cockpit, there was no knowing the history of either the engine or the airframe, and as they couldn't sign any papers, nothing, as far as they were concerned, was legal.

I responded by saying that I was much impressed by their rectitude; nevertheless, provided they could assure me that the engine wouldn't stop and the tyres wouldn't burst, I would fly the aircraft.

As I strapped myself in, all five of them stood alongside, like magpies on a clothes line, shaking their heads.

This time, however, the engine burst into life with a reassuring roar; everything up front seemed very much smoother and, all the temperatures and pressures appearing unobjectionable, I taxied out, crossed myself and then opened the throttle. As I flashed past the small black-and-white control-box caravan, situated beside the main runway, two white faces were pressed against the glass of its tiny cupola, each one registering a mixture of surprise and, I think I detected, regret.

The flight, I am happy to report, was uneventful. Everything worked perfectly, and I wandered about between Rennes and Nantes for a pleasant 30 minutes, even to the extent of flying well into enemy territory, before returning to base. This time, however, although the two white faces were still there, they registered only surprise.

I had other things to do, I recall, for the remainder of the week, but Spitfires, like bad debts, tend to linger in the mind. I took a further hour off to fly it a second time – to keep its morale up, so to speak – and was surprised to see it several days later, still as silent and as lonely as ever, sitting on its hardstanding. Clearly, the owner was not too keen on having it back.

The days of August slid by, warm, wet and sometimes miserable. I flew the C-53 on several occasions, I note, plus the P.51.

Tex Sanders found himself another chateau and we moved across to live with him in comparative splendour near the airfield, surrounded once more by minefields and their macabre signs. The headquarters having set up shop again, I was taking my turn in giving occasional daily briefings but, in the main, flying.

On 25 August, Paris would be liberated, not by the fuming Patton but by General de Gaulle, the tall and taciturn Free French Forces commander, in a contrived political gesture negotiated by the Allies. Little of this, however, was known to us at the time.

Meanwhile the Colonel had found a stream close by his new chateau and was busily engaged, when duty permitted, designing and building what he called a Florida Everglades skim-boat. Having located a small aero-engine and propeller, he was beavering away on his new toy – which, of course, suited me admirably, as it meant I had the P.51 all to myself.

On 10 August, I used it to make a longish trip well beyond Nantes and further down the Atlantic coastline, all alone at 10,000 feet and in the brightest of sunshine. For more than two hours I flew over so-called enemy territory. Not a shot was fired at me and I did not see a single aircraft.

Suddenly, I was struck by the fact that after almost five years of

flying against a tough and resourceful enemy, the war was almost
over. There could well be battles ahead – and indeed there were –
but the end was surely in sight and could only be a matter of months
away.

'Back at the ranch', so to speak, life at Rennes went on much as
before. Freddie Loughran continued to fuss about his grease traps,
Patterson attended to his duties as surgeon, administering potions
and tonics, curing breaks and sprains and lancing a boil or two, his
surgical instruments set out on a pine refectory table, in the open
during the good weather and in a tent when it rained. From time to
time, I would stand beside him to help with the pus and the blood,
but I never felt I had a calling for that sort of business.

And all the time, the war went on to the north and east. Heavy
trucks left and returned on their 'liberating' excursions; crates of
expensive wines and other items were much in evidence and liquor
continued to flow freely.

It was in the latter part of August, I recall, that Jim Haun suddenly turned up flying a new aircraft, a Noorduyn Norseman.

The Norseman I became acquainted with only briefly. I remember it as a biggish high-wing monoplane of Canadian ancestry,
equipped with a Pratt & Whitney radial engine of about 600 horsepower. Accommodating two pilots and eight passengers, it was
slow and ponderous, and, in my jaundiced eye, very reminiscent
of a flying furniture van. I had no particular interest in it and was
mildly relieved when Patterson took a liking to it and insisted on
taking it over.

But sadly not for long, as on about its third flight, it suffered an
engine failure on take-off and crashed in flames with him at the
helm, killing my so helpful southern NCO helper with the speech
impediment, Smitty Minor, and badly damaging Sergeants Smedley
and Johnson. Patterson, too, was severely knocked about, suffering
a broken leg and many lacerations.

I was absent at the time, flying Spitfire 3W-K, but hurried to the
hospital to see Patterson after the accident, to find him heavily
shocked and deeply embarrassed by his inability to keep parts of his
very considerable frame from shaking uncontrollably.

*

On 26 August, the 100th Fighter Wing headquarters was ordered to move forward to the town of Le Mans, about 80 miles to the east of Rennes, and everyone again became involved in their packing and moving routines.

On earlier occasions, and quite by accident, I had been absent when previous moves had taken place, so that my two room-mates, Hill and Bodenheim, had been obliged laboriously to collect my belongings and pack my kit. This became such a bone of contention that we had often laughingly discussed what personal movements I might have in mind, so that they would at least know when the Wing was likely to make another move.

The remaining NCOs of the communications flight, having already packed their equipment, were about to leave when they saw they had a problem. What were they to do about the Spitfire? No one had yet collected it and as most other residents of the air-field had already departed, it would be left for the French peasantry to vandalise, unless of course the Squadron Leader took it into his care. They faced me with silent enquiring looks. How did I feel?

Busy with my own preparations and having forgotten about the aircraft, I had already decided to fly the P.51 to Le Mans when I was forced to consider their dilemma. It took me all of five seconds to make up my mind. The P.51 could be left for someone else to fly and I would take the Spitfire to Le Mans.

Finding a pencil and paper, I scribbled a note for the two white faces in the black-and-white control hut. The note said simply:

'To whom it may concern. Have taken Spitfire 3W-K to Le Mans. Pick it up there.'

And I signed my name.

As I recall, our airfield at Le Mans was a not-too-long strip of muddy and rutted grass from which the Germans had evacuated casual-ties by ambulance plane. There were remains of several burnt-out Feisler Storches around the area to prove it. My Spitfire did not take kindly to the softish turf, as its wheels were small and tended to dig in. The worn tyres also began to look decidedly sad.

My crew soon began to tire of hauling me out of gooey spots and holes, and they spoke to me very severely. I remember the conversation exactly: 'Squadron Leader,' they said, 'you're gonna have to do something about this heap! You're about to kill yourself, and it's not gonna look too good for us. How's about getting someone in your own outfit to check this baby over and get us some paper we can sign?' Also, it was up to me (they felt) whether or not to bring it back, or just leave it somewhere – anywhere, in fact, but here.

I saw immediately the wisdom of their suggestions and a week or so later, decided to fly the Spitfire back to England to find someone to give it the once-over. On 5 September I shook hands with all my 100th Fighter Wing friends and set off to cross the Channel, heading for England and home.

The engine of the Spitfire still being a doubtful item, I was relieved and not a little surprised when I reached the Isle of Wight, where I turned right and flew along the south coast, thinking hard about what to do with this Spitfire.

Then the solution! Of course! I would land at Heston, spend a night or two with my parents at Northwick Park, after which I would telephone RAF Ford and speak to my old Kirton-in-Lindsay chief technical officer mate, Wing Commander Bert Hughes. Eureka!

Two days later, the Wing Commander – all 5 feet 3 inches of him – and I were standing beside Spitfire 3W-K at Ford.

I said carefully, and not without a sideways glance, 'Look, this aircraft was left at Rennes in rather a bad state several weeks ago. I don't know to whom it belongs but it seems to me the owners have forgotten about it. In the meantime, my chaps have since made it serviceable, but there are problems, as it has no travelling servicing documents and therefore no history and nothing for them to sign. In addition to which, it needs two new wheels, a few other bits and pieces, plus a full 40-hour service. So how d'you feel? Is it something you can help with?'

Bert looked pensive. 'We can probably trace the country of origin and the squadron without too much difficulty. Don't you think you ought to contact them first before you consider taking it over?'

'No,' I said firmly. 'I have no intention of getting in touch with anyone. Whoever it was just left it without saying a word and, as I've now had it fixed, the least they can do is pick it up after thanking us. So, once again, is it something you are prepared to do?'

It took my good friend Bert only seconds to shake his head and make his smiling reply. 'You know me! Your wish is always my command.'

Two days later, as the Bible has it, 'Lo, it was done!' and I was able to take off for Le Mans. This time, however, my flight was anything but uneventful.

My Spitfire, as indeed did most Spitfires at the time, came equipped with a 30-gallon slipper tank. This reserve tank fitted under the belly of the aircraft between the undercarriage legs, the fuel being drawn into the engine via a plastic or rubber tube, part of which, for the convenience of those who felt it their duty to check the flow of fuel, was made of glass.

The distance between the Isle of Wight and Cherbourg was (and probably still is) about 90 miles. I had about 8 miles to go before crossing the French coast and was flying quite comfortably at around 5,000 feet when, having been on mains, I decided to use the fuel in the slipper tank.

Bending forward and to my right, I switched on the slipper tank and turned off the two main fuel-tank cocks, whereupon with barely a warning cough, the engine stopped dead.

To be absolutely precise, the engine didn't exactly stop, because at 260 miles per hour and with the airscrew whirling away in front, it was obliged to do likewise. But with the deceleration enormous, I was thrown forward massively as about 1,000 horsepower disappeared with magical suddenness; there was positively no urge.

Immediately, I switched back to mains – nothing! Back to slipper tank – nothing! Back to mains – nothing! I took a quick glance towards the sea below me, all grey and nasty, and decided I was in for a very cold and unpleasant dip. Then, in a flash of inspiration, I

unscrewed the priming pump down to my right and began pumping like mad.

I have to explain here that there were usually two types of priming pump, the first impossibly stiff to operate, the second much
easier. Fortunately, this was one of the easy ones.

With me still pumping as though demented, my engine gave
a series of enormous burps and continued to do so as my aircraft
descended in a series of switchback swoops. I could see the airfield
at Cherbourg (A-15), now about 5 miles away and slightly to my
right, and, losing height rapidly and lowering first the wheels and
then the flaps, I desperately headed in that direction.

Finally, with my fingers raw and with occasional rude noises from
the front, I squeezed over the airfield boundary and dropped the
Spitfire in like the proverbial sack of tripe. As the wheels thumped
on to the ground, the airscrew flicked to a standstill – and that
was that. Allowing my mount to run to a stop, I closed my eyes in
complete, total relief.

When I had recovered sufficiently to move, I climbed down from
the cockpit and went round to the front of my Spitfire. I saw in a
moment the cause of my problem: the small glass inspection tube
that leads from the reserve tank into the fuselage had been broken,
possibly by a rising stone. But who cared? I was down.

As I stood there, I recognised in the distance the large black
shapes of a group of USAAF Northrop P.61 Black Widow night
fighters, reminding me of the common assertion that most American
fighters were nothing more than streamlined bricks. I also saw
several jeeps coming in my direction around the perimeter
track.

When they arrived, their four occupants approached and, after
nodding to me offhandedly, one of them observed, 'Yes sir! That
landing of yours was the damnedest thing I ever did see!'

And before I had time to recover from his barb, one of his mates,
looking at my Spitfire, asked quite seriously, 'Hey, bud! Did you
make this yusself? What is it?'

Nevertheless the Americans were quite nice to me, a little pink-
cheeked, I suspect, from their aircraft recognition gaffe. They

quickly provided another tube for my slipper tank and, after helping me sort out the massive airlock in my aircraft's fuel system, had
my engine going in no time. With their assistance, therefore, I was
able to take off the following morning for Le Mans.

It is at this point that I have to confess I don't really know where
it was I landed before finally arriving at Le Mans half a day later.
This was partly due to the weather being absolutely vile, with rain,
low cloud and poor visibility – I had no radio assistance, as my aircraft was not on any of the local or operational American radio fre-
quencies – but mainly because I was just plain lost. I was also very
frightened.

Flying in the fringes of the cloud and sometimes at no higher
than 100 feet in an area totally new to me, and concerned, too, that
I might fly inadvertently into enemy territory (although I knew it to
be a somewhat ridiculous speculation), it was very trying occasion.
It also turned out to have an amusing aspect, though, which I was
able to appreciate later, but not at the time.

Deciding to land wherever I could, I came across an airstrip in a
wooded area in which there were half a dozen burnt-out wrecks of
German aircraft. Making a quick low circuit, I touched down but
was soon slowed up by pools of standing water and mud. Thankful
that my aircraft had not tipped up, I brought it to rest, stopped my
engine and, sitting back with a sigh of relief, waited.

I had no idea where I was exactly, but I was alive. I suspected,
however, that my Spitfire might be stuck fast in soft earth, which
could prove to be a nasty problem.

As I sat in the cockpit wondering what I might do, a group of
children appeared out of the rain and mist and came racing towards
me. Led by a small boy of about eleven, they stopped, panting and
excited, enabling me to ask in my schoolboy French where I was,
and how far away and in what direction the town of Le Mans might
be. This produced a voluble outburst from the small boy to the
effect that the Germans were not around now, which was comforting but not very helpful.

Climbing down and deciding they might be able to help to unstick
my aircraft, I showed them how to push on the trailing edge of

the wings, trying to explain, meanwhile, what I required. Clearly, however, my French was to them incomprehensible. The situation produced many hand signals and grimaces, suggesting finally that the small boy wished me to follow him. So, closing the hood of my aircraft, I did so, the five children surrounding me like chattering magpies.

I soon found myself being led into a local farmyard encompassed by buildings as ruinous and unkempt as only French farm buildings can be, before ducking through a doorway that nearly took the top off my head, and finally being confronted by a tiny peasant farmer who looked not a day under ninety-five, uniformly grey in colour, with a half-grown beard, wearing the inevitable large flat workman's cap, but grinning. Encouraged, I grinned in return and wished him a good day.

After that, and in whispered silence, another ten faces began to appear singly around the edges of an outer door, all at differing heights and belonging to children and adults of varying age. Finally, a woman, who I deduced was either the wife or the grandmother, joined them, and the whole group continued to stare at me as though I had just dropped in from outer space.

Then, with great ceremony, the farmer climbed rheumatically on to a stool and, reaching into the rafters, produced a cobwebby bottle of clear liquid which, with a palsied shaking hand, he poured into two glass tumblers, before handing one to me. Recognising that I was being accorded a great honour, I raised my drink in a silent toast before sipping it circumspectly.

I probably lost colour: it was akin to swallowing molten lava. Unused to strong drink, I had the greatest difficulty in getting the rest of it down.

After that, as conversation was out of the question, with much bowing and shaking of hands I made my departure as quickly as courtesy would allow, well aware that another five minutes of that sort of primitive hospitality would render me incapable of walking, far less flying.

With the small boy and children still at my heels, I returned to my Spitfire, to find a jeep and two American NCOs standing alongside. They had seen me land, they explained, and wondered who the heck I was and what I was doing there.

So, lying in my teeth, I told them that weather had forced me down and that I was heading for Le Mans. Meanwhile, it would help if they told me where exactly I was and in which direction Le Mans might be.

This produced a lot of pointing and hand-waving, together with the information that I was approximately at a place called Laval and that Le Mans was in *that* direction, about 25 miles away.

After that came the business of extricating my aircraft from the mud, a task which took us all of 15 struggling minutes, with the two Americans and five giggling children pushing lustily from behind, between slipping and falling into the mire occasionally, all amid language that I can only describe as 'earthy'.

Finally, I was pushed free and, my engine starting up on internals (thank the Lord!), I taxied carefully away. After that, with much shouted thanks and waving of hands, I took off.

Within ten minutes, I had reached Le Mans, where I landed – carefully thereafter neglecting to explain to anyone where I had been or what had just happened.

It might be thought extraordinary that I should even think of taking leave, having so recently returned from my brief visit to England. But I did, without consulting any authority, granting myself a fortnight's vacation. After all, I reasoned, as an RAF aircrew member, I was entitled to a period of sixty-one days each year, and I had been flying fairly intensively for the last eight months. However, in making my decision, I had other important thoughts in mind.

Flying the Spitfire again and returning to England, I landed it at Northolt and, after taking the two buses I normally used to convey me to Northwick Park, I stayed with my parents for a day, giving the matter some earnest consideration.

Somewhat to my surprise, my much-favoured friend Miss Hampton had recently written to say that she expected to join me in France in the not-too-distant future. Apparently, she had heard that she was to leave Biggin Hill and be flight officer in charge of five more junior WAAF officers and about 20 female NCOs and other ranks, who were to man the new No. 24 Sector operations room shortly to move to the Continent.

She had also mentioned delicately that she hoped that our verbal marriage agreement could be more formally established and that there would be more tangible evidence of its existence – a hint I immediately took to mean an engagement ring.

Then, of course, there was also the problem of the Spitfire and its all-too-obvious identification markings. If I were to hang on to the aircraft, they would surely have to go. But how to change or obliterate them, and who would carry out the dirty deed?

In moments a solution came to me, as I thought immediately not only of my small, technical officer friend Bert Hughes, but also of Edna, his equally small and helpful wife. How lucky could I get?

My mind made up, I flew the Spitfire down to Ford again, and as Bert and I stood beside the aircraft, I outlined to him what I had in mind. And, I must say, rather to my surprise, he was more amused than concerned.

'What? You want me to take off all the paint, leaving it in its plain metal birthday suit? But that would make it stand out like a sore thumb, as every other Spitfire ever made is camouflaged.'

'You would leave on the roundels, naturally,' I added in a conciliatory tone of voice.

'I don't think that would keep us out of jail, because, not to put too fine a point on it, you've just pinched an aircraft and you want to disguise the fact. If this goes wrong, it could mean a couple of years inside for each of us.'

'Bert,' I replied stiffly, 'I have not *pinched* anything. This Spitfire was unserviceable when it was just dumped in my lap. I got my chaps to fix it, I flew it several times to test it, and I have always expected it to be picked up again by the owners, whoever they may be. But they're so keen to have it back, it seems, that they have left it for more than a month, and if I had not taken it with me to Le Mans, the local French vultures would have vandalized it and picked it clean, and it would be in bits in some French farmyard as we speak.

No, Wing Commander, sir! I have saved a Spitfire, not pinched it! So, having explained all that to you, will you do as I ask?'

I saw Bert shaking his head but smiling. 'You're an incredible young blighter! And you also want my wife to help you choose an engagement ring, I hear. Who is the young lady? And will she be able to cope with you?'

'No, you haven't met her yet. But you'll like her and I'm pretty sure she'll be able to cope. So, if I give you a week, will that be enough?'

'A week?' He was still smiling. 'All right, I'll try to get it done in a week.'

Five days later I drove down to Ford again to pick up Bert Hughes's wife and together we went into Brighton to buy the engagement ring. I remember a remark of hers when I had completed the transaction.

'You look a bit uncertain. Are you having second thoughts?'

And my reply, 'Not really. I'm just thinking: What am I now going to use for money?'

On the penultimate day of my leave, I returned yet again to the airfield, to find the Spitfire ready and waiting, its colour a gleaming silver. Within hours, and after many thanks and much handshaking, I took off again for Le Mans.

Chapter 16
A Nasty Fright

My trip to Le Mans was uneventful. The day fine and bright, I skirted Le Havre, which I thought might still be in enemy hands, and flew at about 4,000 feet and at a gentle speed across a part of France that had so frequently been a battleground for me during 1942 and 1943, thinking, almost sadly, about how much it had all changed.

Approaching the airfield of Le Mans, I lost height and began to make the customary left-hand circuit. As I did so, I glanced over the side. And was surprised – and then shocked.

The airfield was empty. The small area in which our communications aircraft were normally dispersed was totally vacant.

I could scarcely believe my eyes. The 100th Wing element had very obviously gone. Unbelieving, I flew around twice before, feeling totally perplexed, I landed and then taxied almost aimlessly towards the now bare parking area. Where had they gone to and what did I do now, for heaven's sake?

My engine was still running when the inevitable jeep pulled up beside me, this time carrying a young American officer and driver.

Shutting down, I climbed out and approached them, almost preparing myself to be interrogated – which I was. Who was I and what was I doing there? I think the strangeness of the Spitfire rather threw them.

Not exactly in the mood to be questioned, I replied almost truculently that I had landed because I happened to live here (or had until a fortnight ago), and what had happened to the 100th Fighter Wing headquarters, of which I, and all my personal belongings, were a part?

This produced blank looks. The officer said he had never heard

of either the headquarters or the Wing, which was perhaps understandable, as he and his unit had apparently only arrived on the
airfield two days ago.

Recognizing that our rather heated conversation was getting us
nowhere, I suggested that we discuss the situation in a nearby hut,
formerly used by our communications flight ground crew, which,
I recalled, contained a telephone. The proposal had the effect of
calming the atmosphere a little.

Our discussions in and beyond the hut, however, produced no
further information. Two local headquarters were approached
but no one had any news of the 100th Fighter Wing – it seemed
as though my former colleagues had disappeared without a trace.
The only sensible recommendation from one distant American
voice was that, as it was probably 'restricted information' anyway, I
should fly to Villacoublay, on the outskirts of Paris, and consult the
headquarters of 9th Air Force, or the 3rd US Army, or even SHAPE
(Supreme Allied Powers Europe).

All of which left me at screaming point. All I wanted to know
was where my friends had gone to and where my next change of
clothing and a decent cup of tea or coffee were likely to come from.
What was so secret about that?

Within the hour, and very much on edge, I was in the air again
and heading towards Paris, very conscious that I would shortly be
in need of fuel and that Villacoublay was a good 100 miles away.

I knew a fair amount about Villacoublay as, though I was in the
RAF, I had escorted some American B.17 Flying Fortresses returning from a major raid there about a year earlier. So I found the airfield without trouble and even recognised some of the many bomb
craters they had created in the local area.

Landing, I saw many strange aircraft dispersed there, including some French Morane fighters, which looked very small and
insignificant.

Not knowing where to park, I taxied around the perimeter track
for quite some time until my engine began to overheat, obliging
me to stop outside a hutted complex that looked vaguely American.

It was. Inside, there were about six American ground crew, relaxing and 'shooting the breeze', all in crumpled denims, wearing baseball caps and with their feet on an assortment of tables.

After being greeted with affable curiosity, I introduced myself, explaining that I needed fuel and that I wished to speak to someone who might help me find my unit, the 100th Fighter Wing, or even their senior body, 19th TAC. Could they assist in any way, or perhaps advise me?

They said they could certainly arrange for the fuel; they also gave me the telephone number of their local headquarters, adding, however, that they could not promise anything.

The first headquarters I spoke to recommended a higher formation – and it was there I finally struck oil.

Their spokesman admitted that he knew where the 100th Fighter Wing was now based. However, as the new location was very much 'restricted information', he would not be able to tell me.

At this point, courtesy and good manners flew out of the window and I began to protest in very sharp terms indeed. This brought a response from the person speaking to me that it was all very well for me to get hysterical about it, but I could well be a German spy. This quite inane allegation drew my immediate reply that, in that case, I was probably the only German spy in RAF uniform, flying a British Spitfire fighter, at present being refuelled by American airmen on Villacoublay airfield. Furthermore, I would have him know, I had been flying about Europe asking the same questions for a full day, and unless everyone stopped buggering me about and told me where my unit was, I was going back to England 'toot sweet' and he and those he represented could bloody well fight the Germans without me!

After my outburst, there followed a brief interval, during which I heard several muted background conversations, after which there came a change of voice. A new speaker came on to say, almost apologetically, that as the Allies clearly didn't want to fight the Germans on their own, he could tell me that my unit had moved forward and was now on the airfield A-64, at St Dizier.

'St Dizier?' I heard myself echoing. 'Where on earth is that?'

About 150 miles away, I was informed. Towards Bar le Duc and Nancy. If I skirted Paris to the south and flew due east, I would probably find it somewhere in that area.

As it was then approaching evening, I was given transport into the outskirts of Paris and spent the most wretched night ever, in my clothes, sleeping on the marble floor of the Palace of Versailles. I shall never in my life think favourably of the French after those ghastly eight hours.

The following morning, unshaven and having breakfasted on coffee and a single doughnut, I returned to the airfield and took off, 'Bradshawing' my way at little more than 500 feet across the flat and green pastures of eastern France, with the wine areas of Rheims and Chalons on my left, until, after about 50 minutes, the small town of St Dizier, with its airfield, rose like sentinels out of an early mist.

Smiling to myself, with closed eyes and a silent prayer, I most profoundly thanked God, because there had been times I thought I would never make it.

My flying logbook tells me that I landed at St Dizier on 20 September, and that I was to be there for exactly two months.

On the occasion of my first landing at St Dizier, I well recall taxiing in, in my nice, bright new Spitfire, and being greeted almost effusively by a small crowd of smiling, clapping ground crew, the cheerful faces of Sergeant Carter and Smitty Major prominent among them. Once again, I heard Carter smilingly shouting that when I had taken off in 'that heap' (that was the Spitfire), he had not expected to see me alive again. On this occasion he added, 'Hey! What happened? How and where did you get the bird all done over silver?'

Sadly, too, amid all the fuss, I remember missing the face of my friend Patterson, who had still not recovered from his injuries, and those of Smedley, Johnson and, not least of all, dear, dead Smittty Minor.

It was also in late September that my new fiancée, Flight Officer Eileen Hampton, led to France her group of 30 or so WAAFs, who were to be the first female British contingent to take part in the invasion of north-west Europe.

As this was considered to be a newsworthy event, her photograph appeared in most of the London evening newspapers, together with a brief mention of our engagement, and there were publicity shots of the grinning group assembling at Lyneham airfield before boarding the RAF Dakota that was to take them to Amiens Glisy, a French airfield I knew all too well.

Having landed, they were quite comfortably accommodated, rather unusually, in the outer buildings of a trout farm, situated about 5 miles south and east of the town of Amiens – not far, in fact, from the spot where the famous German airman von Richthofen was shot down and killed in 1918.

A day or two following her arrival I took the Spitfire to visit her and found the party happily settling down in their new No. 24 Group Sector operations room, located several miles away from the airfield.

I was to make the same journey many times in the weeks to come; however, I always found it a hard slog walking in my flying boots the 3 miles between the airfield and her accommodation, particularly in hot weather.

I remember, too, that many of the 30-odd members of her group turned out to be distinguished members of society in later, post-war years, some of them becoming notable broadcasters and international journalists, and one a well-known MP, and eventually, a member of the House of Lords.

By the time I arrived at St Dizier, the P.51s, together with the P.47s, formerly at the Kentish airfields of Headcorn and High Halden, had more or less disappeared. At least one of the groups of P.51s at Lashenden and Staplehurst had apparently changed their role as fighters and become reconnaissance aircraft, there being virtually no Luftwaffe left to shoot at. The P.47s had become fighter-bombers, each aircraft carrying two 100lb bombs, and some of the P.51s were attacking ground targets with some new and rather nasty creations named 'napalm fire bombs'.

Some days later, I had the opportunity of examining these fire bombs and, flying my Spitfire, watching them being dropped by P.51s on the German-held forts at Metz. The bombs themselves were merely the normal 100-gallon P.51 drop tanks filled with fuel to which had been added a gelling ingredient and an igniting device. Hurled in the direction of the target at very low level – usually concrete pill boxes or fort-type defences – they would explode into vast seas of spreading flame, so that the aircraft became a type of airborne flame-thrower. A daunting and horrible means of attack for those on the receiving end; strangely enough, because of the bomb's poor near-miss effectiveness, it was not as potent a weapon as was at first anticipated. It was all the rage for a time, but both the bomb and the style of attack fell into disuse within months.

Further north, a different battle raged in those early days of September. Codenamed Market Garden, an 'operation', planned, fiercely supported and encouraged by Montgomery (recently pro-moted to Field Marshal) and employing both British and American airborne forces, was launched as part of a decisive thrust to capture vital bridges over the rivers Maas, Waal and Rhine, the aim being to open up a direct route into central Germany and end the war, possibly by Christmas.

The American airborne forces were successful in capturing the two nearer bridges, but the 1st British Airborne Division, ordered to capture the more distant crossing over the Rhine at Arnhem, as the result of a number of tactical misadventures, bad weather and other reasons, failed in their attempt and suffered horribly, losing half their strength in men killed, wounded and taken prisoner. The setback for a time crippled an important part of the British Army and had the effect of prolonging the war by up to six months.

Although not involved in the battle, those of us further south and watching from a distance were both surprised and depressed by the outcome. The reverse caused dissension at the highest levels and a degree of mistrust between various Allied formations that was never entirely eradicated.

The causes of the disaster at Arnhem were later discussed exhaustively. At the time, at my own lowly level much information was lacking, but our own intelligence and daily briefings gave me, if not a complete picture of events, at least an insight into what was happening.

Briefly, by mid-September, General Eisenhower's command had been increased by other Allied forces which had invaded France from the south in August, bringing his total strength on the ground to more than two million men and around half a million vehicles. This massive force, having fairly raced through France after the German beachhead defences had been breached, was by September fast running out of ammunition and the types of fuel required for armoured vehicles and other means of transport, in addition to the more refined brands of petrol needed for aircraft. However, because of the policy to isolate rather than subdue German-held ports and strong points around the Atlantic and Channel coasts, no major port through which such essential supplies could be passed was either available or indeed suitable – other than Antwerp, which still remained in German hands.

With many options no doubt open to him, Field Marshal Montgomery, the commander of the Allied ground forces, decided not to attempt attacking and opening up the port at Antwerp but instead go for the much more risky option of capturing the Rhine bridge at Arnhem, the benefits, in his mind anyway, being more immediate and beneficial. He was aware, no doubt, that he was risking the whole of the 1st British Airborne Division in such an attack and utilizing a major part of RAF Transport Command; that the target itself was much more distant than the other bridges; and that the weather, the immediate availability of crucial air support and the means of providing reinforcement on the ground would always be critical and uncertain factors.

In the event, the fates were to prove uncooperative. The weather was vile, essential close-support aircraft were mostly grounded, the relieving ground force arrived too late to intervene successfully, and adverse intelligence information, which might have stymied the operation at the outset, was either purposely ignored or not available.

The final outcome was that, over a period of ten days, about 7,000 casualties were incurred (about half the committed force), of whom 1,300 were killed. It was a catastrophic incident in every sense of the word, as

1st Airborne Division, the cream of the British Army, never fought again. In consequence the Allies, on American insistence, reinvented their broad-front strategy, which, to Montgomery's fury, ruled out his 'single thrust' preference and hope of an early victory, besides allowing time for the Germans to regroup and build up their forces.

The failure of Operation Market Garden also resulted in personal relations between Eisenhower and Montgomery reaching an all-time low, and a significant loss of goodwill between Britain and America during the final stages of the war; and, possibly, it was an important factor in fostering the negative attitude of President Roosevelt towards Britain during the 1945 conference at Yalta.

The month of October turned out to be a memorable period of flying. Despite some miserable weather conditions, I flew the Spitfire on twenty occasions, mainly in and beyond the battle area, and the C-53 for about 20 hours, travelling mainly between St Dizier and England, conveying each time up to 25 passengers, returning to the United Kingdom for leave. On each flight in the C-53, I took the peerless Sergeant Smith with me in the second pilot's seat to operate the radios and work the wretched switches.

One particular flight was especially hazardous. Having taken off with a full load of passengers from St Dizier, I deviated to Amiens, planning to pick up my new fiancée and take her very briefly to England. This was very much against the rules, but she seemed keen to go, in order (I suspected at the time) to show her family and others her new engagement ring, which I had presented to her with the minimum amount of fuss a few days earlier.

As I imagined this was somewhat against the regulations, I had warned her to 'look like a man' – to tuck her hair into her WAAF officer's cap, and to be dressed in her new battledress trousers, which were anything but feminine. All this she did, and when we stopped to pick her up, she scrambled excitedly aboard and, having run the gauntlet through lines of grinning male passengers, came to sit with me up front on an improvised seat.

After that, things began to go less well.

Having taken off in pretty poor weather conditions at Amiens, we soon ran into the most brutal of storms, with rain lashing into the windscreen and low cloud obscuring even the lower hills of France and coming down almost to ground level. At first I considered returning to base and calling a halt to the trip, but having reached the Channel, I decided to press ahead.

Now down to around 200 feet above some very grey and unpleasant-looking waves, and with visibility less than a mile, I really began to worry. Although we had radio, there were then no modern emergency landing facilities available to me, and I couldn't climb and commit myself to the cloud, as I would never be able to get down again. With a full load of passengers and a rather precious person sitting wide-eyed beside me, things were not at all looking good. The situation was made the more alarming when, still at 200 feet, I nearly ran full tilt into the cliffs at Beachy Head, which suddenly loomed out of the mist and rain, all white and horrible – and very, very close!

Turning sharply to the right, which must have upset the stomachs of at least half the passengers behind me, I flew parallel to the coast and towards the east. Then, down to 100 feet, and with the rain still hammering against the windscreen, I managed to keep the coastline in view to my left until we came across first the flat fields of Dungeness and finally the higher ground of an area very familiar to me.

Thanking God for his deliverance, I turned left over the town of Folkstone and, encountering the RAF airfield at Hawkinge almost at 'top of the hangar' level, I thumped the aircraft down on the grass runway without warning or making the usual preparatory circuit. As the aircraft bounced and slithered to a stop, I closed my eyes and took several very deep breaths indeed.

Later, and with my small horde of still-grinning passengers lining up for train warrants that would take them the 50 or so miles into London, I found myself surprised and wondering at their sangfroid. The poor deluded creatures: if they only knew how close to death they had been!

To complete the story, Miss Hampton, with her shiny new engagement ring, went with me by train to London that evening, entirely happy with life. The following day, the cold front having passed through and the weather blissfully fine, I picked her up at Heston in the C-53 and returned her to Amiens, still smiling, within the required 48 hours.

But, my goodness! It was a close-run thing and could have been so very different.

It was around this time, too, that I was involved in another minor incident in the C-53, but, on this occasion, it was one with a less dicey conclusion.

Having landed in France, we all soon became aware of the constant stream of visiting Hollywood entertainers who were touring the ETO (European Theatre of Operations), spreading light and joy.

This being a type of war work for millionaires, the names of these prominent actors of stage, screen and radio included Bob Hope, Bing Crosby, Dorothy Lamour, James Cagney, Edward G. Robinson and a score of other stars, male and female, each of whom was normally accompanied by a string of comedians, singers and dancers, and the usual bevy of blonde long-legged lovelies.

Others, who were either cajoled unwillingly into joining the American services or did so out of a sense of patriotic duty, included Clark Gable, who became an air gunner and came to us at Biggin Hill, and James Stewart, who actually flew B.17s (Fortresses). I met him (as I recall) at either RAF Duxford or Debden and he was in later years a regular visitor to my home village in Norfolk.

There were also several of the 'big band' leaders in the group, chief among whom was Glenn Miller, whose rendering of the dance tune 'In the Mood' became a Second World War classic, and who was later tragically killed when on a flight from England to France in a Noorduyn Norseman. However, lest I seem to be overly despising of the genre, there were, of course, scores of other equally patriotic and deserving members of the acting profession I did not ever meet or even hear about.

On this particular occasion, I was invited by Colonel Jim Haun to take the C-53 and fly to another airfield some 50 miles away, to pick up a world-famous group blessed with the title 'Spike Jones and his City Slickers'. The band had been programmed to entertain elements of the 100th Fighter Wing the same evening and the following day.

Delighted to be 'awarded' such a seemingly attractive task, I happily flew north with Sergeant Smith beside me, with not even a single qualm about what might be in store for me.

Having arrived safely at our destination, Smitty and I climbed down to meet our passengers. There was a seething crowd of about 20 of them, plus a pile of baggage and equipment that almost defied description. There were men of all sizes and shapes, and of varying age, most of them either bearded or unshaven and riotously dressed for action in outlandish clothes and Davy Crockett coonskin caps, plus at least two capering and very noisy young females. I immediately became aware that most of them had already been at the 'giggle juice' and sensed disaster on the way.

As Sergeant Smith and I tried, pushing, shoving and lifting, to organise them and their luggage aboard, all of them in high spirits, I was confronted by a bearded person, with a face a colleague later described as 'looking like a ferret peeping out of a bear's bum', who rather haughtily demanded to be introduced to the pilot.

Having told him, with all the charm I could muster, that I was the person he was looking for, the man returned a pantomime glare and said, 'Jesus! I thought you must be the kid who served the coffee and doughnuts.'

I remember smiling thinly in his direction and replying quietly, 'Squadron Leader Neil's the name. And just one more crack like that, sir, and you and your mates will be walking to your next concert party, OK?'

It took Smith and me quite some time to get our passengers to sit and tie themselves down correctly – some of their instruments lodged between their knees and in the passage between them – all amid much noisy laughter and nervous conversation.

After that, having started the engines again, I taxied carefully away, very much aware of what was going on behind me and that there were only two of us up front to fly the aircraft and, perhaps, control the disorderly mob in the back.

My worst fears were realised after a short interval, when the two young ladies appeared over my shoulder, shouting remarks and asking a series of nonsensical questions over the noise of the engines.

With as much tolerance as I could muster, I played the courteous captain for a time, but when one of the girls tried to sit on my knee and began to monkey around with everything within reach, irritation got the better of me, and I ordered them both out of the cockpit. Then when one of the men in charge arrived to question my attitude towards 'important members his band', I told him plainly that if his motley crew continued to misbehave, I was going to land at the nearest airfield and have them removed from my aircraft.

This seemed to reduce the fuss in the rear, but a number of them continued to tramp up and down the passenger cabin, upsetting the fore and aft trim of the aircraft, though always within tolerable limits. Eventually, as the novelty of the flight wore off and, I suspect, some of them began to feel sick, comparative silence was restored, so that when they tottered out singly after we had landed, some of them still clutching their instruments, much of their fighting fervour and zest for adventure had quietly evaporated.

In spite of their early childishness, however, the band's performance that evening was outstandingly good and vastly entertaining, their routine being to commence a well-known ballad or artistic composition in serious vein and then suddenly go berserk, the concert venue ringing with their wild, discordant music.

At the peak of the band's popularity, their records had sold millions, worldwide, as their act was well conceived and they were all brilliant musicians. Clearly, they were a lunatic bunch, and I could understand why. They didn't have to act: it all came naturally!

It was also in October 1944 that a series of incidents occurred at St Dizier, about which I write with some hesitation, as they reflect somewhat unflatteringly on some of my American friends and colleagues. So much so that I devoted much time considering the propriety or indeed the value of including my thoughts and opinions in this book. However, I decided it was important for me to report them, but in as tasteful a manner as possible.

So that I do not appear too priggish, I feel it necessary at the outset to describe my own attitude and habits in the very contentious areas of drink, drunkenness, smoking and the treatment of ladies.

First, the easy one: smoking. I have never smoked, because my father did – not to excess, but continually – and, although we never made a fuss about it, both my mother and I always disliked having the house, carpets and curtains reeking of stale tobacco fumes. However, he was of the generation that treated smoking as a sign of manhood, fashionable and even necessary – during the First World War, soldiers were, I believe, encouraged to smoke, as tobacco (and drink) was said to have a calming effect on those going into battle.

On drinking, I have no special views or objections. I have never imbibed more than a little. I have always enjoyed wine in small quantities, I dislike champagne, and I can't cope with beer other than as a drink to quench a thirst. Moreover, alcohol makes me ill long before it makes me drunk, so there are very few occasions when I have ever felt even close to being 'pixilated' or incapable. All in all, therefore, I have never found the need for the stimulus of drink; nor did it ever become an important part of my life.

For these and other reasons, my appointment to an American military organisation came as something of a culture shock, because my new colleagues smoked a great deal more than I had ever expected, and not only drank what I considered to be excessive amounts, but did so in a manner that seemed to me unnecessarily serious, and much more so than if it was just a lesser social habit.

Not only that: I soon discovered America, in the tradition of the ancient Red Indian tribes, to be a matriarchal society and one where ladies were treated and regarded in a somewhat different manner from that I had experienced as a young officer in the Royal Air Force, where officers' messes, until about the mid-1940s anyway, were refined 'gentlemen's clubs', where wives and other ladies, though often regarded as 'fragrant and gentle creatures', were only allowed to enter by invitation and then usually via the servants' entrance at the back.

There were also two other important factors relevant to this anecdote. First, unlike in Britain, where the women's services, such as the ATS (Army), WAAF (RAF) and WRNS (Royal Navy), had been active since the beginning of the war and were very familiar, there were no equivalent US women's services deployed in Britain – or if there were, I had never come across them. There were certainly none in France, the only American females being the nurses in the local American hospitals.

This meant, inevitably, that, in the United Kingdom, many thousands of relationships developed between American servicemen and young single British women, and probably an equal number of British servicemen's wives, whose husbands had, for up to four years, been fighting in Africa, the Middle East, the Far East and beyond, and had never been given a moment's opportunity to return or see their partners. Although some overall good certainly resulted, many such liaisons caused bitter resentment between members of the British armed forces and their American allies, a current telling description soon bandied about being 'Bloody Yanks! Overpaid, oversexed, and over here!'

From the outset, I was aware that some liaisons existed between several of my closest American colleagues in the Wing and married ladies – relationships they kept up for many months without displaying even an atom of remorse, or so it appeared. Which saddened me at the time, I remember, although I did nothing about it, persuading myself, no doubt, that the married ladies in question were equally to blame.

The second factor was the constant availability of alcohol. There was never at any time a shortage of spirits – mainly whiskies – available to officers in the Fighter Wing headquarters, and after the Allied breakout in France, to these were added vast quantities of every sort of liquor and wine 'liberated' from the Germans or held in the vaults and stores of the many famous French vineyards.

In particular, when the area around Rheims was overrun by the
Allies and set free, stocks of champagne that could only be described
as prodigious fell into the hands of those in the Wing headquarters
whose responsibility it was to deal with such valuable merchandise.
I well remember seeing scores of piled-up cases of Cordon Vert and
Cordon Rouge wine bottles, produced by the famous house of G.
H. Mumm. I recall, too, having the good sense to reserve for myself
three cases of Cordon Vert, which I felt might come in handy for my
forthcoming marriage.

All the ingredients of an enormous binge being so readily available, therefore, when I heard that the nurses of a local American
hospital had been invited to the chateau to liaise with us one afternoon and later take part in an evening of 'relaxation and dancing', I
experienced the smallest feelings of apprehension. It seemed to me,
even at that early stage, that unlimited champagne, together with
some even moderately attractive ladies, could well become a toxic
mixture. And, as events were to prove, I was absolutely right.

Our female guests arrived about mid-afternoon, around 15–20
of them. They seemed a pleasant enough group, most of them
in their 20s and 30s, although their fairly drab uniforms of a
light grey denim material didn't exactly enhance their appearance.
They were greeted cheerfully by an equal number of officers in
the Wing – some of whom, I am bound to admit, I had never seen
before – and there was soon a cheerful and convivial atmosphere
abroad.

Not too eager to take part, I found myself watching from the
sidelines. Only one or two of the nurses spoke to me, each doing
little more than comment on my 'strange accent' and suggesting
I might come from Virginia. Strangely, no one put me down as
British, which I suppose was understandable, as I was wearing a
brown American flying jacket at the time, on which was affixed the
gold-leaf insignia of a major.

After a perfectly decorous afternoon, the ladies sat down to a
meal about 6 p.m., at which time, the laughter and noise of conversation having increased very noticeably, I left to make myself look
a little more respectable by changing into my blue RAF uniform

tunic, before returning later for the 'relaxation and dancing'.

When I did, around 8 p.m., the atmosphere had changed dramatically. The champagne and whisky having clearly been circulated, there were flushed faces and loud laughter everywhere. Dancing had commenced to live music from about five musicians I never knew existed; there were whirling bare arms and raised voices; and many jackets, ties and upper garments had already been discarded. The crescendo of noise rose by the minute.

Then a most curious incident.

First, I have to admit that I am not an enthusiastic dancer. Totally untaught, I have one dance, a sort of half-speed two-step, my rhumba, tango and all the more exotic rest being merely the same little jog, performed either quicker or rather more slowly. Aware of my limited repertoire, I noticed a slightly older blonde nurse sitting quietly to one side and, somewhat to my own surprise, found myself moving in her direction.

On being invited to dance, the young woman merely gave me a glance, stood without a word or a smile, raised her arms, and off we started.

Within moments, I realised she was a far better dancer than I was. However, she made no sign that she was enjoying my company, which prompted me to remark that she seemed rather distant and sad.

This producing nothing more than another shrug, and wishing to draw her out of her obvious misery, I asked if she was married, and was rewarded with a faint smile and the admission that she was.

When I then asked pointedly where her husband was, her reply was she wished she knew.

I persisted. 'Is he in the Air Force and does he fly?'

This produced a wider grin. 'He does fly, yes. In fact, he's one of you lot! A Brit. A Battle of Britain hero.'

'A Battle of Britain hero?' I almost stopped dancing. 'So what's his name? I probably know him.'

She provided her husband's name and rank, which I recognized immediately. However, as the officer had something of a dubious reputation, I decided to plead ignorance and asked obliquely how she had come to meet him.

She explained that after the battle, with some others he had come to the States on a lecture tour, and added, 'We met, I was very young and quite bowled over, and we later married. Just as simple as that.'

'And you don't know where he is now?'

Another shrug. 'He gets around. He could be anywhere.'

'But you're still married?'

'Married, yes!'

'But not very happy?' I ventured.

'Well, he's not an easy guy to live with, put it like that.'

We danced on in silence for quite some time until the band took a break and the music stopped. I suggested that we continue, but she shook her head. 'That's enough for the moment. But thank you, anyway.'

After I had escorted her back to her seat, she did not sit down but gave me a smile and left, leaving me with the distinct impression that we were unlikely ever to see each other again.

But I was wrong, although it would be some years before we did – not once, but twice.

When attempting to describe what went on during the rest of the evening, it is important to say that although I had several drinks, I was never even remotely inebriated, so that I was then, and am now, perhaps overly critical of the drunkenness and uninhibited behaviour that I then witnessed. But nor indeed were several of my closer, more adult friends, including Colonel Hill, impressed with the childish and objectionable antics of many of those around us, both male and female.

It was, moreover, dark, the evening being well advanced, very noisy and altogether distracting, with faces, male and female, flushed and bloated with alcohol, coming in and out of focus beneath lights, some of them coloured and now and then blinding. In short, although used to pretty violent squadron parties in the RAF, for me and others, the function that night, which could have been such a pleasurable occasion, had developed into something altogether different and really rather nasty.

It was against this background of noise, drunkenness, broken bottles and disorder that, about midnight, my friend the Colonel suggested that we leave and go in search of a decent cup of coffee, adding that he had a jeep and driver at the door and that I could meet him there.

Within minutes, in the open but surrounded by mixed groups of party-makers, shouting, cheering and waving bottles, I was seated in the back of an open-topped jeep, with the driver in front and Colonel Hill to his right.

It was at this point that an incident took place that, even now, I can hardly believe happened. It is, moreover, one I must be careful when attempting to describe. Suddenly, out of a mix of revellers, a young woman launched herself in my direction. Climbing into the back of the jeep, she threw her arms around me and, using the plainest and the most obscene language, made a proposal I had never in my life heard a woman utter before, one I could never repeat myself and certainly could never commit to paper.

I was absolutely stunned. The girl was young and attractive, even if tousled and obviously drunk. But she went on: 'Cum arn, Ginger! Your name's Ginger, isn't it? Let you and me give it a whirl, OK?' Then almost confidentially, 'You needn't worry, Ginge, I got my equipment right here with me!'

Above the noise and commotion, I heard Al Hill shouting, 'Hey, lady! Get your butt out of my car, and go wash your mouth out.' And to the nearest group watching, 'And y'all, you get your drunken friend away from here, toot sweet. D'you hear me?'

Amused, yes, but greatly disturbed by what I had just witnessed, I thought when we drove away that it would be the last unpleasant incident of the night. But sadly it wasn't.

At around 2 a.m., and weary beyond belief, I was making my way carefully in the darkness towards my camp bed in the massive bedroom on the first floor of the chateau. Treading cautiously in the gloom, I was forced to step over at least two couples, giggling and writhing on the floor, before I reached it – to find it occupied!

An officer, whose voice I later recognised, was lying there, with his hat on, a young woman by his side, surrounded by champagne bottles, some of them open, some not, the whole area awash with spilt wine.

Looking down at him and deeply annoyed, I said flatly, 'You are in my bed. You know that?'

And the man's response, delivered in a phoney British accent, was, 'We know that, old sport, but don't you worry, old dear, because it's really very comfortable!'

Realising that I would not have a bed to sleep in that night, I turned away, barely resisting the urge to aim a kick at the lout, before wandering about in the dark. Eventually I found two chairs, in one of which I sat, putting my feet up in the other. As I made myself as comfortable as possible, I listened to the muttering, giggling and movements of the pair in my own bed, about six yards away.

After a time, there came a more subdued conversation followed by the sound of the woman snuffling and then sobbing bitterly.

Finally, I heard her raised and shaking voice. 'I know! I know! But we shouldn't have. I was only married last week.'

Perhaps I was just too young and insufficiently worldly to take the whole sordid business in my stride, but I couldn't. For years to come I was to remember that unpleasant night, thinking particularly of that attractive young woman who had been so drunk and so painfully crude. She no doubt had parents who thought of her fondly and lovingly. What a horrible blow for them were they ever to learn of their daughter's so uninhibited behaviour! What, too, if I ever had a daughter of my own, would my own feelings and response be in such circumstances? No, it was all too horrible to consider. War was certainly a beastly thing, which seemed to bring in its train positively the worst possible aspects of human nature.

And the nurse who was the wife of the RAF Battle of Britain hero? I met her again about five years later. Walking into the officers' mess of a neighbouring station in England, I came across her sitting quietly at the bar, a drink in her hand, her appearance very much the same as before.

As our eyes met, I know we recognised each other. But, apart from a faint smile, neither of us acknowledged the other, and not a word was spoken.

Later still, I ran across her again, but this time only from a distance, so that I don't think she was ever aware that I was around.

Her unpleasant husband died some years ago, and if she is still alive, she must now be well into her nineties. Should she read these words, however, I would be happy to speak to her again.

Chapter 17
The End Draws Near

November again, and another Thanksgiving Day in the offing. My near collision earlier in the year still fresh in my mind, I well remembered Group Captain John Hawtrey's remarks at Kirton-in-Lindsay, and my later interview in London, so that I recalled all too clearly that I had been with the 9th Air Force for almost twelve months.

And so much had happened, my goodness! I thought of the faces and voices of my many new American colleagues, the new aircraft I had been introduced to and flown, the doodlebugs, the beachheads and the invasion, the Spitfire, the flying, moving and travelling – and not least of all, my expectations of marriage to a very lovely young woman who now lived 'just up the road', so to speak.

Now totally committed to the Spitfire, I had flown it in and around the local St Dizier battle area for more than 20 hours during that October. I also note with surprise that I had not flown the P.51 even once.

Whereas formerly I had always felt an integral part of the war effort, I was beginning to feel myself a person apart. I was flying the only Spitfire around and had always to take care that I was not misidentified as hostile. There were virtually no Luftwaffe aircraft about, and in terms of the daily battle I felt something of an inter-loper. My aircraft, though still carrying its cannons and machine guns, could not be rearmed, as the Americans did not 'use' my type of ammunition. I was, in short, a warrior without weapons and, for the first time ever, I was beginning to feel superfluous and that I was wasting my time.

However, my relations with General Tex Sanders and other Wing headquarters colleagues had become closer and more intimate by the day. I still shared a bedroom and part of my daily life with Alvin Hill, 'Bodey' Bodenheim and Jim Haun, and found myself much in demand flying cheerful groups of Wing personnel in the C-53 to and from the United Kingdom. With so little to complain about, life was easy and agreeable, but I felt there was something missing.

I found St Dizier airfield, and indeed the whole surrounding area, deeply depressing. War had clearly ruled out even the most rudimentary maintenance of the airfield's runways and buildings, and travelling by road was very much a punishing ordeal, as even the major highways contained a rash of axle-breaking potholes. In short, the whole place was run down and almost exuded neglect and decay, a prime example occurring shortly after my first arrival on the base.

I had just been flying and, still on the airfield and disrobing, was idly watching about a dozen visiting B-24 heavy bombers (Liberators) in the process of landing. As the first six approached, at about 800-yard intervals, each one touched down, ran to the end of the main runway and then, after turning, began taxiing ponderously around the perimeter track. Until, incredibly, the whole group, one at a time, stopped dead in their tracks and I saw that, almost simultaneously, all six Liberators had fallen through the concrete, their wheels disappearing up to their axles and higher.

It was the most incredible sight, and a very expensive one, as not only was the airfield put out of action for more than a day, but the business of heaving the heavy aircraft out of the quite deep holes was a major lifting operation requiring the use of much heavy equipment. I remember six landing; whatever happened to the remaining six, I have long since forgotten.

The end of the war clearly in sight, there were other manifestations of the approach of peace, as back home in England, petty bureaucrats began to appear like worms out of wood.

On one of my fairly frequent C-53 trips into Northolt, as the aircraft captain, I was suddenly confronted by a steely-eyed customs official, who demanded to know whether or not I had anything to declare.

Astonished, I said that I had not, and in a fairly truculent voice, queried the sudden need for all 'this nonsense'. After all, I was a fighting airman, I declared hotly, and had been for more than five wartime years, flying in and out of England on countless occasions without being asked any such ridiculous questions. What was so special about me? I was surely exempt, was I not? Anyway, when did all this nonsense begin?

About 1650, was the unsmiling reply – and the penny dropped: the end of the war was indeed in prospect.

On 4 November, I flew into Northolt again, this time not only with 22 passengers but also with three cases of my precious G. H. Mumm champagne. Beside me in the second pilot's seat I had the peerless Sergeant Smith, who had been carefully briefed to keep a weather eye open for the Revenue men once we had touched down.

Immediately we landed, he gave me the signal that he had indeed sighted the customs jeep, whereupon I kept the C-53's tail in the air and fairly scooted towards the end of the runway, turning then quickly to the left on to the perimeter track, by which time I had a good mile-and-a-half lead on my pursuer.

Taxiing at an incautious speed, I kept well ahead of the pursuing jeep until I stopped with a screech of brakes in front of the dispersal point of a group of ageing Hurricane fighters belonging to Squadron Leader James Storrar, a friend of mine commanding the Courier Flight.

At that point, several of my passengers in the know dropped quickly out of the C-53's rear door bearing my crates of champagne, which they dumped into one of the dispersal huts (greatly to the surprise of those within, I may add), after which, with everyone back on board, I set off again smartly, arriving at our final parking spot outside the main hangar with our faces blank with innocence.

When questioned later, *of course* we had nothing to declare. Anyway, we were Americans, weren't we?

It took me a month before I plucked up sufficient courage to collect my champagne from RAF Northolt, sneaking in and out in my old Morris 10 through the unguarded officers' mess entrance and at the same time feeling an absolute criminal.

*

Towards the end of November, with Colonel Al Hill also in attendance, I stood before General 'Tex' Sanders in his chateau office room.

Considerably to his surprise, I later learned, I informed him that it was my intention to leave the 100th Fighter Wing, explaining that I felt I had 'done my bit' and wasn't now needed, and that I wished to return to my own service and be given a more active command.

I was sorry to leave, I assured him; it had been for me a wonderful experience, and I thanked him for his courtesy and help throughout the past massively interesting 12 months, particularly for allowing me to fly his personal P.51 so frequently.

I recall both he and friend Alvin Hill regarding me with mild unbelieving surprise – this was not the way things were done in the US Army Air Force! In their organisation, a posting, transfer or move had to be ordered, written down, considered at length and then confirmed by higher authority and almost cast in metal. Tex Sanders mentioned that they had not been informed of my possible movement by Air Ministry. Was I certain my departure had been properly sanctioned?

I replied that it was highly probable that Air Ministry hadn't sanctioned it or even that they were unaware that I had it in mind, but I certainly had no intention of telling them now or having them instruct me to do otherwise – after all, I had not heard a single peep from the RAF for almost a year.

No, I would return to the United Kingdom, award myself a few weeks of my normal leave entitlement, before turning up at Fighter Command – or ADGB (Air Defence of Great Britain), to give it its more recent name – to ask for another appointment. Strangely, even at that point, it never entered my head to go to the Air Ministry. Since I had been in the fighter business since the Battle of Britain and earlier, to me Headquarters Fighter Command at Bentley Priory was the natural place to go.

Having ferried my kit and all-important 3-inch sorbo mattress back to England in the C-53, I bade a sad farewell to the General, my long-term room-mates Al Hill and Bodenheim, the doctor Freddie Loughran and a dozen others. After shaking hands so many times that I thought it would come off, I finally climbed into my Spitfire and, after further fond farewells to Sergeants Carter and Smith, set course for England on 18 November.

Landing at Northolt, I left my aircraft in the care of the Fighter Command communications flight, took the now familiar two buses to Northwick Park and joined my relieved and smiling parents. I comforted myself, too, with the thought that all I had to do now was find myself another job – and get rid of the Spitfire.

I can only describe the events of the following several months as utterly confusing. So much so that even now, over 65 years later, having examined every piece of evidence available to me, I have no precise picture of what exactly took place, or indeed when. All I can do, therefore, is describe the events and surrounding circumstances as I remember them.

Unsettled after only several days at home, I drove the 5 or 6 miles from Northwick Park to Stanmore in my old Morris 10 and entered the familiar gates of Bentley Priory. Intent on visiting the Personnel Section, which had always occupied offices in the wooden huts adjacent to the main building, I wished only to introduce myself. I had no particular suggestion to make or appointments in mind; I would just present myself and see what jobs were available and on offer.

I was courteously received by two officers I had never either seen or even heard of before. Each rose respectfully to greet me but expressed surprise on learning who I was, with whom I had recently served and, in the nicest possible way, why I was there anyway. At which point, it became clear to me that, far from being welcomed with open arms by an organisation I had long considered to be my natural home, I was merely a stranger in a foreign land. In the year I had been away with the Americans, the fighter scene had obviously changed greatly – my goodness it had!

Then, in a general way, we began to discuss the state of the nation, the approaching end of the German war, and the effect it was having on those officers intending to leave the Air Force and those others who wished to remain. We also considered the quite unusual degree to which casualties in the recent fighting following the invasion had resulted in the rapid and often extraordinary promotion of some undoubtedly worthy but more junior officers who had acquitted themselves well, whilst others, more senior but just as capable, had, to their obvious dismay, been sidelined.

In short, my companions explained, much of the Air Force was at present in a state of flux, a situation resulting in more than a little heartache. No one knew exactly what the future held, who would be doing what or, indeed, exactly where they would be doing it.

Listening to all their explanations without comment, I felt my morale (and my face) beginning to fall. All this suggested that 'P' Staff did not have a suitable job for me, and if one were to materialize, particularly if it involved promotion, more than likely it would be snapped up by someone already on the spot. *Quel dommage!*

Leaving Bentley Priory, not in the best of spirits, I resolved to have a word with my friend, Group Captain John Hawtrey ('Uncle John', as I would eventually refer to him) in Lincolnshire. He would surely have something to suggest.

When he had listened patiently to my predicament, my favourite group captain was clearly outraged.

'My dear boy! Words fail me! Your bright light must not be concealed under any bushel for a moment longer than is absolutely necessary. I will write a letter now to my good friend Group Captain Loel Guinness, advising him to appoint you as his Wing Commander Flying as soon as possible. I suggest you take an aircraft and fly across to him with my letter. He's somewhere near Antwerp, as I recall. They will tell you where exactly at No. 83 Group headquarters.'

No. 83 Group headquarters, based at RAF Lasham, provided not only the required address but also an Anson to fly me across to Antwerp to attend an interview.

Group Captain Loel Guinness was a pleasant, quiet man who, when he had read Uncle John Hawtrey's letter, made no immediate comment but invited me to dinner that evening to meet several senior members of his Spitfire Wing.

Not exactly encouraged by his silence, I smilingly promised to do so. But, as I somehow suspected it might, the meeting was a disaster.

Arriving at the Group Captain's home, I was introduced to his Wing Commander Flying, whose face I immediately recognised. I was aware, too, not only that the officer I was facing was considerably junior to me in terms of length of service and experience, but also that he was quietly but ruthlessly ambitious. As we shook hands and exchanged a few pleasantries, I sensed at once the evening would be unproductive. The man's face clearly betrayed the thought uppermost in his mind: I was after his job.

At the dinner itself, though it was pleasant in many respects, the three squadron commanders accompanying the Wing Commander, having clearly been carefully briefed, all presented blank faces and produced so little in the way of conversation that I was soon made to feel an absolute outsider. Which, of course, had the effect of hardening my own attitude towards them! All right, to heck with the lot of 'em! If these were the people I might be fated to work with, then I would offer my services to someone else.

I did not speak to the Group Captain again that night, other than to thank him for his hospitality, and I recall retiring later in a very unsettled and resentful state of mind.

So much so that on the following day, when I should have met him formally and perhaps have had a more productive discussion, I chose to return to the airfield at Antwerp without seeking any further meeting, demanding to be returned to England.

As I was on the airfield, sitting on a pile of luggage and waiting for an Anson to collect me, a V2 rocket arrived entirely unannounced and struck the perimeter of the airfield within 1,000 yards of where I was sitting, nearly putting an end to me as well as destroying several buildings, a row of trees and a group of aircraft.

The rocket exploded with a report that almost defied description, and the explosion was followed by a mass of whirling bits in the air and a huge pall of black smoke. I found myself ducking involuntarily and being forced into taking some deep, deep, intakes of breath. Altogether too near and very, very frightening. No, no more of that, if you please, Mister Hitler!

The Anson arrived soon after and, the smoke having drifted away, normality soon prevailed, enabling us to take off as planned for England.

On 14 December, I attempted to fly the Spitfire to Amiens to meet my beloved but had to turn back because of some filthy weather conditions over the Channel. That particular flight was properly recorded in my logbook. What is not recorded is the flight of the following day. Nor is any flight in the Spitfire ever recorded thereafter. The reasons for this will become clear.

It must have been on 15 December that, having failed to complete my journey the day before, I tried again. I well remember flying up the Somme estuary at a very low level and in very miserable weather conditions, before successfully creeping towards Amiens Glisy airfield. Making the usual circuit, I landed safely on the main runway and came to a halt, before turning to observe in the distance two airmen waving me in.

As they clearly intended to have me approach them across the grass, I recall it passing briefly through my mind that this might be a risky business, as the ground, though it appeared firm and green, was probably rain-sodden and likely to cause problems.

And, indeed, this proved to be the case. Within 20 or so yards of where my guiding airmen stood waving in my direction, my aircraft stumbled like a horse gone lame, and before I knew it, my Spitfire was standing on its nose and twisting itself into the ground, to the accompaniment of some very nasty metallic-sounding clicks.

Horrified, and expecting to be turned completely on to my back, I finished up about 12 feet in the air, like a monkey up a stick, staring into the ground and very much aware that much of my airscrew had splintered and disappeared, as had at least one of my undercarriage legs with its fairings and sundry other bits and pieces. In short, my Spitfire was little short of being a wreck.

After being shocked for a moment or two, I undid my straps and, sliding carefully to the ground, surveyed the damage and the cause of my misfortune.

The cause was quite plain to see. A hole, some 10 feet across and 6 feet deep, had opened up, being part of an old filled-in bomb crater undermined by recent falling rain.

An hour later, and with the assistance of the station engineer officer, we had settled on a list of spares that might be needed and, more to the point, discussed who would carry out the repair work and when. Then, as the local expert began to ask some pertinent questions about the home of the Spitfire and to whom it belonged, I thought it best to ask for 'time out' for the sucking of teeth. Clearly, there was much I did not wish to reveal.

Eventually, I was able to persuade him that a friend of mine, Wing Commander Hughes, the chief technical officer at RAF Ford, would attend to the matter and that he need not get involved. I then began to think how I should get in touch with Bert, explain the situation, and perhaps persuade him to help me out yet again.

I finally was able to contact my friend on the 'operational net', and for me our conversation was not easy.

'Bert, I'm sorry to have to tell you that I've broken the Spitfire,' I said.

'You've what?'

'It's fallen down a bomb hole and has been pretty badly damaged.'

'How badly? And where are you?'

'I'm on the airfield of Amiens Glisy, and the local engineer chap says we need the following bits.' I then read out a fairly considerable list of spares, which included a new airscrew and spinner, a new starboard oleo leg, with all its associated fairings, a new starboard wing tip and much else besides – including just possibly a new Merlin 66 engine, if the shock-load test proved to be unfavourable.

After a few moments' silence, my friend Bert responded, 'Look, why on earth can't you have your accidents this side of the Channel? How am I going to get an 11-foot, four-bladed airscrew into an Oxford or an Anson? You really should be more careful.'

Sensing that I was on safe ground, I answered with a straight face, 'Bert, these accidents can't just be prearranged. There's always an element of spontaneity involved. But anyway, how long do you feel it will take to have it repaired?'

After a long silence, there came a word I was scarcely able to hear. Then, wearily, 'All right, leave it with me and I'll see what I can do. Give me about three weeks.'

Stuck at Amiens without an aircraft, I saw my favourite lady only briefly before returning to Northolt as a passenger in an Oxford.

Christmas Day 1944. Twenty-four hours of quiet conviviality sandwiched between four weeks of violent action on the ground and in the air. Also some travelling and other surprises for me – and all amid a period of bitter, horrible weather.

Without the Spitfire to fly and still dismayed by my reception at Bentley Priory, I had fretted in my parents' home on the outskirts of London, unable to concentrate on anything other than the weather and news of the war coming from the BBC – which, on 17 December, was deeply disturbing.

The Germans had apparently launched a massive attack on the Anglo-American lines in the thickly forested Ardennes hills, an area a little to the north of St Dizier, where I had only recently been flying and living. Though this came very much as a surprise, it had long been recognised that if the Germans were ever to contemplate retaliating in force, the Ardennes would be the most likely area for them to choose, as they had used the same route into western Europe for their several recent wars with France.

What was more surprising, however, was that they had chosen to launch their attack in such miserable weather conditions. With snow thigh deep over a wide area and low cloud prohibiting flying, it was strange that so vast a German armoured force should have been committed to so risky an adventure without the availability of adequate air support.

The Allied line, composed mainly of Americans, was rocked to its very foundations by the furious assault by the 200,000 troops of two elite panzer armies. In the worst possible weather conditions, the Americans fell back, first to contain and lessen the effect of the onslaught, before pausing to consolidate and regroup prior to launching a counter-offensive.

By 24 December, the German threat had largely faded and

the Allies had recovered sufficiently to organize and begin their counter-attack.

On the same day, in far-off England, in order to cheer myself up, I had decided to visit my lady friend in Amiens and managed to persuade the communications flight at Biggin Hill to lend me their Oxford. I also have a happy recollection of spending most of Christmas Eve hanging up bunting in the officers' mess at Amiens, but sadly, I remember very little else that occurred during the following festive day.

I do recall, however, the weather clamping completely on Boxing Day, so that I was unable to fly back to England until several days later. I also remember, all too well, having to endure a very unpleasant interview with the group captain commanding Biggin Hill, when I was finally able to return, that aggrieved officer complaining in the most forceful terms that I had pinched his personal Oxford which he had urgently needed over the Christmas period. Oh, woe, woe! Shame on me!

My embarrassment became a thing of the past however, when almost immediately two events of great significance claimed my attention. First, reports of a massive attack by the Luftwaffe against RAF airfields close to the German border on New Year's Day; and the more than welcome information of my next posting. Glory be!

The BBC, not normally given to overstating any situation, reported that about 1,000 German aircraft (surely an exaggeration, I thought at the time) had attacked British airfields in Holland and Belgium shortly after dawn on 1 January, causing widespread damage and casualties and destroying a large number of RAF aircraft. However, many of the attacking aircraft had been shot down or otherwise destroyed and the situation, much affected by the bad weather, had since been restored. The impression was conveyed that both the land attack through the Ardennes and the air attack on the airfields, though damaging and most unpleasant, had now petered out and that no lasting harm on the Allies had been inflicted.

Listening to the reports with a fair degree of scepticism, I nevertheless felt relieved that a similar attack had not been made on the airfield of St Dizier or indeed, on the 100th Fighter Wing's place of abode.

It later became known that the German attacks on land and in the air in December 1944 had been planned several months before, Hitler being obsessed by the need to push the Allies as far back as possible from the borders of Germany.

Such was his obsession that he failed to keep his generals either informed of or even persuaded by his shifting intentions. He insisted, for example, that the massive attack in the Ardennes by 24 divisions of Nos 5 and 6 panzer armies, in all involving almost a quarter of a million men, should continue to take place even if adequate air support became unlikely because of unfavourable weather. Such adverse weather conditions being experienced, the result was, within 48 hours, his various generals were forced into regrouping and ordering a retreat.

Similarly, Adolf Galland, the German fighter leader (whom, with Johannes 'Macki' Steinhoff and others, I met and with whom I discussed these very operations after the war), had by as early as 10 November made his own arrangements to attack the Allies with up to 3,700 fighters and bombers as soon as suitable weather conditions existed. His carefully husbanded and trained force was, however, never used, as Hitler intervened and instructed him to use the majority of his strike aircraft to assist the Ardennes advance, a task which Galland became unable properly to carry out, being hamstrung by unfavourable weather, which reduced all flying to an absolute minimum. Instead, as a sort of second-best compensation exercise and as part of Operation Bodenplatte (Ground Plate), he felt obliged to instruct a reduced force of 800 fighters and fighter bombers to attack 17 bases of the RAF's 2nd Tactical Air Force, which, at the time, were crammed tight with many squadrons and most types of fighter aircraft.

At about 9.30 a.m. on 1 January 1945, his aircraft roared in at tree-top height, destroying 144 aircraft, seriously damaging a further 84, setting aflame fuel stocks, buildings and supply dumps, and killing 46 personnel and wounding a further 146.

The cost to the Luftwaffe, however, was huge, about 300 aircraft with their pilots being lost, many of them being squadron or flight commanders. Additional losses resulted, too, from the sheer inexperience of some

*younger pilots, who became involved in collisions, as well as being the vic-
tims of accurate anti-aircraft fire, bad tactics and poor flying discipline. In
short, the whole exercise, though very damaging for the RAF, was, for the
Luftwaffe, an enormously expensive fiasco.*

*Hitler's insistence on the maximum employment of Galland's force in
the Ardennes during the Führer's last desperate attempt to ward off the
Allied advance into Germany from the west was, in Galland's own words,
'the final dagger thrust into the back of the Luftwaffe'.*

It was with a light heart that I drove the 5 or so miles between
Northwick Park and Fighter Command at Bentley Priory, and I
swear that the gates of the priory welcomed me with a morning
smile. It was, I recall, Thursday, 4 January 1945.

My 'P' Staff friends greeted me cordially and sat me down with a
mug of their infamous tea, which, as it normally tasted like sweet-
ened bull's blood, I found impossible to drink. Their attitude suggested that good news was about to be delivered.

I sat there patiently but all agog. What did they have lined up for
me, I wondered? Where was I likely to go?

The news of my new appointment was spelled out in detail. A
new establishment, the School of Air Support, was in the process of
being formed at RAF Old Sarum in Wiltshire and I was one of the
first to be selected as instructor and lecturer. The school was a tri-
service establishment and only the most experienced and capable
officers were being considered as members of the Directing Staff
(DS).

Mindful of the clear intention to butter me up with the description and apparent importance of my new appointment, I was nevertheless pleased to hear Old Sarum mentioned as, having flown
from Boscombe Down during the early part of the Battle of Britain
and later, I knew and was very fond of Wiltshire and particularly of
Salisbury.

I was further informed that my official posting date was 8 January.
It would take about a month for the school to organise and arrange
its procedures and methods before its first students arrived, probably during the first week in February.

It was also explained that there would be regular demonstration air exercises and displays as part of the curriculum, so there would be masses of flying to be organised. A fair amount of travelling by the DS was also envisaged, as the syllabus would cover the war in the Far East, and unless those chosen to instruct were sufficiently knowledgeable about the very nasty battle in that particular war zone, someone would have to go out to India, Burma and even further afield, to gather information and experience.

The first step was for me to make myself known to the new commandant, Air Vice-Marshal L. O. 'Bingo' Brown, and his second in command, Brigadier P. H. W. 'Pip' Hicks of the Parachute Regiment. Both, it seemed, were even now at Old Sarum. It would be up to me to introduce myself and learn what they might have in mind for me to do.

The next day I drove my old Morris 10 down to Old Sarum with mixed feelings. The possibility of an overseas visit to the Far East was not exactly appealing, but otherwise the job sounded exciting and more than a little fulfilling.

But there was the wretched Spitfire to consider, too – a permanent cloud on my horizon. Would my new job offer a solution? A possible way out?

Chapter 18
A New Beginning

I found Old Sarum a joy to behold. The day was crisp and cold but unusually fine for January; the rolling all-grass airfield stretched away towards the rising mound of the old castle, just as I remembered it. The officers' mess was unusually large with lots of elegant spacious rooms, oak panelling everywhere, and seemingly quietly and well provided for with elderly striped-coated mess servants and smiling WAAFs. Stretching away to the south was the large, sloping expanse of the mess rose garden, the flowers not in bloom at the time, of course, but offering prospects of a colourful, scented summer to come.

Suddenly, it was all exciting and life so well worth living – a far cry from the rigours of living in a tent in some muddy mine-ridden French field or broken-down chateau and balancing my bum on a pole over a ditch.

In addition to the normal scattering of officers and airmen going about the business of running the Old Sarum station, I noted a sprinkling of more senior officers of all three services here and there, who, I deduced, were members of the new Directing Staff of the school to be.

There was also, I was pleased to note, a group of aircraft parked in the near distance beyond the most westerly hangar, an assembly which included several Spitfires (one of which appeared to be a Mark 12 of No. 41 Squadron, the unit I had so recently commanded), a large naval Grumman Hellcat, something that looked like an American Beechcraft Traveller, with its rather odd, back-staggered wings, a Dominie (DH.89a), a Proctor and one or two other minor 'phut-phut' aircraft.

Wow! My eyes must have fairly sparkled. This was just the place.

My silver Spitfire would fit in here without too much of a problem. All I had to do was to persuade the commandant, or whoever, to take it on.

My first official meeting was with Group Captain Peter Donkin, who commanded the Offensive Support Wing of the school. A tall, rather lugubrious-looking officer, he had a sharp tongue, an off-putting turn of phrase and so decidedly an offhand manner that I found it, and indeed him, upsetting at first. However, later, as so often happens with such people, I discovered him to be a helpful and understanding colleague.

In a dreary monotone, he explained that the other half of the school, termed the Transport Support Wing, would deal with the purely Army contribution to the course, including the employment of parachutists, gliders, air transport, air supply generally, plus the control of all similar Army elements.

He then listed a whole series of Air Support Wing lectures and exercises and displays he had in mind for the various two- and three-week courses; and he enquired to what extent my own experience might enable me to make a worthwhile contribution to the running of the curriculum.

Oh (he added this with a casual wave of a hand), and if I wasn't already conversant with the war in the Far East, it might be necessary for me to go out and have a quick look at what was going on in India and Burma.

More than a little dazed by the catalogue of requirements my senior had outlined, I said that although I was probably as experienced as most officers of my age and rank, there was clearly much I needed to learn. Which prompted the immediate instruction that, in that case, I was to arrange for a driver and transport in which to tour the whole country, if necessary for the next three weeks, until I had gathered sufficient information to speak and write convincingly on at least five of the subjects he had mentioned. Also, I should know that he had me in mind to organise and run the fortnightly air displays and demonstrations.

Five subjects, plus air displays and a possible visit to the Far East! I must have blanched and swallowed. There was clearly not going to be much time for me to attend to the future of my Spitfire.

My mind still in a whirl, I went in search of the commandant, Air Marshal Brown, and within minutes was ushered into his office by his adjutant. Stiffening to attention, I knuckled my forelock in the approved manner before removing my forage cap and sitting down.

The Air Marshal was quiet, grey-haired and smiling. We exchanged polite remarks about my recent arrival and method of travelling to Old Sarum, followed by a few further words about my background and history since the war and my assertion that I was looking forward to making a worthwhile contribution to the school.

I was then forced to clear my throat (which suddenly had become very tight and dry) before introducing the existence of the Spitfire, how it had dropped in my lap by accident, so to speak, when I was with the Americans, and how circumstances had more or less obliged me to look after it for the last eight months. I finished up, 'So, I ... er, well, I was wondering, sir, if it might be possible to include it here in our communications flight?'

After which, I waited for five seconds that seemed like five hours.

Finally the verdict – delivered with a slight but knowing smile. 'No, I don't think it would be sensible to add a further Spitfire to the two we already have.' He picked up a paper and examined it. 'You see, we already have a Mark 12 from the RAF and also a Seafire from the Navy. I think another Spitfire would be altogether too much of a good thing, don't you?'

Two minutes later, I stood outside the head man's office, feeling as though I had just been punched between the eyes. What in heaven's name was I going to do with the wretched aircraft?

At this point, a few details about Spitfires in general would not go amiss. Such information would also be helpful when considering my so-called 'Silver Spitfire', explaining the reasons for some of the problems I experienced when flying it for more than a year and the need to get rid of it.

About 22,000 Spitfires were built during the Second World War. There were 24 Marks of the type, from the Mark 1, built and used before and during the Battle of Britain, to the Mark 24, which appeared and was flown in 1945 and later. There were, moreover, some 50 variations within the 24 Marks – for example, the most numerous Mark 5 had a series of slightly different engines, supercharger ratios and maximum power settings, plus three or four different types of wing and various combinations of armament.

Within Fighter Command during the war, the life of any Spitfire was theoretically 240 flying hours. Assuming an aircraft survived (and most didn't), a brand-new Spitfire could be expected to remain in an operational squadron for a maximum of no more than eight or nine months and the average monthly flying time was 30 hours. However, like the Lancaster bomber, which had a 'life span' during the war of about 44 hours (six trips to Berlin and back), the average life of a Spitfire was about the same – 40 hours or less. This meant that although a few aircraft flew for their full life span, most did not, some being shot down or irreparably damaged on almost their first sortie or flight.

Assuming that a Spitfire was lucky enough to survive, like a well-maintained car it was inspected every day (usually at dawn in an operational squadron) and, thereafter, serviced at regular 40 hour intervals.

Then, when its life of 240 hours came to an end, it would be removed from the squadron and sent to a maintenance unit, where its engine would be taken out and completely refurbished, its airframe inspected and, if necessary, a series of modifications incorporated. Thereafter, the whole Spitfire then became a 'second life' aircraft and was usually employed on second-line duties.

Every Spitfire had its own logbook, termed a 'form 700'. The main document was kept on the squadron or unit and a 'travelling 700', a lesser document, was kept in the aircraft to record all details of refuelling and minor incidents. The main 700 contained all the flying times and a complete service history of the aircraft, including all details of its unserviceability and repairs. Understandably, the travelling 700 was always removed before any operational sortie, so that the aircraft's squadron, unit or base was not revealed to the enemy should the aircraft be shot down.

The first indication of any flight was normally contained in the squadron or unit's 'authorisation book', in which were written details of 'the duty' to be carried out before being countersigned by a flight commander or squadron leader. At the conclusion of the flight, the exact times would be recorded with any further relevant details, all such information then going to the orderly room of the unit concerned and recorded yet again in other squadron documents, from which the pilots normally made up their flying logbooks at monthly intervals.

From all of this, it can probably be deduced that possessing no identifying aircraft or squadron number, and coming from no known unit or base, my Silver Spitfire was anonymous. Its history unknown, it had no permanent form 700, and only a sketchy travelling document; its flights never appeared in any authorisation book; and its pilot (me!) was responsible to absolutely no one and able to fly it whenever and to wherever he liked.

I cannot recall when exactly it was that I picked the repaired aircraft up from Amiens Glisy, although I suspect it was on or about 10 January. I do remember, however, the station commander at Amiens, having air-tested it himself, being full of 'insatiable curiosity' as to who owned the Spitfire and where it had come from. I responded by stating rather loftily that the aircraft was American owned and that I flew it now and then only because I was attached to the 9th USAAF – which, of course, by mid-January 1945 was an absolute fib.

After that, although after my arrival at Old Sarum I estimate that I flew the Spitfire around the country for an additional 30–40 unrecorded hours, for the time being my Silver Spitfire sat among a dozen other aircraft of the communications flight at RAF Northolt and was never flown, as I, its dubious owner and pilot, was otherwise engaged.

*

In fact, until 13 February, I was very busily engaged indeed. Travelling widely around the country by car and sometimes by air, I visited a score of airfields and places of interest, collecting a variety of weapons, objects, documents and maps, plus any other item that might provide a background for the lectures and talks I had been scheduled to give. It was interesting work but wearing, my goodness – a burden lightened, however, by frequent opportunities to fly some of my favourite aircraft.

From Old Sarum, among others, I flew the Mark 12 Spitfire several times in late January and early February. This was the aircraft formerly in my old command, No. 41 Squadron, and having the large 37-litre Griffon engine, it was a very fast mover low down. I was to use it many times in the months ahead.

I also able to fly two splendid aircraft of the Royal Navy, the big but very successful Grumman Hellcat fighter and the very plush four-seater Beechcraft Traveller – the aircraft with the unusual back-staggered wings.

On one of the several occasions I visited the Air Fighting Development Unit at RAF Wittering, I was able to take a short trip in their captured German Me.109. It was, I recall, the G2 version, but I may be mistaken. I remember the cockpit being a bit small for even my normal-sized rump, but the aircraft was very nippy and pleasant to fly, although the thumping great 39-litre Daimler-Benz engine up front was somewhat rougher than the Merlin or even the Griffon engines in our Spitfires.

During the first few days of February I gave the first of my several lectures. Not to an assembly of students, but in an empty lecture hall and in front of the AOC and about twelve of a very critical and discerning group of the school's Directing Staff. It was an unnerving experience.

I am happy to say, however, that it went off well. So well, in fact, that the Air Marshal came up to me at the end and, tapping me lightly on the arm, said briefly, 'A very good talk. You have a gift!'

Which made my day, of course – a day only slightly marred when Group Captain Peter Donkin, my immediate senior, informed me that I would be going out to Burma for at least a month, and that I was one of a party of four who would be leaving within days.

And believe it or not, my immediate thoughts were not about the impenetrable jungles, poisonous snakes and elephants, but of my lonely Silver Spitfire. I was being obliged to leave it for weeks, if not months, on end. What on earth was going to happen to it?

Chapter 19
India and Burma

My trip to Burma had little to do with my Spitfire. However, so much occurred during the visit that for me was new, interesting and sometimes downright amusing, that I will mention one or two of the more unusual incidents.

There were four of us in the party: Brigadier 'Pip' Hicks, of the Parachute Regiment; Major David Powell, a gunner and so-called army liaison officer; and another major, a strange man whose name escapes me now, who was formerly one of Brigadier Orde Wingate's Chindits, operating in the faraway jungles of Burma.

Pip Hicks was a large, solidly built, rather pompous-sounding officer in his early 40s. As brave as a lion, he was even so a dreadfully nervous passenger when flying over the sea. Apparently during the invasion of Sicily in 1943, his glider, being towed by an American C-47, had been cast off prematurely and without warning while over the Mediterranean, resulting in most of his fellow passengers being either drowned or given a nasty fright.

David Powell, a delightful person, was about five years older than me. A territorial officer before the war, he was a highly qualified accountant by profession and went on after 1945 to become a 'big wheel' in the City of London. He was also something of a thespian and an author, and had a grand sense of humour. He and I always got on famously and enjoyed many laughs together during our Burma visit.

Our other major passenger was always civil, friendly but quiet. He had little to say for himself until we arrived in Burma, at which point he seemed positively rejuvenated. Springing out of the aircraft and waving his arms about, he disappeared into the jungle and I don't think any of us ever saw him again for the rest of the visit. Apparently, Wingate's Chindits produced that sort of person.

Flying in an RAF Dakota, which was pretty slow and very much a military aircraft, we had only half a dozen not too comfortable seats. This meant that the 135 hours we were to spend in the aircraft during our trip to Burma and back were acutely uncomfortable as well as boring.

Anticipating such a possibility, I had bought myself several substantial books and also an embroidery kit, wool and needles, enabling me to make cushion covers – a diversion which produced lots of sniggers from my rugged, manly Army colleagues. After untold hours in the air, however, gazing down on vast expanses of seemingly endless desert and sea, and becoming bored almost to the point of losing the will to live, my travelling companions were later forced to admit to harbouring second thoughts about my unusual pastime.

The aircraft itself had a crew of four: the pilot, a rather elderly flight lieutenant, a more junior co-pilot and two NCO airmen. All nice enough chaps, they were helpful in every way, although they began to lose patience with our rather pompous brigadier towards the end of our very long journey.

We were also obliged to spend at least another 30–40 hours flying in various other types of aircraft, not all of which were as comfortable as even the Dakota. No, my rear end will remember my trip to Burma for the rest of its life!

And there was one incident at the end of our long flight between Bahrain and Karachi that was not in the least amusing.

As we reduced speed and let down to circuit height near the airfield at Karachi, I remember gazing out of my window towards the distant landing ground. At which point there came a prodigious, thudding bang from up front, so violent that I was later able to swear that our aircraft had halted in mid-air for just a moment or two. Realising that we had hit something very substantial, I rose from my seat and moved quickly forward to open the crew cabin door – and the sight that met me was most unpleasant.

A massive black something-or-other had struck the windscreen and fuselage just in front of the pilot, so that the poor man, as well as the instrument panel, was covered in a mass of blood, entrails and feathers. An enormous bird, a vulture-type flesh-eating creature, had flown into our Dakota, smashing the windscreen and making a substantial hole in the nose of the aircraft, through which the wind was now whistling and howling.

Covered in slimy red goo, feathers and entrails, the flight lieutenant captain was clearly in a mild state of shock and unable to attend to his controls and fly the aircraft. However, as our Dakota did not appear to be seriously damaged, the co-pilot, within about ten minutes, was able to make a safe landing and allow the rest of the crew begin the unpleasant task of clearing the cockpit of all the blood and mess.

The damage, however, was considerable. It would clearly take some time for repairs to be carried out, which suggested an immediate change to the programme of our visit.

Naturally, we passengers began to discuss the incident excitedly, seeking local advice as to what precisely might have happened, what sort of bird was involved and if such an incident was a frequent occurrence. The news we received was given in a fairly off-hand manner. Our aircraft had apparently flown over a local but very important area where human remains were normally disposed of either by fire or with the cooperation of the admittedly very unpleasant creatures that had damaged our Dakota.

Such an accident as ours was not, we were assured, a frequent occurrence, although similar incidents did occur from time to time. The birds, however, would never be discouraged, as they provided a vital service by consuming the mass of rotting bodies that was always available. Gorged on an unending diet of human flesh, it was small wonder they could be huge and very heavy, often with a wingspan of more than 6 feet.

Having so recently being chilled by the sight of all the blood, feathers, guts and damage one of them was capable of causing, I was inclined to accept the local, rather pragmatic view of the birds and their important role in life, but with little enthusiasm.

As the pilot of any aircraft, I would never wish such a thing to happen to me.

With our own aircraft unserviceable, we were obliged to use another Dakota for our journey from Karachi to Rawalpindi, situated on the north-west border of India and the ancient gateway to Afghanistan. We were going there to see a demonstration of the use of parachute troops in a rugged, high-mountain area.

I was delighted with the arrangement, as, since I was brought up on the books and stories of Rudyard Kipling about the North-West Frontier Province, its skirmishes and battles, the East India Company and the British Raj, which for 200 years had been the dominant controlling force in that part of the world (and, in 1945, still held sway there), India and its colourful peoples had always held an enormous fascination for me. That I was at last going to visit the area, with its fierce, dark-eyed and bearded warrior tribes, was for me an enormous treat.

And I was not to be disappointed, as the colours, the heat and talcum-power dust, the scents, the atmosphere, the cardboard cut-out scenery of the area and the sheer vitality of life were all so strikingly unusual that they were to remain vividly in my mind for years to come.

The local landing ground was not an airfield in the strict sense of the word, merely a wide area of impacted clay and rock on to which aircraft were pulled out and dispersed each morning, having been guarded behind walls or in hangars against the ever-present threat of malicious tribal hands, guns and bombs.

On a late morning, during which we wilted under a clear sky and a brilliant sun, our party was confronted by a group of crimson-hatted Parachute Regiment officers and NCOs, and a company of Gurkhas, headed by an older, serious and weathered VCO (Viceroy Commissioned Officer).

Having had it explained to us that it was the intention to introduce the Gurkhas to the manner in which a parachute drop would normally be executed, we were told that a Dakota would soon be airborne with a small group of them, and asked if we would like to fly in the aircraft and witness the exercise. I recall being the only volunteer and scrambling aboard.

After taking off, we flew around for a while with the fuselage door of aircraft open and with me standing aside and admiring the scenery. There were about five in the parachute group, plus the Gurkha officer and several of his NCOs. Although there was much smiling and talking together, it appeared that only the Gurkha officer spoke and understood English.

Turning and then straightening out, the aircraft made its first run in at about 1,000 feet above ground level, which the Gurkha officer watched carefully before making remarks to one of his Parachute Regiment instructors. Unable to hear what was said because of the noise of the engines, I was quite surprised when the aircraft turned away before losing height and came in again some 500 feet lower, all the Gurkhas, meanwhile, studying the ground below very carefully. After this run, however, they seemed altogether happier, as there was much grinning and conversation, and even one or two hugs.

The flight over and the Dakota having landed, I asked the instructor what all the chat was about and if he was satisfied with his little exercise. To my surprise he grinned widely and, shaking his head, explained.

Apparently, his Gurkha students thought the first run at 1,000 feet to be a little too high and had asked for it to be reduced to 500. When he, the instructor, tried to explain that 1,000 feet was normally the minimum jumping height to ensure that the parachutes would properly develop, his students were all greatly surprised. Apparently, they had thought they would be jumping *without* parachutes and although 1,000 feet seemed a bit high, they were perfectly prepared to jump from 500 feet.

I simply could not believe my ears. 'Do you really mean that those little chaps were prepared to jump out of an aircraft flying at 500 feet, without a parachute?'

'That's what they said.' The man was still grinning. 'That's Gurkhas for you!'

Among many other pleasant memories of Rawalpindi is one of

being able to buy a beautiful Persian Shiraz carpet in the souk for 'peanuts'. The same carpet stills adorns a floor in my eldest son's house today.

The next place we were programmed to visit was Eastern Air Command (EAC), a combined British/American headquarters sited near Calcutta, on the east side of India. It was a very long trip indeed: it took us many hours of flying in our repaired Dakota, with intermediate stops at Delhi and Allahabad. I spent a lot of time on my cushion covers.

Unless my memory is at fault, the headquarters was situated to the south of Calcutta in a particularly unpleasant low-lying area in which snakes and creepy-crawly things abounded.

Our visit coincided with a severe (or apparently severe) rice famine in that part of the world, resulting in hundreds, even thousands, of maimed and deprived poor dying in the streets before our astonished and outraged eyes: they had been denied the life-saving rice, which for most of the population was the staple diet on which they depended, when local rapacious and grasping 'food barons' refused to make their enormous supply mounds available, 'until the price was right'. It was agonising to see. With so much available to us Europeans, I and others, many times after a hearty evening meal, offered life-sustaining food to those lying and dying on the streets, but it was always refused or rejected, as it was unnatural for them to eat what we were pressing upon them.

Our visit to EAC headquarters, in order for us to examine and learn of their methods, was also an opportunity for me to meet again a very old colleague and friend, James 'Nick' Nicolson, VC, of No. 249 Squadron – his being the one and only VC awarded to a pilot of Fighter Command during the Second World War. Nick, my flight commander during the Battle of Britain and a good mate with whom I had kept in touch over the years, was three years older than me. Now a wing commander, he had earned himself a further DFC and, having flown Mosquitoes in Burma, was now a staff officer in Eastern Air Command.

He was still his charming, noisy, garrulous self, and we enjoyed a riotous weekend together, with him telling outrageously untrue stories to his American colleagues about my being so successful a Battle of Britain fighter pilot. We ate stomach-searing curries, drank a lot of wine, put dead snakes in each other's beds, and generally behaved like a couple of adolescent delinquents. I have blurred and unpublishable photographs of the pair of us in our pyjamas, taken the morning after one of our memorable 'late night parties'.

Poor, dear Nick! Under a bit of a cloud at the time because he had been involved in a road accident in which an Indian civilian had been killed, he quietly informed me that he was anxious to get away for a time if he possibly could. He managed to do so by becoming a supernumerary crew member on an RAF Liberator (B-24), but, alas, when engaged on a bombing mission to Burma, the aircraft was forced to ditch in the Bay of Bengal when an engine caught fire. Although apparently seen alive in the water, he was one of several crew members who, very sadly, were drowned – all this a matter of days after our final, happy reunion.

Within days we were droning endlessly south and west in our Dakota – a very long trip this time, first to Madras, in southern India, and then across the sea to Ceylon, or Sri Lanka as it is now known.

We landed at an airfield close to Colombo, on the west coast of the island, in a tropical rainstorm so violent and heavy that it was positively frightening. Then, as so often happens in that part of the world, a clearance came with miraculous suddenness and we found ourselves in an area of unbelievable beauty, where the thousand greens of the vast jungle areas were sprinkled with millions of gaudy tropical flowers.

After two days in Colombo itself, we set off by road for Kandy, in the centre of the island, in order to meet Admiral Lord Louis Mountbatten (the head man), and his deputy, Air Marshal Sir John Whitworth-Jones, in their South East Asia Command headquarters.

For some reason or other, I don't recall meeting the Admiral, but I had a long conversation on matters of strategy and tactics with Sir John Whitworth-Jones, whom I had met before when he was air officer commanding No. 9 Group, Fighter Command, in England.

In the late summer of 1942, when I was with No. 41 Squadron and flying Spitfires from Llanbedr in Wales, he had spent more than a day with me as squadron commander, and I remembered him well. A pleasant man, he was also down to earth, punctilious and very unforgiving of woolly assertions and facts that could not be absolutely established. I had learned at lot from him that day. More than two years later, he remembered me (he said with a smile), and fortunately, our long discussion in Ceylon went down well and was very productive.

Strangely, though, when I think of Ceylon, my mind immediately dwells on the almost unbelievable beauty if the place, and on another quite trivial but memorable incident.

When we were at Kandy, I recall visiting one RAF airfield in the area and it was there (I believe) that this story was recounted.

Apparently, a group of ground-crew airmen, at a loose end and wandering about in the fringes of the jungle, came across a thumping great snake, no less than 20 feet long, with a sizeable lump in its middle. They deduced that it was a sort of python or boa constrictor, which having made a kill was digesting its meal and was likely to be in a quiescent state for between two and four days, after which it would probably be up and about again, searching for its next victim.

Standing over the quietly sleeping animal, and deciding it represented no immediate threat, three or four of them picked it up (it was pretty heavy, apparently) and carried it back to base as a trophy, where they laid it out on the floor and then wondered what to do with it.

I would like to be able to report that they either knocked it on the head or, more humanely, took it back into the jungle to squeeze some other poor wretched creatures to death. Regrettably, I can't. I only include this tale because snakes do not appeal to me in the least, and the picture in my mind's eye of three or four unadventurous 'erks' picking up a dangerous brute that size and taking it home with them like a lost dog almost beggars belief.

But the British are like that, it appears. I later heard tell of an

NCO pilot in Burma who, pretty ordinary in the air, was, apparently, an absolute miracle man with 4-ton Indian elephants!

Our plodding Dakota crossed the Bay of Bengal and took us to the airfield of Akyab in the area known as the Arakan, on the west coast of Burma. The Arakan was later described by Mr Churchill in his book *The Second World War* as being 'a tangle of jungle-covered hills with its narrow coastal strip of rice-fields and mangrove swamps, and a monsoon rainfall which sometimes reached twenty inches a week!' – in short, not a comfortable place in which to fly, fight or even live.

From the airfield of Akyab Squadrons Nos 1 and 2 of the Indian Air Force flew Mark 2 Hurricanes – a snippet of information which sent my heart plummeting, for after flying Hurricanes in Malta during the last months of 1941, I had earnestly prayed to the 'person up there' that I would never see another Hurricane for the rest of my life. And here I was in Burma, about to fly not only a Hurricane but one maintained by chaps who normally were said to use string and sticking plaster when servicing their aircraft.

My main purpose, however, was to see how the Army (No. 15 Corps, under General Christison) and the Air Force (No. 224 Group, under Air Commodore 'Paddy' the Earl of Bandon, a unique character whom I was to meet later at RAF Staff College) collaborated when fighting the Japanese, and the day-to-day methods they employed. To do so, I would have to attend their daily meetings, talk to the officers involved who were actually engaged in the jungle fighting, and listen to their chat; my intended flights in the Hurricanes were regarded almost as incidental. Happily, I was able to do both, and learned a great deal which was to form the basis of my later lectures at Old Sarum.

My two bombing sorties in Hurricanes flying from Akyab were uneventful but not pleasant.

Our targets, Japanese headquarters' bashas or huts, hidden in a series of jungle ravines, were almost impossible to find – if you happened to be a novice like me. On each occasion, the weather grey and threatening, as one of a squadron of 12, I flew over about 100 miles of the nastiest-looking jungle imaginable and, as I recall, we each carried two 250lb bombs.

Over the targets, I just followed my leader. From about 5,000 feet above jungle level, we each dived steeply into each ravine before releasing our bombs at the lowest possible height, and then climbed at full power up the side of the steep jungle-clad cliff-faces, praying that we had enough speed to totter over the top, the trees meanwhile seeming always to be reaching out to snatch at us as we limped by.

I never did see my targets or the effect of my bombs, and I'm sure the Japanese were not in the least inconvenienced by my bombing efforts. After that would come the blissful return journey – of a further 100 miles of swamps, water, endless trees and, needless to say, poisonous snakes by the score.

As I say, they were not a few days I enjoyed.

During my time on Akyab airfield, I lived in a nearby tent alongside trees that to me amounted to jungle but to the local inhabitants would probably be described as a tropical garden.

I was allotted a bearer, or personal servant, who, apparently, was of the Dogra sect or tribe, a small dark chap, who grinned at me unendingly but did not speak or understand a word of English. As I only spoke English, we conducted our affairs by sign language and by pulling faces at each other.

For the week or so I was there, he never left my side, following me around like a dog, squatting mostly within 10 feet of wherever I was and springing up constantly to attend to my every need. Not only did he fetch my food, wash and clear away the dishes and cutlery, but he wanted, too, to feed me, wash me, brush my hair and teeth, look after all my clothing, make my bed and do everything possible to make my life worth living. He also sat outside my tent, even when I had retired for the night, presumably to remain on guard. In short, he was quite a servant.

There were, however, occasions when his attentions were unnecessary and even embarrassing, a point I made quietly to a resident officer when I asked him why my bearer was apt to follow me into the nearby jungle loo.

With a smile the man replied, 'Probably to scare away any snakes you might inadvertently sit on, but most likely to wipe your bum.'

Wipe my bum! I was always to remember that! Gunga Din, move over!

When I was there in about the middle of March 1945, the Japanese advance beyond Imphal into India was collapsing and in the ensuing fighting they were to lose as many as 64,000 men, killed and missing. The hard fighting over a period of six months was also to cost the British imperial forces 225,000 men in sickness alone. It was a bitter war fought in, and over, the most trying of terrains and in utterly debilitating tropical conditions.

An added factor, new to soldiers of Western origin, was that the Japanese warrior never gave up. If defeated and not killed in battle, he committed suicide – capture by the enemy was regarded as unthinkable and not an option.

I mention this as shortly before I was there, one Japanese soldier had been captured and was being taken by air to Delhi in India to be interrogated. As he sat in the aircraft, escorted by two Indian soldier guards, he apparently snatched a bayonet from one of them and committed suicide there and then, causing an unpleasant mess in the middle of the passenger cabin.

Towards the end of my time in Burma, I was being flown northwards from Akyab to Cox's Bazaar, further up the coast. Seated on one side of the passenger compartment of an RAF Lockheed Electra, to my horror I found myself facing another single Japanese prisoner, guarded by two slightly dozy Indian soldiers, equipped with rifles and bayonets. As the two guards nodded off, for the rest of the flight I couldn't take my eyes off the young Japanese captive, expecting the suicide business to begin at any moment.

When we landed and I had moved on to another aircraft, I thought I'd seen the last of him. But no! At a further comfort stop on our way to Delhi, I found myself sitting down to a meal with the Japanese prisoner sitting next to me. It was unbelievable: the poor little chap had probably never used a knife, fork or spoon in his life and some half-wit had placed him next to me at dinner. Whatever next?

When I protested, I was told that the prisoner looked pretty harmless, they couldn't think of anywhere else to put him, and I was probably the best person around to keep an eye on him.

I remember shaking my head in disbelief. The British were probably the strangest people in the world. I am also happy to record that the Japanese prisoner did not commit suicide during, or even after, our meal together.

As a final gesture of hospitality, a day or so before I left, the RAF Wing Commander Flying at Akyab (whose name, sad to say, escapes me now) invited me to take a quick tour of the local villages.

It was a delightful experience, the primitive houses and unpaved streets hot and dusty, but the people slow-moving, smiling, barefooted and attractive, most of them – the young women especially – glowing with friendship.

At one point, I was asked quietly if I wished to purchase any precious stones – apparently rubies and jade could always be obtained, as Burma was noted for them. The suggestion left me wide-eyed and faintly embarrassed as, having so recently bought an engagement ring, I barely had enough money to pay my monthly mess bill. Smiling, therefore, I declined the invitation, giving the impression (I hoped) that, although I had the resources to do so, it was just a little inconvenient at the moment. Rubies and jade – wow!

They were indeed moments to treasure.

We finally arrived back in England on 15 April, after a long but uneventful journey in the Dakota, although there were moments of tension from time to time.

At Karachi, on our way westwards, the Brigadier suddenly turned up in a truck with enough Indian and Persian carpets to furnish the liner *Queen Mary*. Our long-suffering flight lieutenant captain, who had been insisting that his aircraft was already overloaded, dug his heels in and refused to accept even a small pile of letters destined for England. This so infuriated 'Pip' Hicks that an argument started, which developed into something of an unseemly row.

My opinion being sought, although I thought it too trivial an additional item to fuss about, I expressed the view that our captain was right. He was the person who would get the blame if an accident occurred and the overload business was revealed. In short, he was the boss man of our particular ship and his rule was law – or should be considered as such. The Brigadier was not at all pleased – with neither the flight lieutenant nor me.

When we were over the Mediterranean again and near the place where he had been dunked in the water and nearly drowned, the Brigadier became excitedly agitated again and, sadly, created quite a stir, poor man.

Otherwise, things went well and we all agreed that our visit had been very useful. However, it was jolly nice to be home again.

Chapter 20
The Final Picture

The six months that followed my return to England from Burma in early April 1945 were a period so loaded down with international incident and, for me, personal change that, looking back, it is difficult, even now, to realise and accept that so much of stunning significance could happen in so short a time.

One of my first discoveries that memorable April was that my fiancée, Flight Officer Hampton, had moved from her rather unusual billet at the trout farm on the outskirts of Amiens to Ghent, where, apparently, she lived in much more salubrious circumstances, being quartered in a comfortable hotel in the centre of the town, not too far from her place of work, again 'down the hole' but this time for the Sector Operations Centre of No. 85 Group, 2nd Tactical Air Force.

Not only that: she was based almost within walking distance of the local airfield of Ghent, which was already under the control of the RAF. Remembering all too well the long walks I had had in my uncomfortable flying boots when I used to visit her in Amiens, her posting to Ghent was certainly an advantage for me, if for no one else.

During the third week in April all eyes and minds were focused on the death of President Frankin D. Roosevelt. Although it had been known that he was gravely ill, his death was something of an unwelcome surprise. None more so, it was thought, than for his successor, Harry S. Truman, the Vice President, a small, physically unimpressive man whose only redeeming quality, it was said, was his smile. But the Democratic Senator from Missouri turned out in later months to be a lion in sheep's clothing. A former clothing-store manager in the Midwest, who was bankrupted during the Great

Depression of the early 1930s, as President of the United States Mr Truman was to demonstrate firm leadership and great courage in the immediate post-war years.

The mid-weeks of April also saw the massive but still highly disciplined German Army well nigh give up trying to defend the borders of the Reich from its western enemies and, instead, concentrate its remaining strength on attempting to prevent the Russians from overrunning their country from the east. The Russian hordes, already sweeping across eastern Germany, had already surrounded Berlin and, conscious of their massive strength on the ground, showed every sign, despite the presence of the Western Allies, their obvious military might and their successes, of intending to take over entirely the rest of Europe.

Throughout shattered Germany, and aware of the imminent collapse of their nation, the guilty members of the Nazi hierarchy were already fingering their poison pills and re-examining their contingency plans for escaping to South America. Recognising their enemies in the west to be a far better alternative to those from the east, many defected to the British and American forces.

Then on 29 April came the news that the Führer, Adolf Hitler, had committed suicide in his Berlin bunker by shooting himself, and that his mistress, Eva Braun, had taken poison and lay dead beside him.

At about the same time, Hitler's squalid, undersized mouthpiece, Dr Goebbels, had poisoned his six beautiful but innocent children, before ordering his SS guards to shoot both him and his wife to death. Later, there were pictures of Russian soldiers taking grim satisfaction and pleasure, apparently, after lining up the tiny night-clothed dead bodies, as if exhibiting and viewing a row of slaughtered lambs.

Ten days later, at midnight on 8 May, the Germans finally capitulated and the war was over.

It is perhaps surprising, whilst all these dramatic events were taking place in and around Germany, that I should feel sufficiently detached to be able to attend to my own duties and responsibilities. But I was, and to a very considerable extent.

For weeks on end, I found myself lecturing, writing, collecting weapons and items of interest for my talks, organising displays and visiting other RAF stations. I was also flying a great deal.

At the Air Fighting Development Unit at RAF Wittering (a favourite haunt of mine), I was always able to gather much important information and to make use of some of their aircraft from time to time. And I always made a habit of flying the Old Sarum Mark 12 Spitfire over each weekend when the school normally stood down, invariably taking it to Northolt, where my Silver Spitfire was parked (it seemed to me very uncomfortably) in the Fighter Command communications flight hangar.

The Silver Spitfire had been there throughout my six weeks in Burma and although nothing thus far had been mentioned officially, I was nevertheless aware that there had been many dark glances and questions about to whom it belonged, who was supposed to be looking after it and why it should be there anyway. The wretched aircraft was really keeping me awake at night. I just had to get rid of it – but how?

But then I suddenly found myself with another serious problem on my hands.

Having been invited to an 'official' party by my fiancée, I had flown my silver Spitfire across the Channel to Ghent. Sadly I now have no record of the date, but it is more than likely that it was shortly before 8 May.

The occasion was a celebration. The local army units and other military formations in the area had decided to mark some of their recent successes in Germany by organising a monster gathering, 'tarting' themselves up in their scarlet jackets, bear-skin hats and kilts, and bringing with them their pipes and drums and other musical instruments. A thumping great party had been planned, and, in the event, it was indeed considerable.

I have fond memories of the occasion. I recall being lodged in a comfortable wartime hotel, drinking a fair amount of wine and dancing endlessly with my favourite lady, among others. In fact, the party was so good, I remember being there for at least two days.

The time coming for me to leave, I was transported to the airfield and climbed into my Spitfire with a smile on my lips. My lady and I had talked at length and we had discussed possible wedding dates when the war with Germany was finally declared over. Yes, things were really looking good.

Ghent, a grass airfield, had a PSP (pierced steel planking) runway. I had landed on similar runways a hundred times before, so to me they meant absolutely nothing. After checking around my cockpit and making sure I was properly strapped in, I taxied out and prepared to take off. Finally, after spending an extra moment or two running up and clearing my engine, I turned into wind and opened the throttle.

As I accelerated away rapidly, everything was going well until, at about 70 miles per hour, with the engine howling away in front like a tethered watchdog, we began to slow down and, rather surprisingly, veer to the right. The Spitfire then seemed to get down on its knees, there was a protracted, nerve-jarring screech from somewhere underneath, accompanied by streams of sparks, and the airscrew began to grow smaller by the second.

Sensing something very serious was amiss, I closed the throttle, my aircraft stood on its nose with a twisting jerk and, once again, I did my 'monkey up a stick' act.

Somewhat shocked, I was forced to take 'time off' to recover both my breath and my composure, so that it must have been a good several minutes later that I noticed a van speeding urgently in my direction, bearing a man wearing a round hat.

So beside himself with rage that he could hardly speak, the man – the station commander – was, as the saying has it, 'fit to be tied'. Eventually, gathering himself, he was able to scream, 'Just look at what you've done! You've made a right bloody mess of my airfield, you half-wit!'

And indeed I had. My Spitfire had apparently lost a wheel, and one undercarriage leg had dug into the PSP, which had been torn up for more than 50 yards and was sticking up like a well-constructed hawthorn hedge.

The man was right in exclaiming he needed a new airfield. I needed a new Spitfire. For the next several minutes we indulged ourselves most eloquently, exchanging a series of half-hysterical insults.

It took me some time to reach Bert Hughes at RAF Ford. I may be mistaken, but when he heard my voice, he sounded resigned.

'You will never believe this,' I cried.

Bert, showing great restraint, said that he probably would. Where was I *this* time and what precisely had happened?

Having been advised at length by him and the local engineer officer, I decided we needed a new engine (probably), a new airscrew, two new undercarriage legs, new wheels, a starboard wingtip and radiator (most likely), etc. Bert reckoned it would take him several weeks to sort out.

Later, physically weary and mentally crushed, I was obliged to borrow an aircraft and pilot to fly me back to Old Sarum.

For me, the need to rid myself of the Spitfire had been underlined earlier in the year when I read that a prominent air commodore had been court martialled for misappropriating an old Gloster Gladiator fighter. A clapped-out Gladiator, for heaven's sake! And here was I with a comparatively new Mark 9 Spitfire, which I had been using as a private run-about for almost a year.

The need clearly urgent, when the repaired aircraft was back at Northolt, well within three weeks, I knew that I would to have consult, very seriously indeed, my most intimate friends to discuss and decide on a means of disposing of the wretched aircraft.

As ever, the name of Group Captain Uncle John Hawtrey sprang immediately to mind. Contacting him at his new Group headquarters office in Grantham, Lincolnshire, I suggested a meeting during a weekend early in May. I flew the Spitfire up to Cranwell, and then travelled by car the 10 or so miles to Grantham.

John was delighted to see me and greeted me warmly. We had dinner together, during which I was able to introduce the subject of the Spitfire and the problems I was having with it. Perhaps he might wish to travel up to Cranwell the following day, I suggested craftily, in order to inspect the aircraft? To which proposal he agreed; and he promised to bring some of his friends to join us. I was vastly encouraged. Things were going well.

The following morning we all drove up to Cranwell airfield, where I introduced the Spitfire much as I would a prized racehorse.

Deeply impressed by its unusual silver finish, the Group Captain remarked on its uniqueness but added, in a rather offhand manner, that it did not appear to carry any sort of identification letters or numbers – a perceptive observation that rather floored me.

However, after talking more about the aircraft and remarking on its high rate of serviceability, I came straight to the point: the Spitfire was immediately available for some other careful owner. Did he want it?

My offer was greeted with a few seconds of stony silence, after which my good friend Uncle John responded with all the diplomatic aplomb of a well-brought-up Old Etonian.

Mine was a generous offer indeed, he admitted, which he much appreciated. However, he was getting a bit long in the tooth for my sort of Spitfire. A tired old Mark 1 or 2 he could probably cope with, but this one looked altogether too lethal for him – all those nasty cannons and things! Moreover, how on earth had I managed to get an all-silver one?

Realising at once that I was getting nowhere, I let my face betray my dismay, causing my sensitive Group Captain friend to have an apparent brainwave.

After smiling gently at my discomfiture, he told me quietly that he had another friend, Group Captain 'Bruin' Purvis, who now commanded the RAF airfield at Netheravon, in Wiltshire. Had I considered him? Apparently, this particular friend was a chap who did not have much time for King's Regulations and all that sort of thing. He might be interested in my Spitfire, so why didn't I give him a try?

I was enormously relieved. Bruin Purvis sounded just the person.

★

I flew the Spitfire down to Netheravon later the same day and found
Bruin Purvis in a hangar.

Tired of messing about, I came straight to the point: did he want
the Spitfire?

The Group Captain was downright surprised. He had been in the
Air Force for 25 years, he said, and no one had ever offered him an
aircraft before.

But, a man after my own heart, he looked it over as though
examining a prize Jersey bull, gave the tyres a kick or two, and said
all right, he would have it. If I stuck it in the hangar, I could forget
about it.

Mightily relieved, I arranged to have it pushed away without
delay, and, with a light heart, began to ask around for the times of
buses that would return me to Old Sarum.

After that, for a week or so, nothing happened. I lectured away
quite happily at the School of Air Support. I also flew the Hellcat
and, now and then, the Beechcraft and the naval Seafire. Life was
good and uncomplicated. The future looked rosy.

Then one Monday morning at ten minutes to nine, I was preparing to start the week off with my customary weapons lecture – a
rollicking, knockabout 40 minutes of good clean fun – when I was
summoned to the telephone.

It was Bruin Purvis's adjutant, speaking quietly but quickly, and
the gist of his message came like a blow between the eyes.

There was to be an inspection by the air officer commanding that
very morning and his visiting staff officers had already been enquiring closely about the Spitfire. In short, I was to come immediately
and remove it without delay.

'Without delay?' I echoed faintly.

'Without delay,' hissed the adjutant. I was expected, he added,
within the hour.

I cried off my lecture, pleading morning sickness, and hurried up
to Netheravon by air, being piloted in the Dominie.

I found Bruin pacing up and down, nervously whacking his thigh
with a vanity cane. We hardly exchanged a nod or a word.

The Spitfire was out and ready for off. I climbed in, started up, taxied quickly away and took off. I didn't even look to see if there was sufficient fuel in the damn thing. I recall, too, that I was bare headed, not even wearing my flying helmet, and that it was all very noisy.

As I climbed up over the broad green expanse of Salisbury Plain, I felt very much alone and quite desperate. What, in God's name, was I going to do with the aircraft?

Then I suddenly experienced terrible pangs of remorse. There it was, buzzing away as docile and as friendly as you like, and there was I thinking black thoughts about how I was going to get rid of it! It would be like shooting the family dog.

It was a beautiful day, bright and clear, with only a little cloud. I climbed up to 10,000 feet and drifted south towards the Channel coast. Far below the sun shone on the sea and the Channel looked endless, warm and friendly.

Then, in a flash, I glimpsed the perfect solution. I would simulate engine failure, give a Mayday call and bale out.

But almost immediately, caution prevailed. When and where was I going to do it? Suddenly, the sea below looked far less warm and friendly, and I realised that not only was I not wearing a Mae West or carrying a dinghy: I was even without my 'electric hat', so that I couldn't speak to anyone anyway. In any case, no one of any consequence knew I was airborne, so that by the time the people down below had sorted everything out, I would be bobbing about in the sea but as dead as a mackerel.

Chastened by my bleak review of things, I flew over the Isle of Wight, turned towards Southampton, and saw below me the small airfield of Worthy Down.

Worthy Down! I imagine my eyes lighting up. I had landed there several times before and remembered it as a friendly grass airfield situated on a hill.

I had met the test pilot, Jeffrey Quill, there a year or so earlier, when he had shown me round a new type of Spitfire they were producing that was shortly to enter the service. I never quite knew whether it was a Supermarine Company airfield or if it belonged to the Royal Navy. What I did know was that it was mostly quiet, often deserted, and that it had hangars. Yes, Worthy Down was clearly the place for me.

I descended as quietly as a Rolls-Royce Merlin would permit, dispensed with the usual circuit and touched down gently on the grass. I then taxied up the hill towards one of the hangars and stopped my engine. Absolute silence. Not a soul about. A few unidentified birds sang to each other. Otherwise, all was peaceful, and delightfully quiet.

Quietly undoing my straps, I suddenly had the urge to walk away and vanish. Then I remembered I had forgotten to bring my hat, and that I would have my parachute with me, and an RAF squadron leader without a hat and lugging a parachute would look pretty strange on a bus.

As these various thoughts plodded through my mind, a man appeared in the distance and strolled towards me. He turned out to be a Royal Navy petty officer.

With a sigh, I plonked my parachute back in the cockpit seat and, turning to the man and forcing myself to smile, told him that I would be staying for a day or two and would he kindly put my aircraft in a hangar until I returned?

It was all too easy. The petty officer returned me a jolly-tar-type naval grin, said that he would be happy to do so, and that was that. Then, however, he rather spoiled my day by inviting me to visit the duty pilot in Flying Control and tell him who I was and where I had come from.

I remember closing my eyes in despair. But what else could I do? With a heavy heart, I clocked in, left my parachute in a locker and went in search of the next bus to Salisbury. And, I have to report, I have never felt quite the same about buses since that day.

About a week later, I received a telephone call from Worthy Down.

A voice said that a group he identified only as 'they' were relieved to have found me. What about the Spitfire and how long was it likely to be with them? Furthermore, as no one was looking after it, was it all right to leave it standing about?

I said hastily that no one needed to bother themselves about it, and could they not hang on to it for a little longer?

The voice sounded a bit doubtful but decided that whoever it was probably didn't really mind, but wouldn't wish to have it sitting about for too long.

Back in my office at Old Sarum, I sat for quite some time, figuring out possible solutions. Dropping the Spitfire into the Channel was high on my list.

Then suddenly, I had a brainwave. What was the point of having a WAAF officer girlfriend in Europe if you couldn't make use of her? Eureka!

It took me quite some time to get through to her in Ghent, but I succeeded eventually. Would she get in touch with some of her mates in Germany, I asked her nicely (it must have been after 8 May but before 3 June). The German war having ended, there must surely be masses of Spitfires, Typhoons and Tempests on German airfields as part of the occupation forces, so that an extra Spitfire among that lot wouldn't even be noticed.

She replied artfully that she would see what she could do – but it would cost me.

A day or two later she called back. An old acquaintance, Group Captain Barthold – 'Bats' to those of us who knew him – would be happy to have it. He commanded a German airfield with some unpronounceable name, she explained, and would send someone across to pick it up. Could I make suitable arrangements?

Could I make arrangements? She must surely be joking! I could, indeed, and with the greatest of pleasure.

I telephoned Worthy Down immediately.

There followed a few days of silence. I continued to give my lectures on weapons, tactics and strategy, and busied myself endlessly with displays and other essentials connected with my duties as instructor.

Then Worthy Down again on the telephone, explaining that they had an officer with them who didn't speak English too well. They thought the chap might be Polish but he could be something else.

He had apparently said that he had come to take the Spitfire away. Was it all right to let it go?

I recall raising my eyes to heaven before answering in a voice I barely recognised as my own, 'Yes, give it to him – immediately!'

Two days later, just before midnight, I answered a telephone call in my pyjamas and dressing gown.

A voice explained that it was hoping to clear up some confusion in connection with a Spitfire that had taken off from Worthy Down, at a time my informant then provided, in order to fly to Germany. The said Spitfire had not arrived in Germany at the time it was expected – in fact, nothing had been heard of it since.

It was now assumed it had gone down in the Channel and the air and sea rescue services – some six aircraft and boats – had been out for more than a day searching for it. Sadly, nothing yet had been found, but they intended to keep going for another 24 hours. Meanwhile, in order to help them, could I provide any details they didn't already possess?

When the voice then told me what they knew, it was plain to me they didn't know very much.

In the silence and darkness of the empty hall of that officers' mess, I felt the net closing in around me and smelt the damp, stale odour of the dungeons. I wanted to sit down but there was nothing around to sit on.

Three days later I was again called to the telephone. Thinking it was the police, I picked up the receiver with a none-too-steady hand.

It wasn't the police, however, but another voice, which announced in quite cheery tones that its owner was pleased to inform me that the Polish pilot had now been found, and was now, in fact, in Wales. Yes, in Wales! Pixilated – or, in other words, as drunk as the proverbial skunk.

He had taken off for Germany, it seemed, but, on impulse, had decided to visit some friends in Llanbedr, near Harlech. There they had all been involved in a wild Polish party, after which he had been in no condition to fly for several days. I should not be concerned, however, as he should already be on his way back to Germany.

Relieved beyond the power of words to describe, I hurried away to light a candle for him.

And that, I thought at the time, was the last I would ever hear of the Silver Spitfire I had 'owned' for more than a year and flown for 120 hours, if not more.

And if the original owners were still wandering about Rennes looking for their Spitfire 3W-K, they would probably be better employed searching the back streets of Warsaw or Lvov.

And the rather special WAAF officer who was instrumental in finding a home for the Spitfire in Germany? Well, I had to marry her to keep her quiet.

Flight Officer Eileen Hampton and I were married on Sunday, 3 June 1945, in the attractive parish church of St Mary-the-Virgin, Kenton, Middlesex. The bride was 26 and I, the bridegroom, just a month short of 25.

Our two-week wartime honeymoon was not a sparkling success! Our hotel in Sennen Cove, Cornwall – the only one we could find in the whole of western England not taken over by the military – was small, expensive and utterly fifth rate. It also rained so heavily for at least 12 of the 14 days we were there that we seldom even saw the prominent rocks of Land's End, lying within a mile of us.

Although the German war had formally finished on 8 May, the Japanese war raged on, only coming to an end on about 14 August, after the dropping of two atom bombs a few days earlier on Hiroshima and Nagasaki finally convinced the Japanese that they faced annihilation. My new wife applied to be released from the service shortly after our marriage but continued to serve 'down the hole' in Ghent and was only able to return to civilian life in late September.

Readers may be forgiven for believing that when the Silver Spitfire disappeared over the horizon heading for Germany on some unspecified date between June and late July 1945, that would be the last I would ever see or even hear of the aircraft. But they would be wrong – dead wrong!

Having taken up writing as a minor hobby in the 1960s, I often produced articles describing my flying experiences during and after the Second World War. One such article was entitled 'The Saga of the Unwanted Spitfire', appearing in *Aeroplane Monthly* in August 1982. With a circulation of roughly 30,000 copies, the magazine was read in all corners of the world and the article resulted in many letters appearing in the 'Readers' Correspondence' section as well as my own mailbox in Norfolk.

Naturally, I read all the letters with interest and often with amusement. Some observations and remarks were helpful and interesting, others absolute nonsense, and more than a few just plain wrong – particularly those which alleged that my story of the Spitfire, its existence and its fate was fanciful fiction.

As I was never one to involve myself in discussion or arguments arising from my writing, after several months the subject faded away, peace was restored in the land and nothing was heard or spoken of the Spitfire story – for about another 20 years!

Then, in the summer of the year 2000, quite out of the blue a letter from Poland arrived. A gentleman named Mr Wojtek Matusiak, describing himself as a military aircraft historian, informed me that he had read my article in *Aeroplane Monthly*, had been vastly interested in its contents, and for some long time had been investigating not only the truth of my account but also, if and when its veracity was confirmed, the final fate of the Spitfire. Happily, he was now able to tell me that, although he was still short of some important details, he could provide not only an explanation of what actually happened to the aircraft but also pictures.

Delighted, and scarcely believing my good luck, I wrote back immediately, and for the next year or two we exchanged letters, pictures and logbook details, before finally agreeing to meet at the Imperial War Museum Air Show at Duxford in July 2006.

Our meeting was both pleasant and instructive. My new Polish friend, at about forty years of age, was younger than I had expected, but clearly very knowledgeable and full of enthusiasm for his chosen subject. He had brought with him several of his Polish friends, who seemed equally well informed, and we had a long and agreeable discussion, during which he explained that he expected shortly to complete his research into the Spitfire's precise ownership and final movements.

After that, there followed silence of a year or so. Until, in the February 2011 edition of *Aeroplane Monthly*, Mr Matusiak published his findings in the form of a comprehensive article, illustrated by photographs and pictures. As he also let me have a separate but slightly amended copy of his findings, I feel free to include the information in these pages.

The Spitfire that landed at Rennes with its number obliterated but showing the squadron markings 3W-K turned out to be from the Dutch No. 322 Squadron.

Strangely, the squadron's commanding officer, Squadron Leader H. F. O'Neil, was an old acquaintance of mine, who, when he read my magazine article, had stated in a letter to *Aeroplane Monthly* that 322 did not possess any Mark 9 Spitfires at the time. This, of course, was not the case, as Mr Matusiak was able to confirm.

As he later discovered, 322 had moved to RAF Hawkinge in Kent on 9 August 1944, to exchange their Griffon-engined Mark 14 Spitfires for the Merlin-engined Mark 16s, having been given some old Mark 9s, formerly used by No. 350 (Belgian) Squadron, to use as a stop-gap measure for a day or two.

Two Dutch pilots, Flying Officers Burgwal and Jonker, took off on 12 August in two of the old Mark 9s (one of which was 3W-K), presumably to fly over, or seek targets in, the more northerly British and Canadian operational areas of France and Belgium. Not more than one hour and thirty minutes later (the normal sortie length of a Spitfire carrying a 30-gallon overload tank), Jonker landed 3W-K at Rennes, having (it was said) been heading for the beachheads. This is odd, as Rennes is at least 100 miles south and west of the nearest American beachhead, so what Jonker was doing down there has never been properly explained.

At this point Burgwal disappeared and was later pronounced missing. It seems that Jonker, having asked later to be collected, was picked up in Rennes, not by a Dakota, as was alleged, but probably by an Anson, that aircraft type looking very much 'like a greenhouse with wings', as described by my former dear friend Smitty Minor.

As for the unserviceable Spitfire never being recovered, in all probability, that was due to paperwork being either ignored or lost, or simply that Rennes was too far away for a British-based salvage team to regard the collection of an obsolete aircraft as of sufficiently high priority.

Sadly, as Jonker died in about 1982, the exact circumstances of his landing at Rennes and his short stay there may never be revealed.

I have no explanation to offer about the picture of Spitfire 3W-K, taken apparently in Rennes. It was certainly not taken by me, nor any of my associates, and as the Spitfire always stood next to other aircraft of our communications unit, the photograph may well have been taken elsewhere and at some other time. It does, however, show the aircraft exactly as it appeared shortly after it had landed at Rennes.

For me the flight of the Spitfire from Worthy Down to Germany (via Llanbedr) has always been real enough in my memory, although its exact timing has always remained uncertain. The name and rank of the person who eventually took over the Spitfire once it reached Germany were equally uncertain. Several possible candidates were considered, apparently, until only one wing commander was singled out.

That particular officer was Wing Commander Martin Duryasz, who held a non-flying appointment at 2nd TAF headquarters. It was he, it seems, who arranged for the identifying letters MB-D to be painted on the side of the Spitfire, plus the Polish emblem and a wing commander's flag. Although in a non-flying post, there is evidence that he did, in fact, fly the Spitfire for about 70 hours and was instrumental in persuading the engineers of No. 131 Polish Wing to change the engine and remove the cannons and machine guns.

After that, the plot thickens.

When the Wing Commander was posted from Europe to Britain

in February 1946, he apparently handed over the Silver Spitfire to Flight Lieutenant (later Squadron Leader) Ludwik Martel, a former Polish Battle of Britain pilot, who had some adventures with the aircraft himself before spending some time trying to get rid of it, as its appearance – the presence of the wing commander flag but no identifying number – had begun to excite comment.

My industrious Polish friend Wojtek Matusiak was also able to produce a catalogue of other discoveries.

First, that the elusive number of Spitfire 3W-K was MK 520; that the aircraft had been made in Castle Bromwich, England, probably late in 1941 or 1942; and that it had seen service not only with the Dutch No. 322 Squadron but in four other Allied squadrons as well. Small wonder it arrived at Rennes looking decidedly second-hand!

He was also able to reveal that one of the distinguished officers to whom Martel tried to 'sell' the Spitfire was the then Wing Commander Johnny Kent, who had formerly been with No. 92 and 303 Squadrons, RAF. A colleague of mine in 1940, Kent had the good sense to turn the offer down, warning Martel that they would both go to jail if such a deal came about and became common knowledge. According to Martel, Kent did, however, introduce Martel to an American officer named Lieutenant Colonel Winkel, a former Eagle Squadron member. And it was to Winkel that Martel finally sold the Silver Spitfire for either 200 or 400 cigarettes – Martel could never remember which.

It is also a fact that shortly after taking possession, Winkel (to the absolute disgust of Johnny Kent) crashed the Spitfire on landing. Whether or not it was irreparably damaged is not recorded, but the general belief was, and remains, that it was eventually written off.

Unlike the proverbial cat, the Silver Spitfire did not have nine lives and probably had the misfortune to run out of its quota of lives some time during the summer of 1946. Or on the other hand, perhaps there are still pieces of it hidden away in the dark corners of some overgrown backyard in downtown Los Angeles.

Epilogue

The 100th Fighter Wing

Looking back over the years, it has become increasingly apparent to me that the comparatively short but memorable period of time I spent with the 100th Fighter Wing in 1944 not only was reflected in my later service career but also powerfully influenced my future life.

In part I believe because of my productive association with many of the senior officers of the Wing, it doubtless became known in the Air Ministry that my ability to cooperate with Americans generally was a quality worth exploiting. Consequently, with just a little help from several friends, I was posted to America on a number of occasions, first to Wright/Patterson Air Force Base, Dayton, Ohio, as a service test pilot in 1948, and later, in the 50s and 60s, as a pseudo-diplomat in the British Embassy, Washington DC, and as a junior delegate at the United Nations, New York.

Living in the beautiful Virginian countryside, my wife and I enjoyed ourselves enormously, although, being separated from our three growing sons, then being educated in England, was a long and bitter hardship. In fact, because of our pleasant association with America and its people, we decide to emigrate, and did so – partially anyway – in the middle 1960s.

However, after living there for a total of almost seven years, for reasons I need not enlarge upon here, it eventually became necessary for me to return to England and plough a new furrow in the broad acres of Norfolk.

Having left the 100th Fighter Wing at the end of November 1944,

I kept in touch with General 'Tex' Sanders and, more constantly and more frequently, with my old room companion Lieutenant Colonel Alvin Hill. The 100th Fighter Wing itself, consisting of the headquarters element and several hundred fighters, P.51s and P.47s, had, according to Colonel Hill, by the late spring of 1945, advanced into Germany and almost ceased to operate. General Sanders had moved on to command 19th TAC, and even the 9th USAAF was in the process of reducing, disbanding completely in the December of 1945.

Meanwhile, the officers I had worked with so agreeably were posted away by degrees, either back to the United States or to the Far East. By 1946, nothing of the 9th Air Force, the 19th TAC, the 100th Fighter Wing, nor indeed any of my companions, remained.

Brigadier General Sanders

Homer L. 'Tex' Sanders, with his dark, glittering eyes and sinister-looking pencil-line moustache, looked for all the world like a well-dressed Mexican hitman when first I met him. As he came from Texas, a part of the United States where Mexicans have always been thick on the ground, I heard it suggested more than once that the Anglo-Saxon 'Sanders' was merely a corruption of the Mexican name 'Sanchez', which appeared to me, early on anyway, more than likely.

Like many other American generals over the years, he cultivated a hard-man image and his intemperate remarks were often uttered in an off-putting flow of very unbiblical language. In short, until you knew him better, he often displayed a façade that was sometimes hard to understand and even harder to tolerate.

Fortunately, he always treated me with great respect and our association grew easier and more companionable with time. Moreover, in his more restrained moments, he could be a charming and interesting companion who not only had views on almost any subject but always explained them in a balanced manner and with a keen sense of history.

After leaving him in France, I met him again several times in Washington in the late 1940s. Working in the Pentagon and living locally, I well recall him proudly showing me round his quite substantial home, in which he had incorporated all manner of gadgets he had designed and built himself.

I also met him again a year or two later when he visited Boscombe Down in Wiltshire, where I was employed as a service test pilot. Our commandant, Air Commodore 'Sam' Patch, learning of our previous association, handed him over to me, enabling me to spend most of a day showing him round the A&AEE, and to introduce him to one of our latest jet fighter aircraft, the de Havilland Vampire.

Rather to my surprise, when I asked him lightly if he would like to fly it, he immediately jumped in and, after I had given him a quick explanation of the cockpit, took off and flew the aircraft for about thirty minutes. Which, I thought, was a brave thing to do, as jet aircraft were at the time very new and he must have then been in his later forties and probably not in full flying practice.

No, my friend Tex Sanders was never without courage!

Both of us close friends of Colonel Alvin Hill, the General and I always kept in touch with a message or a letter now and then.

When my wife and I were visiting Arizona in the 1990s, by which time I had heard that he was then living in New Mexico, I telephoned to say that we would visit him if we had time. Sadly our visit did not take place, as when we tried to make final arrangements, his wife explained that 'Tex' was then very frail and not quite up to a meeting. However, he would be happy to speak to us.

When we did, for me it was an unhappy moment. The old, sharp, decisive voice was gone, having given way to barely a whisper.

He said very quietly, 'Hi, Ginger! Good to hear your voice again.'

Then, when I explained why we did not have the time to make such a long journey, he whispered, faintly and with obvious regret, that he quite understood.

And that, really, was that. He died shortly after in 1998, aged 94.

Lieutenant Colonel Hill

Alvin Martin Hill came from a farming community in Omaha, Nebraska, an area noted, apparently, for its utter dreariness and lack of anything special.

A middle-sized, well-built man, he had the face of a bruiser but at heart was a kind, gentle and sensitive person, who formed an immediate friendship with me but had an aversion to flying. Some of his family spoke to me later of his 'barnstorming' past, but nothing was further from the truth, as Al never enjoyed being in the air – or perhaps it was just my piloting.

The right-hand administrator of 'Tex' Sanders, Al Hill kept the 100th Wing headquarters very much in order. A National Guard officer, called up during the war, he went on to serve in the Pentagon, Washington DC, and elsewhere, for some years beyond 1945, before retiring and finally making his home in Arizona.

As a civilian he went into insurance and undoubtedly made a success of it, as he became fairly affluent and made frequent visits to Europe and England, on which occasions he would always insist on calling in to 'see the kids', as he was wont to refer to my wife and me, at our home in Norfolk.

For our part, besides meeting him frequently in the Washington area, when we lived there, we later made several visits to Arizona, where we stayed with him at his splendid home in Green Valley, a little south of Tucson. Always a US Air Force man at heart, during my visits to Arizona he would always escort me around the area, showing me the defensive underground rocket installations and the almost untold masses of new aircraft cocooned and dispersed in the open on the vast unmanned desert airfields.

The attachment my wife and I enjoyed with Al Hill and Genevieve, his second wife (the first, Gartha, having died), was deep and enduring, so much so that when, in their nineties, they both finally passed away at their second home in Seattle, Washington State, we felt we had lost very much more than just two close American friends.

Captain (later Major) Patterson

Dr Robert A. Patterson, MD, whom I have described as large, noisy and capable, was certainly all of that, as, staying on in the service, he finally became Surgeon General of the United States Air Force.

He was about 29 years of age when first I met him. Although I was five years his junior, because of my past flying experience and record, he always regarded me as very much the senior chap around and tended to follow me about in the hope of cadging a flight or two, either with me or in the aircraft I flew. In short, he just plain enjoyed flying. Before he had his flying accident in the latter part of August 1944, in which he was badly injured, we flew many times and did many outrageous things together, both in the air and on the ground, finally becoming great friends.

After his accident, I lost touch with him for a time until, rather surprisingly, he turned up in about 1947 at Boscombe Down, in Wiltshire, where I was flying as a service test pilot. The next thing I knew he was in my home on the outskirts of Salisbury, looking over the fields beyond our small back garden, shaking his head and muttering, 'Ginger, you got it made here!' Which was a remark I did not understand at the time, although I always knew he was very fond of my wife.

When I met him later in Washington, I realised he was a some-what lonely young man. He appeared to be without a permanent base, and I met several young ladies of his in Washington and New York, which rather surprised me, as I had earlier been told that he had already married and had a family. However, as I never consid-ered his personal affairs to be a concern of mine, it was a subject we never discussed.

Throughout my time in America we continued our friendly asso-ciation. He came with me to the National Air Races in Cleveland, Ohio, in 1948, and from time to time he would get in touch and invite me to fly with him as he had 'gotten himself a B.45', or some similar reserve aircraft, we could use for the weekend.

After that, I again lost contact with him, for a long period. Eventually through Al Hill I heard of his advancement in the Air

Force and his many movements throughout America and Europe. Finally, when at the point of his retirement, or even later, we again managed to speak, I recall our conversation all too well, as it personified absolutely the Patterson I knew fifty years earlier.

After exchanging a few introductory pleasantries, I said, 'Pat, I've been hearing a lot about your shooting expeditions in Africa. Are the rumours correct?'

He replied, 'Oh, absolutely correct. Yessiree! I shot me a whole bunch o' crocs and tigers in Africa.'

'But Patterson, there aren't any tigers in Africa!'

'There aren't now,' came his quick reply, 'because I shot 'em all!' And finally, 'Say, why don't you come across and have dinner with me so that we can discuss old times together?'

'Patterson, you are 2,000 miles away! I have neither the time nor the money to do that, so you will have to join me here in Arizona.'

'OK then! So let's make a date.'

Which we did – but he never turned up.

After which, and very sadly, my old medical flying mate died, I believe, in 2008, at which time he would have been in his late nineties.

Lieutenant Colonel James Haun

I shall always cherish the happiest memories of Jim Haun. When I think of him I shall always see in my mind's eye his hat at its usual rakish angle, almost obscured by a lingering cloud of blue tobacco smoke from his ever-present pipe. I shall also hear his southern drawl and his amusing tales of Tennessee 'Mountain Men'. But mainly, I shall remember him as a very nice person and a good friend, who was also a splendid pilot.

As head of the A3 Operations Section, he was nominally my immediate superior, but he exercised his authority so gently and with such discretion that, throughout the momentous year we served together, he never issued an instruction or order that caused me the slightest embarrassment or to be in any way offended.

We both soon became aware that he was not a natural 'fighter boy', so that from the start, he allowed me absolute freedom to fly when and where I pleased and in any of the Wing's fighter aircraft. More than that, as an older, less volatile person, he always seemed to derive quiet satisfaction and pleasure when instructing me in the art of flying the heavier, twin-engined aircraft.

As the war in France progressed and the Wing's fighters became less involved in combat, we tended to drift apart, although he was always 'the chap living in the next bedroom to me'. So much so that when I finally left at the end of November 1944, I don't remember his face being around to bid me farewell, although I am sure it must have been.

The war having ended, over a period of years I received the occasional letter from him in America, telling me of his continuing activities in the Air Force, how much he now enjoyed flying the larger four-engined DC6s and even bigger aircraft, and also how he hoped soon to get back into the civil flying-instruction business again.

That aim he was soon to achieve, apparently, as in 2001, I accepted a letter sent on from the editor of *Aeroplane Monthly*, with the news that 'Colonel Haun, The W.W.2 flying ace and Smyrna instructor' had died at the aged of 89 at his home in Donelson, Tennessee. The letter also revealed that, born in Memphis, he was survived by two sons, who lived locally, five grandchildren, five step-grandchildren, three great-grandchildren, and nineteen step-great-grandchildren.

Sad, sad news! I will always miss him. With his hat, his pipe, his flying and his amusing tales of the 'Mountain Men' of old Tennessee!

Colonel Frederick Loughran

I was never an intimate of Freddie Loughran, MD, who, almost a generation older than me, was a quiet, rather intense Irish-American from Boston, Massachusetts. As principal medical officer in the Wing, it was only as Patterson's senior that Freddie and I officially rubbed shoulders with each other. But although our separate functions seldom brought us into contact other than occasionally, he and I were able to remain quietly friendly for our year together.

I was well aware of his dislike of 'Tex' Sanders, whom he gloweringly loathed, mostly because 'Tex' was from the south and normally expressed strong Republican opinions, which I suspect did not accord with those held by Freddie, who, I have to admit, kept his own political leanings very much to himself. However, throughout the year, although there was much muttering and seething from Dr Loughran, nothing that really could be described as subversive became generally obvious. His attitude was rather like the perennial Irish attitude towards the British: merely a private, Fenian hate.

No, more than anything else, although he had to cope with constant problems arising from German landmines, it was Freddie's almost passionate devotion to his 'grease traps' that became the standard joke among those of us not that concerned about such mundane, though essential, aids to health.

Having parted towards the end of 1944, in 1948 I happened to be in Worcester, Massachusetts, and within 40 or so miles from Boston. Learning that he was in private practice there, I rang him up and we were able to chat together.

At first he seemed surprised to hear from me, and we had an agreeable conversation, only becoming on the verge of being jovial when I mentioned his grease traps, the very existence of which he had entirely forgotten. But that was about all we discussed. Our conversation lasted less than five minutes, and I did not ever see or hear from him again. And as he was born on or about the turn of the century, I dare say he has now been dead for quite some time.

Top Sergeant Smith

About my own age, Sergeant Smith (Smitty Major) not only flew with me many times in the C-53 but became a much-valued friend. But when his name now crops up in my mind, I immediately recall an almost incredible coincidence.

In 1948, I had been in the United States for little more than a day.

Al Hill had met me from the *Queen Mary* in New York, we had travelled down to Washington together by train, and I had spent my first night in America at his home in North Columbus Street, Arlington, Virginia, which was within a few miles of the vast military establishment called the Pentagon.

The following morning, Hill having already departed for his office at an early hour, I was instructed to walk 100 yards to the end of the road, wait for a bus, put my quarter (25 cents) into the machine by the driver and then ask to be offloaded at the Pentagon.

It was raining slightly, I recall, and I was wearing a blue RAF raincoat, which in those days did not have rank-bearing epaulets attached. I had been waiting for no more than 20 seconds when a car swerved in my direction, a door was thrown open and I was hailed by a voice within.

'OK, get in, Squadron Leader!' came the instruction.

Ducking my head and scrambling in, I was amazed to be confronted by the smiling face of ex-Sergeant Smith.

I was so surprised I could hardly speak, but somehow managed to get out a few words of greeting, after which came the questions.

'So tell me, Smithy, what are you up these days and do you live round here?'

'No, I live about 500 miles away in the Middle West. When I looked up and saw you, I was just passing through on my way to Georgetown University to try and get me a place. I've never been to Washington before in my life. But I might ask you the same question: what are you doing in this neck of the woods?'

'I'm on my way to the Pentagon. Do you happen to know where it is?'

'No, but like in the good old days, I reckon the two of us together can find it!'

Fifteen minutes later he dropped me at one of the many entrances, after which, with a smile and a wave, he drove off.

Since that moment, and to my everlasting regret, I have neither seen nor heard of him again. Such an unhappy and unfortunate ending to so successful and personal a wartime relationship.

*

I have left to the last the two RAF officers whose efforts and help in 1944 so sustained me. Neither one of them is alive, now, alas, but each will live in my memory for ever.

Wing Commander E. B. Hughes

Having served in the First World War, 'Bert' Hughes was at the age at when he would normally have been expected to retire in the mid-1950s. As a much decorated chief technical officer at RAF Ford, he was in post when I damaged the Silver Spitfire in Ghent on or about 8 May 1945 and, as ever, proved to be so helpful.

However, although he had again come to my rescue, for a score of quite valid service reasons I was not able to thank him personally at the time; nor was it possible for us to meet beyond the summer of that year.

Moreover, because I spent a further eight years overseas, either in the Middle East or in America, somehow our paths never crossed, and, greatly to my sorrow, he and his small, delightful wife faded into the distance and I was never to see either of them again.

Bert, for reasons he never was able, or wished, to articulate, was devoted to me for the many years I knew him. An age later, or so it now seems, I remain deeply conscious of his concern and regard for me, and only wish I had been more responsive to his obvious feelings of what can only be described as parental affection and love.

I missed him greatly during and after the war, and though I often tried to find him, I never succeeded. Having served in the First World War, he no doubt has long since passed away. I think of him often, particularly in November, the month of rememberance.

Group Captain (later Air Vice Marshal) John Hawtrey

John Hawtrey, whom I called 'Uncle John', was one of nature's gentlemen and a person who became a powerful influence in my young life.

Not everyone's 'cup of tea', being 'well connected', he had in the late 1930s served as personal staff officer to the then government's Air Minister, a gentleman of considerable wealth but also a rather questionable lifestyle. Later, he had apparently served as station commander in France at the beginning of the war, and (according to John) incurred the displeasure of his seniors when, surrounded by the fast-advancing German army in the spring of 1940, he had ordered a retreat without official sanction.

Later still, and still smarting from his rebuke, he was station commander at RAF Habbaniya in Iraq, when the German-assisted Iraqi insurrection occurred in 1941. He returned to Kirton-in-Lindsay, Lincolnshire, in the autumn of 1943, with a filthy cold and still in his tropical uniform plus a long Afghan woolly coat stretching down to his ankles, his other kit having been lost on the journey.

He was again in Iraq, this time as air officer commanding, in the early 1950s, at which time, while I was serving at Abu Sueir in Egypt, I visited him several times in his quite magnificent home in Habbaniya, flying there via Amman in Trans-Jordan, with my two flight commanders in our Mark 9 Meteor jets.

I found my friend John's lifestyle to be truly awesome. Living alone in his magnificent mansion, he had as his only companion a huge mastiff dog (an absolute sweetie), and employed a whole company of Iraqi levies (with their military band) as guards, cooks, house servants and musicians, the last named to perform before, and during, dinner each evening and for the benefit of visiting guests when appropriate. It was luxury and grandeur in the style of the Arabian nights.

Some time in 1954 (if I remember the date correctly) he wrote to tell me that he was intending to retire and that he wished to visit Abu Sueir to inspect my unit, which was at the time No. 208 Meteor FR Squadron.

He arrived and it was a formal yet joyous occasion, during which, over a long and memorable dinner, he informed me that he had recently purchased either a small Greek island or at least an important part of one. There, he explained, after retirement he would return and, with a few selected friends, would drink fine wines to his heart's content and eat only the most exotic foods from the finest Chinese porcelain dishes. All that remained for him to do was visit the Air Ministry and sign on the dotted line.

Sadly, it was not to happen as he had planned. Having reached London, I heard soon after, he collapsed and died of a heart attack.

Section Officer Cynthia (Ogie) Oglethorpe

Having moved across France in July 1944, I did not see or hear of 'Ogie' Oglethorpe for quite some time. Some three years later, in 1947, I did however hear mention that she had left the Service and was then an Air Traffic Control Officer at Rochford airfield (now Southend Airport). Hoping to see her again, I flew from Boscombe Down, where I was then stationed, to Southend in a Vampire jet fighter. Unfortunately I missed her as she was not on duty and to my everlasting regret, I was never to see her again.

Soon after, I was told that she had joined a new fledging airline and had gone out to Australia with great expectations of starting a new life 'down under'. Sadly however, the airline failed and she not only lost her job but, refusing to return to the United Kingdom, spent some years trying desperately to make ends meet, eventually being reduced to 'doing the books' at a local Chinese restaurant.

This information was passed to me many years later when I happened to sit next to an Australian colleague at a Battle of Britain luncheon at the RAF Club. Upon being asked if he had ever heard of my good friend 'Ogie' Oglethorpe, to my great surprise, he said that he had indeed come across her in Australia, before going on to describe, in the most guarded of terms, her lifestyle as 'most unusual and distressing'.

But after that, and for many years, I heard nothing! Until one morning, my wife came across her name in the obituary columns of the *Daily Telegraph*. Eager to learn more about our former colleague and friend, my wife and I eventually discovered that a younger brother of hers, a retired solicitor, lived within a few miles of us in

Norfolk and he was able to give us at least some details of what happened to her in Australia and her later life.

For some years following the failure of the airline, she did indeed have a very difficult time, although her brother was not specific with the details. She was however persuaded to return to the United Kingdom where, as still a single lady, she settled down in Sussex and lost her heart to a rather questionable gentleman whom she later married, much to the dismay of at least one member of her family.

But ever a rebel at heart, when after only a few years of marriage, her husband died as the result of an accident and she continued to live on her own; first in London where she held down a minor appointment in the local government and then later in Lewes, Sussex.

'Ogie' finally came to a somewhat lonely end in a Sussex nursing home on 1st June 1998, aged 78 years, which greatly saddened both my wife and me. We would always remember her with affection as a most attractive, if unusual, young WAAF Section Officer who, during that memorable evening in the summer of 1944, was able to toss a senior American Colonel over her shoulder like a sack of apples!

A Final Acknowledgement

Between January 1944 and the end of the German war in May 1945, I met and served with countless men and women, in and beyond the military forces, whose courage and devotion to duty was truly magnificent and humbling. Sadly, the number is so great that I could never properly do them justice in these pages should I even attempt to describe their contribution to the Allied victory.

In particular, however, I would especially mention the bravery of the parachutists and glider troops who, on the dark and terrifying night of 5th and 6th June, took part in the initial airborne assault on the German coastline defences in France, and the courage of those who, shortly after, waded ashore and stumbled up the mined sand

and mud of the five beachheads in the face of withering fire from the entrenched German defenders.

Then there was the skill and persistence of my many pilot friends in the 100th Fighter Wing, who were so successful in the air against the Luftwaffe, together with the Typhoon squadrons of the RAF who, in the face of rising curtains of flak, with their rockets and cannons, destroyed almost completely the armour, guns and indeed the morale, of an entire German army at Falaise.

The courage and fortitude too, of the thousands of victims of the German Vengeance bomber attacks on the southern counties of Britain, and the patience and stubborn endurance of the civilian population as a whole, who after burying their dead, with set and grieving faces continued to go about their daily business.

And last but certainly not least, the many silent non-belligerents who, with friendly smiles and without reward, just helped out – the NCOs of 'the line' who serviced the many aircraft I flew, my officer colleagues and others, who fed me, laughed with me, made my bed, mended my car, or, working in their various departments and offices, kept the Wing headquarters operating successfully and maintained order behind the scenes.

To all of them – American and British alike – I offer a final salute. Well done ... and thank you.

Photograph Credits

Portrait of author with sword ©Tom Neil

Portrait of Flight Officer Eileen Hampton ©Tom Neil

My first P.51B, taxiing out: *Archives of Alan Wright*

King Peter of Yugoslavia on his visit to Lashenden airfield: *Archives of Alan Wright*

Marshal of the RAF Sir Hugh Trenchard: *Archives of Alan Wright*

General Patton of the US 3rd Army: *Archives of Alan Wright*

General (later President) Eisenhower smoking a cigarette: *Archives of Alan Wright*

A line up of P.51Bs at Lashenden: *Archives of Alan Wright*

A P.51B at Staplehurst, fitted with the new Malcom Hood: *Archives of Alan Wright*

The much decorated P.51D, belonging to Lt. Col. Eaglestone: *Archives of Alan Wright*

A P.47 from High Halden: *Archives of Alan Wright*

Been there, done that!: *Archives of Alan Wright*

The P.47 engine 'wot did it'!: *Archives of Alan Wright*

Lt. Cols. Bickell and Eaglestone pose for a photograph beside a Lashenden P.51: *Archives of Alan Wright*

Pilots of the 382 Fighter Squadron at Staplehurst pose for their photo: *Archives of Alan Wright*

Flight Officer Eileen Hampton leads the first group of WAAFs: *Archives of Alan Wright*

A wedding photograph of Miss Hampton and me ©Tom Neil

The first picture taken of Spitfire 3W-K, as it was when it landed at Rennes airfield in France on or about 20th August 1944: *(above) Harry van der Meer collection via Wojtek Matusiak (left) GeertJan Verheij Collecion via Wojtek Matusiak*

The same aircraft after having the camouflage paint removed some
   months later and the initials of the new owner painted on in 1945:
   Wing Commander Marian Duriasz via Wojtek Matusiak
Mark 14 Spitfire of No 322 Squadron with its Dutch pilots: *Harry van
   der Meer collection via Wojtek Matusiak*
The silver Spitfire with the armament removed and two Polish
   airmen in attendance: *Rock Roszak family archive via Dan Johnson/
   Wojtek Matusiak*
A group of high-ranking Polish officers: *Gabszewicz family archive via
   Wojtek Matusiak*
Another group of Polish officers with Squadron Leader Ludwig
   Martel standing on the left: *Szymankiewicz family archive via Wojtek
   Matusiak*

Index